TAATHIRA ZA KIARABU KATIKA KISWAHILI PAMOJA NA KAMUSI THULATHIYA

(KISWAHILI—KIARABU—KIINGEREZA)

تَأْثِيرَا زَا كِعَرَبُ كَتِكَ كِسُوَاحِلِ پَمُوجَ نَ
كَامُوسِ ثُلَاثِيَا (كِسُوَاحِلِ - كِعَرَبُ - كِنْغِرِزَا)

التَأْثِيرَاتُ العَرَبِيَّةُ فِي اللُّغَةِ السَّوَاحِلِيَّةِ مَعَ مُعْجَمٍ
ثُلَاثِيّ (سَوَاحِلِي - عَرَبِي - انْجِلِيزِي)

The Influence of Arabic Language on Kiswahili With a Trilingual Dictionary (Swahili—Arabic—English)

I. BOSHA

Edited by: A. S. NCHIMBI

Dar es Salaam University Press
P.O. Box 35182
Dar es Salaam

ISBN 9976 60 201 4

DEDICATION

I dedicate this Book to my mother Aïsha A.A. Al-Badawy, God blesses and gives her a long life.

PREFACE

Less than fifty years ago, many linguists particularly from the West and the Middle East had established the idea that Swahili language was of Arabic origin. Their contention was based on the fact that the name "Swahili" originates from Arabic and that the Swahili language itself has a lot of words of Arabic origin. It was because of these linguistic facts that some believed the language to be an "Arabic pidgin" or an "Arabic dialect". Surely, such conclusions founded by such linguistic data are scientifically unsatisfactory since the name of a language and words commonly found in two or more languages are a common phenomenon for all human languages.

In this research, Ibrahim Bosha Ahmed has elaborated not only the research methodology but also the analysis of his research findings leading him to draw very logical conlusions. He argues that since there was interaction between Arabs and the East Africans for many hundreds of years, naturally there were linguistic interferences from both sides. Phonology was the most affected domain of the two languages: Arabic and Swahili. His present research has only tried to illustrate the influence of Arabic language on Swahili language; it is hoped, however, that the next task would be to illustrate the influence of Swahili language on Arabic language spoken by the Arabs who came to stay in East Africa.

His research ends with a list of Swahili words believed to have originated from "Arabic" which he translates into Arabic and

English languages. Moreover, he transcribes phonetically the Arabic word to facilitate a comparative and contrastive analysis with the corresponding Swahili word.

It is high time a detailed scientific research on the origins of Swahili loanwords was undertaken as such loanwords increase geometrically as science and technology advance with time. Here is a scholar well informed of current linguistic trends and with a wide personal experience of bilingual situations. Here it is.

ATWAYA NCHIMBI

30th October, 1990.

CONTENTS

ACKNOWLEDGEMENT

Many people have helped me in various ways in my course, and I am grateful to all of them. It is very difficult for me to mention all but I can mention a few.

I'm profoundly indebted to my lecturer and my supervisor Mr. D.S. Ngonyani for unlimited assistance not only in supervision but in all Linguistics problems as a whole and for opening his door everytime. In addition I am deeply grateful to Prof. H.M. Batibo for his lectures, consultations and guidance in all branches of Lingustics and also to Dr. A.S. Nchimbi for his enormous help from the beginning in resupervising the whole work and in revising the lexical section of this reseach.

I am also grateful to my all lecturers in Kiswahili Department, particularly Professor E. Kezilahabi(Head of Department), Professor C. Maganga and Mr. R. D. K. Mekacha who have given me invaluable advice and guidance in undertaking this research.

I would like also to thank DR. T.S.Y. Sengo, Mr. M. R.Alidina, Mr. Y.M. Kihore and Mr. C. Bwenge from the Institute of Kiswahili Research for their valuable assistance.

I should like to acknowledge my indebtedness to the following:-

1. The Institute of Kiswahili and Foreigh Languages, Zanzibar where I began studying Swahili Language.
2. The University of Dar es Salaam for accepting me as a short course student.
3. The Library of the University of Dar es

Salaam, particularly the Africana Section for allowing me access to all relevant references.

4. The National Kiswahili Council for helping me in various areas of Swahili language.

and

5. All compilers of the Dictionaries which are listed at the end of the Lexical Dictionary.

To all, I can say this Arabic Proverb: (مَنْ عَلَّمَنِي حَرْفًا صِرْتُ لَهُ عَبْدًا) which means: "I declared myself a servant to he who has taught me but one letter."

For Mrs. E. F. Mwanuzi, I thank her profusely for typing this work using the Latin characters.

Last but not least, I thank my wife, Mariam Ahmed Adam who was constantly a source of moral encouragement and other supports including the typing of this work in Arabic.

Finally, I bear full responsibility for any deficiency in this work.

BOSHA, I.

MARCH, 1989.

INTRODUCTION

No language is an island in itself. It comes to contact with others. Amongst those languages is Arabic language which made contact with Swahili.

The relationship between them goes back to the First century A.D. as stated by Polomé (1967:9)

"The first reference to definite commercial relations between Arabia and the East Coast of Africa dates back to the end of the First century A.D."

1.1 STATEMENT OF THE PROBLEM:

Some people nave often thought that Swahili is an Arabic language or has developed from Arabic. Often this has been caused by the presence of many words of Arabic origin. This study wants to study Swahili words of Arabic origin and specifically to answer the following questions:-

1.1.1. Is the Swahili language an Arabic language?

1.1.2. What are the percentages of Arabic loanwords in Swahili and which areas are influenced by Arabic words more than others and why?

1.1.3. Are there problems of pronunciations and why?

1.1.4. Which is more related to Arabic, Swahili in general or standard Swahili?

1.1.5 Are the loanwords Arabic words that have come to Swahili from other languages through Arabic language?

1.2 **OBJECTIVES:**

The study will examine:

1.2.1. The extent to which Swahili borrowed from Arabic and the factors behind the whole process.

1.2.2. The degree of assimilation of loanwords where complete and partial assimilation will be examined.

1.2.3. Semantic features where differences in meanings between the original and adopted meanings will be studied.

1.3. **SIGNIFICANCE:**

This study will shed some light on the origin of some Swahili words:

1.3.1. Swahili speakers will be able to know exactly the origin of some Swahili words.

1.3.2. Arabic speakers who learn Swahili will be able to make their learning easier by knowing the Swahili words of Arabic origin.

1.3.3. Lexicographers can compare direct and indirect origins of words.

1.3.4. It will be useful to both Swahili students and teachers of Arabic language, especially in studying poetry with Arabic loanwords, e.g. Rasi-LGHULI.

1.3.5. It will help dictionary makers who might wish to know the etymology of different words which they include in their dictionaries.

1.4. METHODOLOGY:

The methods which I used to collect data from different areas included:

1.4.1. Reading publications of the "National Swahili Council": (magazines, journals, Newspapers and books).

1.4.2. Talking to people. This was important because some words are not found in the books; so I collected them from the field through verbal interviews as some people do not know how to read and write.

1.4.3. Trying to trace the origin of different words. A comparison of forms in original language (Arabic) and Swahili has been made to discover phonological, morphological and semantic differences.

1.5. SCOPE AND LIMITATIONS:

Due to time limit, I will confine my research findings of borrowed words from the phonological, morphological, semantic and script data.

2.0 LITERATURE REVIEW

2.1. <u>What has been done so far</u>. Really, not much work has been done in this area, inspite of the close relationship between the two languages:

2.1.1. In Khartoum University (Institute of African and Asian Studies).

T.S.Y. Sengo established a programme for preparing a Swahili-Arabic dictionary. This dictionary only shows the meaning of words, and as I know, the work was discontinued at Alphabet (D).

2.1.2. Y.M. Kihore wrote many topics about the Arabic script, but his research was of general nature rather than intensive in various areas.

2.1.3. Some dictionaries have been written which mention some words of Arabic origin. Words of Oriental Origin in Swahili are mentioned by Krumm. He mentioned some words but unfortunately, he has made some mistakes: e.g. when he talks about the word "Swahili" from "Sahil" (ساهل) he wrote (هـ) instead of (ح) which, in this way, means "<u>easy</u>" but (ساحل) with (ح) means "<u>Coast</u>", the sense which he wanted to convey.

2.1.4 M. Al-Hallugy wrote a Concise Swahili-Arabic Dictionary and Arabic-Swahili Dictionary (1987): but he did not use modern Swahili, and also some words are not correct in spelling. May be, some works have been done but in Zanzibar and Dar es Salaam library, I didn't find any. The above literature review calls for some more research to be done in order to give solutions to the lacunes. This is the reason why my present research is important.

2.2 WHAT IS TO BE DONE:

2.2.1. To add to this dictionary (or Lexicon dictionary) the words which are not found at all in all Swahili dictionaries which the people use them daily. e.g. dhifa, awamu, mamluki, makubadhi, etc.

2.2.2. In poetry

(i) Some words are not explained clearly because the authors misundarstand the original Arabic word itself e.g. (In Utenzi wa "Rasi-LGHULI" by Kessel)

(ii) We shall differentiate in writting between the Arabic <u>wa</u> and the Swahili <u>wa</u> (preposition) which also occurs in proverbs.

2.3. HISTORY

2.3.1. <u>History of Arabic</u>

Arabic is spoken by Arabs who originate from Arabia. The border of Arabia in the past extended to the Southern west of the Asian Continent, to North Syria, to the East of (Al-Furat) Euphrates river up to the Persian Gulf and the Indian Ocean. To the South it borders the Indian Ocean, and to the West, the Red Sea.

Arabs belong to the Semitic Group (son of the Prophet Noah). The Bible mentions that the Semitic Group at the beginning dwelt in Arabia: others say in Ethiopia. In the 1900s some people in Egypt discovered in a monument that Arabs established their Kingdom about 2,460 B.C. Anyhow Arab history is not known exactly. (Al-Rafii"1940:40)

2.3.2. History of Swahili

Likewise, the history of Swahili language is not fully known. Polomé (1967:8) says: "Though the history of penetration of Swahili from the coast inland practically coincides with that of Arab trade towards central Africa, the origin of the language itself remains disputed."

When we see the term 'Swahili' in Arabic, it means 'Coasts', the singular is 'Sahil'. The Swahili language is modified from this Arabic word. The name of the language has this origin.

According to Polomé (1967:9-11), the trade relations between the coast of East Africa and Arabia goes back to the First century A.D. Early links with Persia are implied by the active commercial relations between the Persian Gulf and the East Coast of Africa, but inspite of the assumed Shirazi origin of the founder of

Kilwa and the claims of Shirazi ancestry for the tribal forebears of the Tumbatu People, early Persian Loanwords in Swahili have been introduced through Arabic, since the Arab settlers from Oman and Hadramaut had been strongly influenced by Persian elements.

2.3.3 The Theories About the "Origin" of SWAHILI.

It is very difficult to know how and when the language started; moreover, Kiswahili has been used as a spoken language for a long time before it was written by the Arabs and even before the first Arabs came to East Africa. Many theories have been suggested to show the origin of Kiswahili:

2.3.3.1. The theory by C. Meinhof and C. Rohl says that the Shirazi ruled parts of East Africa from Kilwa up to Bagamoyo. The Shirazi and Swahili became one tribe through intermarriage with the Wazaramu. These people interacted socially and commercially with Arabs, Indians, Portuguese and so on.

2.3.3.2. Steere and Taylor say that the Swahili are creoles from Arabs and many Bantu tribes who were converted to Islam. Many words were borrowed from Arabic, Shirazi and Indian languages to be used for trade purposes.

2.3.3.3. R. Reusch agreed with Steere that Kiswahili was a creole from Bantu tribes from Somalia, Kenya, Tanzania and Mozambique after the Zenj countries were converted into Islam and intermarried with Arab-Swahili who were found in this area.

2.3.3.4. F. Johnson says that the Arab refugees who dwelt in Lamu contacted the citizens of this Island who spoke Bantu languages; after that they created Swahili language which spread in East Africa.

2.3.3.5. B. Krumm also says the same thing, but he adds that the Shirazi were included, and they together used the language especially in trade and navigation.

2.3.3.6. Chiraghdin believes that the language created from the Kingdom of Pate was originally a Bantu language with some words from other foreign languages.

2.3.3.7. Guthrie did a scientific research for more than 20 years during which he compared about 22,000 words from 200 Bantu languages. He found that about 2,300 words were similar in different Bantu languages. From this, he found 500 words that were common in all 200

Bantu languages. He discovered that if he descended towards the South, the words were different. Moreover, he found from his study the following:

(a) Many of the words which are of Bantu origin and with vowels /a,e,i,o,u/ and even those words which had been borrowed from foreign languages: such as words from the Arabic language: fahamu (vt) "understand" or fahari (N) "grandeur" "glory".

(b) The derivation in Swahili language is the same in Bantu languages, e.g. "piga", pigo, pigana, mpigo, pigania, pigio.

(c) The classification of Nouns (Ngeli) is also found in Swahili: e.g. nyumba ya (sing.) nyumba za (pl.).

(d) Bantu languages always have open syllable structure: V, CV, CCV, ...

2.3.4. The original meanings of some Arabic words and how they change through time.

2.3.4.1. Ras:

The original meaning of the word Ras in Arabic language is "head". From this word, Arabs derived many words of various meanings, and the Swahili borrowed the word Ras to mean Cape, Promontory, Rais, etc. as follows:

SKETCH 1:

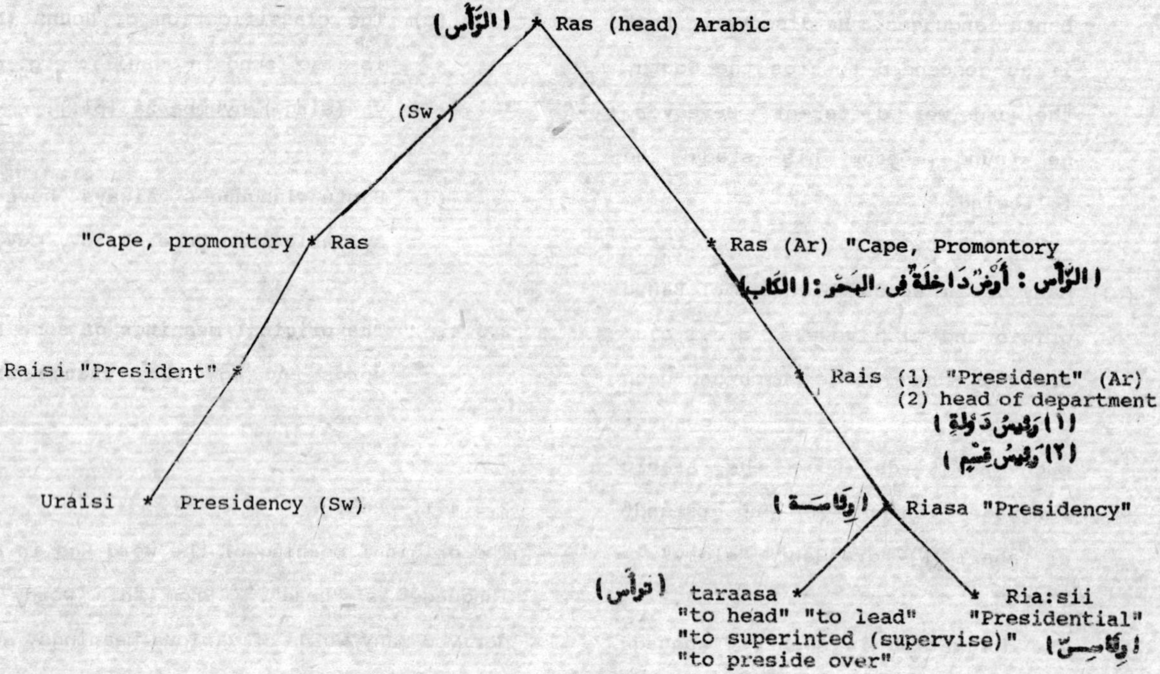
(الرَّأس) Ras (head) Arabic
(Sw.)
"Cape, promontory Ras
Raisi "President"
Uraisi Presidency (Sw)
Ras (Ar) "Cape, Promontory
(الرَّأس : أرضٌ داخلةٌ في البحرِ : الكاب)
Rais (1) "President" (Ar)
(2) head of department
(١) رئيسُ دَولةٍ
(٢) رئيسُ قِسْمٍ
(رِئاسة) Riasa "Presidency"
(ترأّس) taraasa
"to head" "to lead"
"to superinted (supervise)"
"to preside over"
Ria:sii
"Presidential"
(رِئاسِيّ)

SKETCH 2:

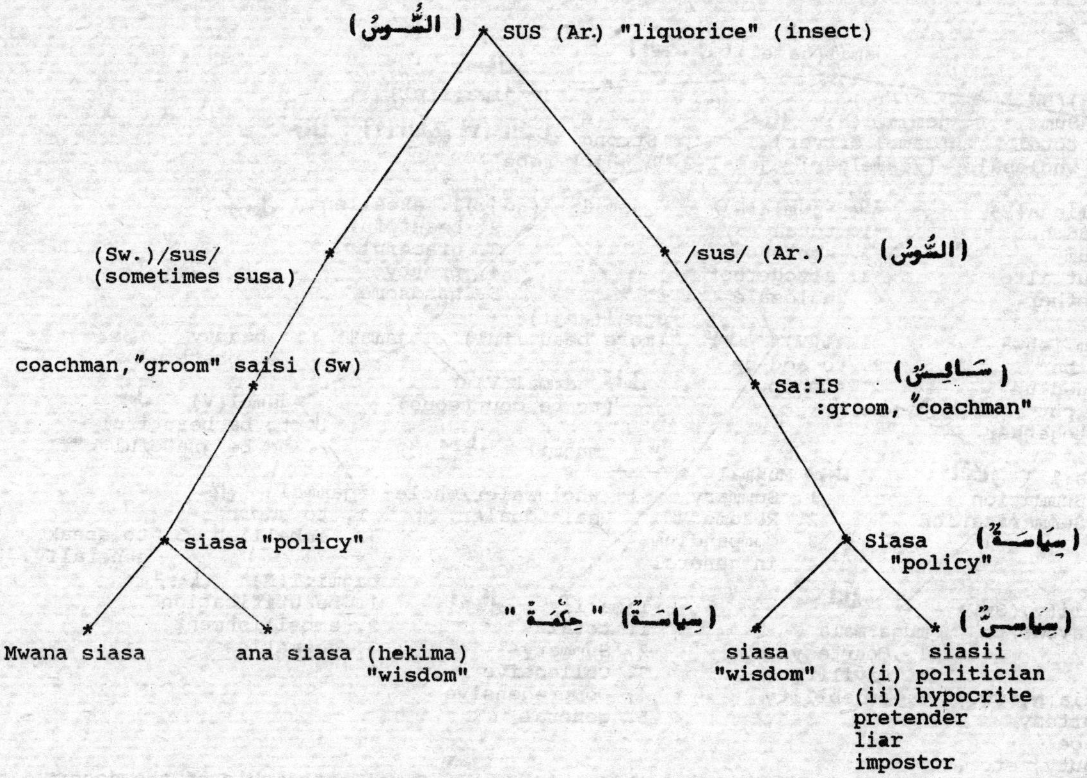

(السُّوسُ) SUS (Ar.) "liquorice" (insect)
(Sw.)/sus/
(sometimes susa)
/sus/ (Ar.) (السُّوسُ)
coachman, "groom" saisi (Sw)
Sa:IS (سَائِسٌ)
:groom, "coachman"
siasa "policy"
Siasa (سِيَاسَةٌ)
"policy"
" حِكْمَةٌ " (سِيَاسَةٌ)
(سِيَاسِيٌّ)
Mwana siasa
ana siasa (hekima)
"wisdom"
siasa
"wisdom"
siasii
(i) politician
(ii) hypocrite
pretender
liar
impostor

SKETCH 3:

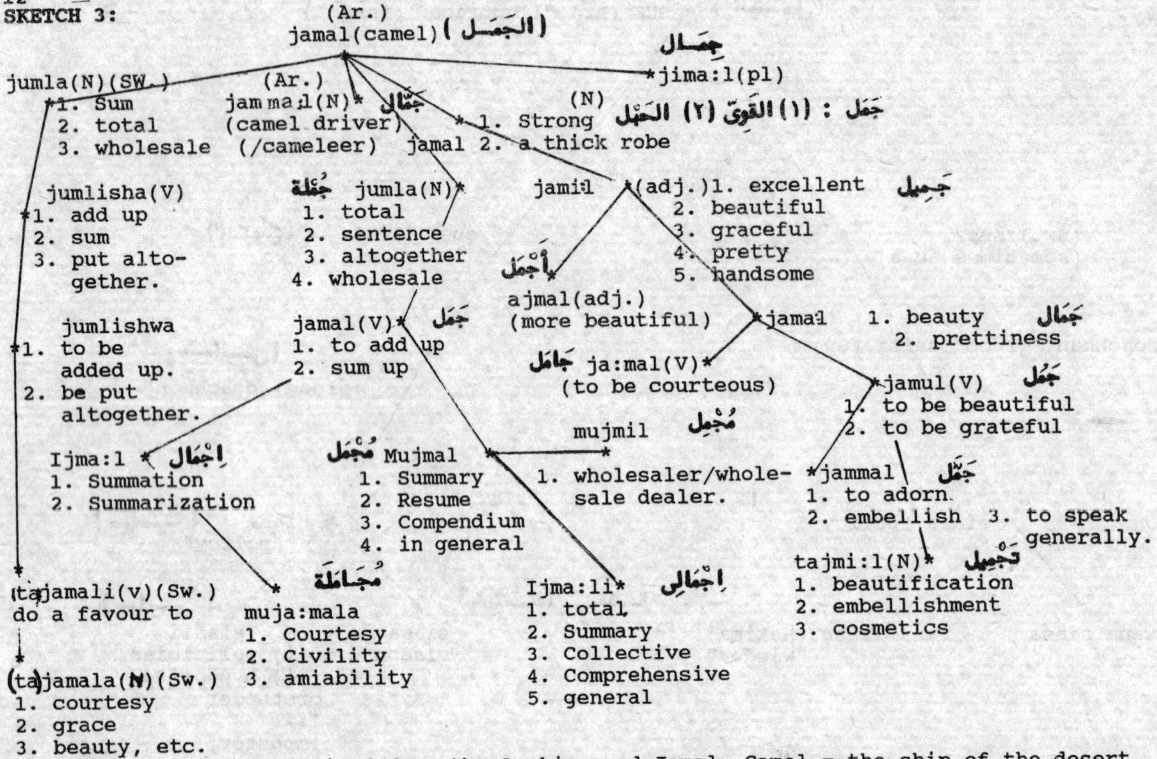

All these words were derived from the Arabic word <u>Jamal</u>, Camel = the ship of the desert.

De Hammer compiled some Arabic vocabularies which concern the word <u>Camel</u>, its synonyms and derivations. He found there are more than 5644 words. (See V. Renan, Langues Sémitiques :387)

Siasa (policy):- It has been derived as shown in the above Sketch 2: Sa: IS means, Coachman because the groom/coachman himself has many ways to deal with an unschooled horse; he can choose the best way to deal with it. From this, they derived another word, Siasa which means Policy and Siasii Politician because he (a politician) has many ways to deal with his public; but he should choose the best way to deal with it.

What is a politician nowadays?

Some people say that if a man promises and fulfils his duty, then such a man knows nothing about politics, and he will not know it in the future; but if he promises and does not fulfil his duty, then he is really a politician; as he knows how to use this word in different manners such as:-

(1) Mwanasiasa

(i) Who knows politics

(ii) Who promises but does not fulfil his duty.

(2) ana siasa (i)he who has wisdom and knows how to deal with people.

2.3.4.3. The word/Jamal/(Camel) (جَمَلٌ)

Arabic Derivations (see Sketch 3)

(1) [Jamal] means, (A thick robe)

(2) [Jumla] (i) "total"

(ii) sentence

(iii) altogether

(3) [Jamal] (v) "Strong"

(4) [Jami:l] (adj.)

(1) Excellent

(2) Beautiful

(3) Jammal/(v)

(i) to adorn, ambellish

(ii) to speak generally

(5) [Jama:l] (N) beauty.

(6) [Ja: mal] (v) to be courteous

The word camel came to Swahili as follows:

(1) Jumla: "the sum", "total", "lot", "all together", "wholesale" (adj.)

(2) Jumlisha: "add up", "Sum up", put "altogether"

(3) Jumlishwa: be added up, be put altogether.

(4) tajamala(v) to do a favour to.

(5) tajamala(n) elegane, grace, beauty, manners, behaviour, affability, propriety, decorum, kindness, complaisance and gracious. Arabs derived many words from this word because they said: "The camel is a ship of the desert" (الجَمَلُ سَفِينَةُ الصَّحْرَاءِ).

There are many words like this in Arabic language, but the following are only a few:-

(1) Dhahab (gold)(ذَهَبٌ) in

Swahili dhahabu(gold) also. From the verb dhahaba which means: to go away, depart, to send away, derives from dhahaba which means: to transfer from somebody to another by inheritence or by other means.

(2) [qima:r](قِمَار) (gamble), in (Sw.) kamari was derived from qa mar]("قَمَر" هِلال) (crescent), because somebody who gambles can lose or gain as many times as the crescent does because it also becomes bigger and returns to smaller size.

(3) [Aql] (Ar.) (عَقْل) in Swahili) akili, is originally from the robe called [Ϛiqa:l] which is used to tie the camel). Also the word akili means: to keep the human being from doing useless things.

(4) Adhama (عَظَّمَ) (Ar.), which in Swahili means: adhimisha (glorify) is originally from [adhm] (عَظْم) which means bone.

(5) mkabilishamsi (mi-) is the Swahili for mqangani which means: sunrise; and the Arabic word is [Ϛabbada ʃʃams](عبّاد الشَّمْس) The word is decomposed as: Mkabili (Sw.) meaning "to face" is from the Arabic word[muqa:bil] and [ʃams] which means sun.

2.3.5. Some Characteristics of Arabic words

2.3.5.1. If the word is not in the matrical way of Arabic words like/Ibrisim (ابْرِيسِيم) it is not an Arabic word.

2.3.5.2. No word in Arabic language has the initial consonant/n/ followed by /r/. For example, the word: [nirjis](نِرْجِس) is not an Arabic word; it is a Persian word. (Al-Rafii 1940).

2.3.5.3. If the word ends with /dz/, then it is not an Arabic word e.g.Muhandz is a Persian, so that it became <u>Muhands</u>, and from Arabic to Swahili language, it became <u>Mhandisi</u> or <u>Muhandisi</u>.

2.3.5.4. /ʤ/ (ج) and /ṣ/ (ص) are not found together in Arabic words, like: sihri:j (صِهْرِيج) meaning "tank" is originally a Persian word; or [ṣa:j] (صَاج) is also a Persian word.

2.3.5.5. /q/ (ق) or (ك) and /ʤ/(ج) never come in one word like <u>Minjiniq</u> (مَنْجَنِيق)

2.3.5.6. If the root of the word has more than three letters, one of the following letters /f,r,m,n,l,b/ must be in the root of that word, if not, then this word is not Arabic; e.g., the word [ʕasjad](عَسْجَد) which means "<u>gold</u>" is a Persian word. (f,r,m,n,l,b,= فَرَّمَنْ لُبّ).

2.3.5.7. /ʤ/ (ج) and /ṭ/ (ط) are not found together in one Arabic word e.g. [ṭaʤin] (طَاجِن)

2.3.5.8. /t/ (ت) and /ʤ/ (ج) are not found together in Arabic words like [Al-jibt] (الجِبْت)

2.3.5.9. /ṭ/ (ط) and /ṣ/ (ص) are not found together in Arabic words; like [sira:t] (الصِّراط) originally [ṣ] is [s]. <u>Sirat</u> which means "a <u>way</u> or <u>road</u> used only by Muslims when referring to the way, to heaven or hell".

2.3.5.10. It is rare to find /r/ (ر) and /l/ (ل) together in Arabic words like [kural] (كورل).

2.3.5.11. /d/ (د) and /ð/ (ذ) are rarely found together in one word like Baghdadh "(Baghdad)" (بغذاد) which is the capital of Iraq, is a Persian word.

2.3.5.12. No Arabic noun ends with the vowel /u/ except one word only: [rabu] (رَبُو), which means asthma.

2.3.5.13. There is no /ʃ/ after /l/ (ل). That means Swahili words with non-Arabic features mentioned hereabove are not Arabic in origin. They may nevertheless have been borrowed by Swahili through Arabic.

2.3.6 Arabic Script

2.3.6.1 Arabic Alphabet

ARABIC	ROMAN	PHONETIC	OLD-MOMBASA
أ	(a)	[a]	
ب	(b)	[b]	w,mb,p,mp,pw
ت	(t)	[t]	t,t,tw
ث	(th)	[θ]	
ج	(j)	[ʤ]	j, nj
ح	(ḥ)	[ħ]	
خ	(kh)	[x]	
د	(d)	[d́]	d, ɗ, nd, nɗ
ذ	(dh)	[ð]	
ر	(r)	[r]	
ز	(z)	[z]	z, nz
س	(s)	[s]	
ش	(sh)	[ʃ]	sh, ch, ch
ص	(ṣ)	[ṣ]	sw
ض	(ḍ)	[ḍ]	
ط	(ṭ)	[ṭ]	
ظ	(dḥ)	[ð̣]	
ع	(a) or (ʕ)	[ʕ] [á]	
غ	(gh)	[ɣ]	g, ng, ng'
ف	(f)	[f]	f, v, vy, fy
ق	(q)	[q]	
ك	(k)	[k]	k, kw, k', kw'
ل	(l)	[l]	
م	(m)	[m]	
ن	(n)	[n]	
ه	(h)	[h]	
و	(w)	[w]	β (bi-labial fricative)
ي ى	(y)	[j]	y, ny

2.3.6.2 The Sounds which are not found in Arabic Script

ROMAN	PROPOSED ARABIC SCRIPT
1. nd	ند
2. nj	نج
3. ny	ني
4. ng	نغ
5. ŋ	نغ
6. c	چ
7. g	غ
8. p	پ
9. v	ڤ
10. p^h	
11. K^h	
12. t^h	
13. t^h	
14. e	
15. o	

These sounds are not found in Kiswahili,

1.	[ṣ]	(ṣ)	ص
2.	[ḍ]	(ḍ)	ض
3.	[ṭ]	(ṭ)	ط
4.	[ḍ]	(ḍh)	ظ
5.	[ʕ]	(ʕ)	ع
6.	[q]	(q)	ق
7.	[ħ]	(ḥ)	ح
8.		[ð](dh)z	ذ
9.		[θ](th) -s	ث
10.		[ɣ] (gh)-g	غ
11.		(ə)-A	أ

Appear only with loanwords from Arabic but have not always been pronounced as required.

VOWELS

Swahili (Mainland)

Proposed Arabic Script

a- اَ ـَ

e- ـٖ

o- ـٗ

i- يِ ـِ

u- وُ ـُ

Swahili (Zanzibar)

a- اَ ـَ

e- ـٍ

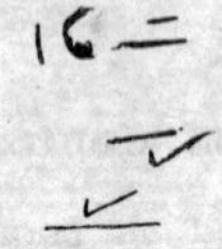

o- ـٌ

i- يِ ـِ

u- وُ ـُ

Let us see the difference in Arabic Script between the Mainland Swahili and Zanzibar Swahili: "Ndugu Waislamu nakuusieni, enyi waja wa Mwenyezi Mungu pamoja na kuiusia nafsi yangu kumcha Mwenyezi Mungu. Mwenyezi Mungu amesema katika Qurani kimbilieni kwenye maghfira yanayotoka kwa Mola wenu kwa kufanya mazuri ya kukupatieni pepo."

(i) Mainland Swahili:

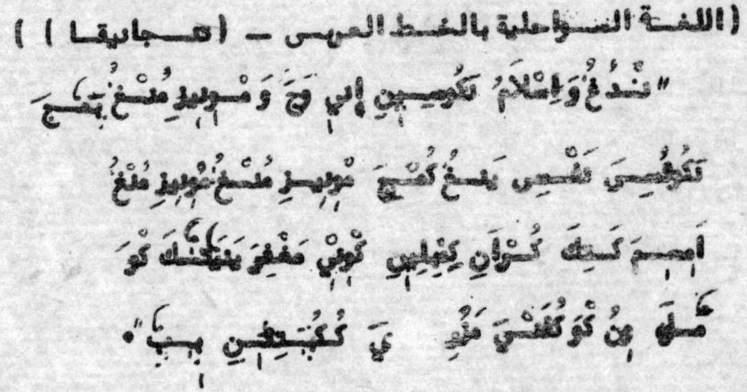

(اللغة السواحلية بالخط العربى - (افريقيا))

[illegible]

[illegible]

[illegible]

[illegible]

(2) Zanzibar Swahili:-

(اللغة السواحلية بالخط العربي — (زنجبار))

«ندغ واسلام نكوصين انى وج ومونيز منغ بموج نكنو اصي

نفس منغ كمج مونيز صنغ. مونيز منغ اميم كتك قرآن

كمبلين كيوني مففرينيت كومل ون كوكفني مزور

يكبتئن» ييب.

Notice the difference in vowels and consonants in Zanzibar Swahili; the Quranic people pronounced all the Arabic Alphabet as they are pronounced by Arabic speakers when they speak Swahili. Swahili is characterised by the fact that it was first written in Arabic script and then transliterated into Roman script by Taylor (Mohamed H. Abdul-aziz: 1979:70).

3. THEORETICAL FRAMEWORK

3.1. GENERAL:

Anttila (1972:154) observes that borrowing is one of the important factors behind changes in lexicon. There are a number of things that can be observed:

3.1.1. The Relation of borrowing to other mechanism of change e.g. In misspelling like, ila (in Kiswahili) is used to denote two different meanings:

(i) defect, blemish, drawback, disgrace, stain, blot: mtu huyu ana ila.

(ii) Conjunction: (except, unless, but) e.g. hana ila mke mmoja ("he has but one wife")

This is misspelling of the word because the Arabic word to mean defect is written (عِلّة) and that which means except is written (إلّا).

3.1.2. Loans are the easiest to observe in vocabulary from culture to culture. e.g. sakafu is "floor" in Swahili, but is "ceiling" in Arabic.

3.1.3. Often borrowing increases sychronic variation.

3.1.4. Loan words may be taken over with the foreign morphemes unchanged e.g. su:q (Ar.) while in Kiswahili it becomes soko.

3.1.5. The direction of borrowing the items occur in neighboring languages, e.g. /Saxara/ [Persian] > /sukkar/ (Ar.)>/sukari/ (Sw). This word came to Swahili through Arabic but its origin is Sarskrit.

3.1.6. Borrowing as evidence of change and

of earlier stages, is illustrated by the following example: /ʃa ṯ r/ (Ar.)> /tʃotara/ (Sw.). /ʃ/ is older than /tʃ/ like in French and English: e.g. chaise (Fr)> chair (Eng.)/ʃ>tʃ/.

3.1.7. Borrowing as evidence of cultural contact is illustrated by the following examples:

3.1.7.1. Government and social order:-

Rais, Makamu, Naibu, Waziri, Katibu, Kalamu, Kitabu, Karatasi, etc. [see appendix).

3.1.7.1. In law: sheria, hakimu, mahakama, hukumu, rufaa. mdai, mdaiwa, hatia, adhabu, haki, dhuluma, ...etc.

3.1.7.3. In Commerce:- faida, hasara, rasilimali, riba, biashara, mizani, soko, rahani, kasoro, bidhaa, hafifu, forodha, etc.

3.1.7.4. In Mathematics: nusu, robo, thumni, thuluthi, sita, saba, tisa, ishirini, thelathini, arobaini (40), hamsini (50), sitini (60), sabini (70), themanini (80), tisini (90), mia (100), elfu (1000).

3.1.7.5. In medicine: dawa, zahanati, tibu, tiba, matibabu, maradhi, homa, utibabu, afya, mauti, uhai, mahtuti etc.

3.1.7.6. In social life: akidi, talaka, hedhi, damu.

3.1.7.1. In Arts and skills: sanaa, mshairi, sanii, sanifu, jinsi, marhamu, sumu.

3.1.8. Various kinds of borrowing: are evidenced in mixed words, for example: Biashara (commerce) is formed of "bia" which means sell and "shara" which means buy.

3.1.9. Reasons for lexical borrowings are evident from the following:-

3.1.9.1. Lexical innovation in general which calls for the need:

(a)- to designate new things, concepts, places.

(b)- to show how and what language has borrowed from another (Weinreich: 1964:56) e.g. kiswahili has imported Arabic designation mostly in commerce, Religion, culture and poetry.

3.1.9.2. Morphological Change of Word - Form can easily be noticed from the relationship between the original morphological forms and the newly formed word:

e.g. in Synonyms

(a) Badili/ badilisha (v) where

Badili > badilisha (v) and

(b) ghairi/ghairisha (v) where

ghairi > ghairisha (v)

so structurally, Swahili is Bantu.

3.2. DATA ANALYSIS

In analysing our data, we shall examine: (a) the data from different areas; (b) the problem of word analysis; (c) the results of the morphological changes and (d) the percentages of loan-words in different domains.

3.2.1.   DATA FROM DIFFERENT AREAS

3.2.1.1.   Ministries and Administration

ENGLISH	SWAHILI	ARABIC (in Latin Script)	Arabic
1. Ministry of Education	Wizara ya Elimu	Wiza:ra(t) At-taali:m	وِزَارَة التَّعْلِيم
2. Ministry of Energy and Mineral	Wizara ya Nishati* na Madini	" At-ta:qa wa " At-taadi:n	" الطَّاقَـة و التَّعْدِين
3. Ministry of Finance	Wizara ya Fedha*	" Al-Maliyya(t)	" المَالِيَّة
4. Ministry of Commerce	Wizara ya Biashara*	" At-tija:ra	" التِّجَارَة
5. Ministry of Health	Wizara ya Afya*	" Aṣ-ṣiha(t)	" الصِّحَـة
6. Ministry of Justice	Wizara ya Sheria*	" Al-aḍl	" العَدْل
7. Ministry of Communication	Wizara ya Mawasiliano	" Al-muwa:ṣala:t	" المُوَاصَلَات
8. Ministry of Tourism and Natural Resource	Wizara ya Utalii* na Maliasili*	" As-siya:ḥa wa Al-Mawa:rid aṭṭa-biạya	" السِّيَاحَة و المَوَارِد الطَّبِيـعِيَّة
9. Ministry of Lands	Wizara ya Ardhi	" Al-àra:ḍi	" الأرَاضِى
10. Ministry of Social Walfare	Wizara ya Ustawi* wa Jamii	Wiza:ra(t)Al-shuū:n Al-ijtima:iya	وِزَارَة الشُّـؤُون الاجْتِمَاعِيَّة

11. Ministry of Culture	Wizara ya Utamaduni*	Wiza:ra(t) A-thaqa:fa(t)	" الثَّقَافَة
12. Ministry of Information	Wizara ya Habari*	" Al-iila:m	" الإعْلَام
13. President	Raisi	Rai:s	الرَّئِيس
14. Vice-President	Naibu /Makamu* wa Rais.	Na:ib Ar-rais	نَائِبُ الرَّئِيس
15. Minister	Waziri	Wazi:r	الوَزِير
16. Deputy Minister	Naibu waziri	Naib-wazi:r	نَائِبُ الوَزِيـر
17. Assistant	Msaidizi	Musa:id	مُسَـاعِـد
18. Secretary	Katibu	Ka:tib(Amin Assir)	كَاتِب (أَمِينُ السِّـرِّ)
19. Admiral	Amiri Jeshi	Ami:r Aljaish	القَـائِدُ الأَعْلَى للقُـوَّاتِ المُسَلَّحَةِ

The Swahili words are Arabic in Origin.

Please see the following words in the Lexical Dictionary: nishati*, fedha*, biashara*, afya*, sheria*, utalii*, maliasili*, ustawi*, utamaduni*, habari*, and makamu*

3.2.1.2. **figures: (1,2,3,4,5,6,7,8,9,0)**

(1) These figures ar Arabic in origin but the figures which are used nowadays in Arabic script are Indian: (1), <, or (٢), ٢ or (٣), ٤, ٥, ٦, ٧, ٨, ٩, ٠

(2) Numerals: sita, saba, tisa, ishirini, thelathini, arobaini, hamsini, sitini, sabini, themanini, tisini, mia, elfu are words of Arabic origin, otherwise: moja(1), mbili(2), tatu(3), nne(4), tano(5), nane(8) and kumi(10) .... are of Bantu origin.

3.2.1.3. <u>Medicine</u>: dawa, afya, siha, matibabu, bakalhadi, tibu, (v) jeruhi, jeraha, shashi, vidudu, etc. are words of Arabic origin.

3.2.1.4. <u>Religion</u>:- dini, sheikh, sadaka, dua, sala, Ijumaa, kafara, and mwenye + ezi (عز) + Mungu which is composed of (Sw. word) + (Ar. word) + (Sw. word, wakati, mimbari, (pulpit) Mwalimu, nikahi, talaka, kasisi, kanisa, Askofu, thawabu, mirathi, Kurani, Imani, dhuluma, haki, hayati, adhabu, shetani, ... etc. are words of Arabic origin.

3.2.1.5. <u>Domestic Animals</u>: like: farasi, bata, tausi, are words of Arabic origin.

3.2.1.6. <u>Plants</u>; such as: figili, bamia, biringani, are Arabic words.

3.2.1.7. Parts of the body, such as: dhakari zubu, damu, are words of Arabic origin.

3.2.1.8. <u>Technical words</u>; such as:

lla (aberration), sifuri halisi, (absolute zero), thamani halisi (absolute value,) dhahania (abstract) aljebra (algebra) kiziada (accessory), ukabilihali (acclimatization), mrekebisho, (accommodation) are words of Arabic origin. (Ohly: 1987:1)

3.3. PROBLEMS OF WORD ANALYSIS

There are two domains in which problems of word analysis occur:

3.3.1. Confusion in poetry and proverbs; such as the use of:

(a) wa in Arabic which means "and" (وَ) and

(b) la in Arabic which means "no" (لاَ) while the compound word formed by the two words wala (وَلاَ) simply means and not.

In Kiswahili wa is a preposition in statements like: Mtoto wa which means the son of.

3.3.2. A word may seem to contain a familiar Arabic base but it is not Arabic in origin.

e.g. (a) /sukkar/(سُكَّر) is Arabic from Persian /saxara/ whose original meaning is "grain of sand". Then it was used to mean "sugar" (cf. Annandale, p. 677, the year is not mentioned.)

(b) falsafa/ is a Swahili word from Arabic, but its real origin is Greek: Philosophos where - Philos means Loving, and sophos means wise. Therefore "A person versed in or devoted to philosophy" (Annandale year not mentioned p. 503).

3.4. RESULTS AND MORPHOLOGICAL CHANGES

Arabic has elements which are known as bases: root, or stem, prefixes, initials and suffixes. These are used in various combinations to form different words. In this research, we can see the Arabic words in Swahili derivatives, for example, from Arabic ktb we get:

3.4.1. Maktaba "library" from the root (ktb) which bears the sense katab (v) "to write"

3.4.2. Kita:b(u) from the root(kitb) "book (Sw) and (Ar)

3.4.3. Katibu "Secretary"

4.3.4. Mkataba "contract", "engagement" Muka:taba (Ar.) (مُكَاتَبَةٌ). means correspondence.

In (Sw.) u --► ϕ/N - becomes mkataba

-There are different processes in borrowing from (Ar.) to (Sw.) which occur, such as:

(a) Opposition of meaning:

e.g.(i) sakafu (Sw.) "floor" in (Ar) /saqf/ (سَقْفٌ) "ceiling"

(ii) Kuhani Swahili verb which means console, to give condolence whereas in Arabic - it means to congratulate

(b) Opposition of Number (Singular/Plural)

sometimes Swahili borrowed the word from Arabic in Plural form, for example: sahaba is plural in Arabic, but singular in Swahili.

Its plural is masahaba which means Followers of Prophet Muhammad (S. A. W)

(c) Misrepresentation:

Biashara (commerce) had been borrowed by Swahili from two Arabic words:

(i) "bia" (بَيْعٌ) which means to sell and

(ii) "shara" (شِرَاءٌ) which means to buy.

The two words put together in that order form the word biashara to mean commerce.

(d) Assimilation:

(i) Prefix assimilation MU --▸ m-

e.g. Musaid (Arabic) becomes msaid; and by the suffixation of - izi to the same word msaid bears the word msaidizi to mean in both languages "assistant".

(e) Dissimilation is evidenced in the following example: samli(Sw.), but samn(Ar.) (سَمْنٌ)

Where: n > 1

Also, you can find this case in Arabic language itself: e.g. ʕu nwan (عُنْوَان) which means "address" is sometimes pronounced by some people as ʕulwan(عُلْوَان) in standard Arabic, where again: n > 1

3.5. PERCENTAGES:

It is very difficult to get the exact percentages of loan words in a language because of the analytical procedures involved in getting them. Percentages are therefore only approximate:

e.g. in English, more than 80% are loanwords because of the chain of the origin of the borrowed word. D. Ayers(1986: 196) states:

"...If we consider loanword in this sense, then more than eighty percent of the English language consists of loan words." And in Kiswahili according to the BAKITA records, the words in different areas have enabled us to calculate the following percentages:

Commerce and Economics	.....72.17%
Commerce and Economics(Ar. sing)	...35%
Poetry (Arabic Single)	.....70%
Agronomy and Animal husbandry	.....14%
National assembly/Parliament	......55%
Mathematics	......44%
Mathematics (in another book from BAKITA)	.......49%
Library and Bindery	.......61%
Post Office	.........56%
Geography	.........37%
Language Science	.......61%
Language Vocabulary	........22%
Education Research and Evaluation	...63%
Administration/Management	........56%
Agricultural Engineering	.......16%
Punctuation Marks	....50%
Psychology	....53%
Plant, Animals Diseases and Pest	....20%

Motor Mechanics 15%

Photography 17%

Physics 51%

Ministries, Institutions, Departments

Post, etc. 58%

This data gives us an average of ..44.3% of all the Swahili words whose origin is Arabic.

4.0 CONCLUSION

4.1 LANGUAGE IN CONTACT:

There is nc doubt that Swahili has been influenced by Arabic language to some extent. As Polome(1967:13) states: "The influence of English with the new institutions and products of civilization brought in by the British, has considerably enlarged the vocabulary, stuffing it with innumerable loans, but Swahili remains as it did when it was similary exposed to over whelming Arabic influence, strictly a Bantu Language in its structure." We find that Swahili has been influenced more in the commercial area because of the contact between Arabs and Swahilis since the First Century A.D. In the administration and in Religion most of the words are Arabic in origin because the Islamic Religion and Administration dominated in the coasts of East Africa for a long time.

4.2. OBJECTIONS TO THE CONTENTION THAT KISWAHILI IS AN ARABIC LANGUAGE:-

As we said in the introduction, some people postulate that the Swahili language is a Bantu language, while others "regard it as an Arabic pidgin". (Fuller: 1967). Although some Swahili speakers say that Kiswahili is from the Arabic language because of the origin of the name "Swahili" and because there are a lot of "Arabic words" in Swahili language, I don't agree with that idea. From the little investigation which I did, we can see that the Swahili language is not an Arabic language, because of the following reasons:-

4.2.1. I can't take a "name" and say that this name originally belongs to "that thing because of the "name". The following examples refute the argument:

(a) "<u>Phillippines</u>" derived from Philip (II) (1527 - 1598) the king of Spain, but the people living in the Phillipines aren't Spanish.

(b) The name "<u>Africa</u>" was derived from a Tunisian tribe called Africa. When the Europeans touched the continent of Africa for the first time in the north,they found this tribe "Africa' living in what is today Tunisia. They thought that there were no other tribes in Africa except this tribe -"Africa" - and for this reason they called the whole continent <u>Africa</u>. We can't say that all the continent of Africa belongs to this tribe alone because of the name. Nowadays, the name has completely changed its original meaning; when we say <u>Africa</u> it means "<u>the black people</u> while the tribe itself is not black!

4.2.2. The second reason is the structure of the Swahili language itself; it is different from the Arabic language. It has the structure of Bantu languages in general, inspite of the many words borrowed from the Arabic language. For example: <u>Kiswahili</u>: Taifa(nation) --▸ Taifisha (to nationalize, to cause to be a national property) --▸ Taifishwa to be nationalized). But the Arabic language's structure has quite a different process by which it arrives at these verbial concepts from the noun "taifa" which means "nation" in both languages.

4.2.3. Almost in every language, you find the names of the parts of the human body from the vernacular language. In Swahili, the parts of the body of a human being are taken from the Bantu languages, except dhakari, zubu, (both are taboo words) and damu which means blood.

4.2.4. Sometimes you find that the name is taken from a complete Swahili sentence. e.g. "Mgeni haji" is the name of a village in Zanzibar which means "foreigner does not come". Why does the name derive from a complete sentence. So, what is the relationship between the "name" of this village and "mgeni" (foreigner) in this case?

4.2.5. Sometimes the name is chosen wrongly e.g. the name "malaria" is originally an Italian word which apperred in the 18th century. It means bad air, and after that it entered into the French language as it is, and also into English in the 1900s and, into many other languages there after. But later on, it was discovered that there is no scientific relationship between the name and the disease itself. They thought that the disease was caused by bad air; but really, it is caused by a virus which is spread by mosquitoes called anopheles. And so, the name "Swahili" has nothing to do with the idea that "Swahili language" is Arabic by nature.

4.2.6. English words were taken from either French or Latin. If the word ends with -ion or begins with Pre-, these words are mostly of French origin. However, we know that French belongs to either Romance or Italic group while English belongs to Germanic group. Therefore, we can't say that English is a French pidgin or French simply because the English language has borrowed many words from the French language.

5.2.7 People also can develop the name: e.g. Libya was developed from the Berber tribe called Lwata. It was developed as follow:-

Lebu --▸ Libya --▸ Lebata --▸ Levata ---▸ Lvata --▸ Lwata (the tribe):-

We observe that changes from plosive voiced [b] > fricative voiced [v] > semi-vowel [w]. So the name can be changed or disappear to suit the local language. And so, "Sahil" (Ar.) was modified to "Kiswahili" by Swahilis to mean the name of their language.

4.2.8. According to the Daily News TZ 21.8.88

According to the Oxford English

Dictionary, the English language has borrowed many words from other languages (about 425,000 words). For a language to borrow from another language does not matter, but how to use the loanword in the new language structure is what matters. His excellency, the President of the United Republic of Tanzania Ally Hassan Mwinyi (at that time Chairman of the Swahili National Council) said: "Kuna ushahidi kuwa maneno mengi ya Kiingereza yameazimwa kutoka lugha ya Kifaransa na Kilatini wakati Uingereza ilipotawaliwa na dola hizo; hali kadhalika nchi za Ulaya ya Mashariki zimeazimwa maneno mengi ya Lugha za Kilatini na Kiarabu kutokana na utawala wa Warumi na vita vya kidini kati ya Wakiristo na Waislamu" (BAKITA):Toleo la 32, April 1977.)

"More than eighty percent (80%) of the English language consist of loan words" (AYERS 1987:196). But is English Latin or French? No, it remains to be English up to date and continues to borrow from other languages.

4.2.9. The word Swahili itself had a metaphorical meaning when it entered into Swahili language. The Arabs used it to mean "The Black People". Why didn't they use this word in the coasts of America, India, China, etc? Let us see this word itself in the Standard Swahili Dictionary

(Kamusi ya Kiswahili Sanifu): From the word Swahili we get a "Mswahili" which means:

(a) The person whose mother tongue is Kiswahili language.

(b) The Person who dwells on the East African coast.

(c) A sly, a smart, a deceitful, a clever person in a cunning way.

4.2.10. The word "Swahili" is not standard Arabic because, if something is pertaining to something else, you should return it to its singular form according to Arabic forms. For example, "sawahil" (pl) (سَوَاحِل), you should say "Sahily" (سَاحِلِيّ) (sing.), but not "sawahily" (pl.) From "sahil" (sing.), the plural form in Arabic is "sahiliyyun", (سَاحِلِيُّونَ) but not "sawahil:yyun" (سَوَاحِلِيُّون) according to the standard Arabic Rules. In this case, it may be exceptional because it is a proper name and not an adjective.

From these points, I agree with Minnebusch B. 1976, Nurse and Spear 1985 who say: "According to our analysis, the original Kiswahili language in its vernacular form as a descendant of the Sabaki complex probably spoken in or around the Lamu archipelago. ...... acquaired substantial neologisms from Arabic and other languages "in their new robes".

4.2.11. Our research has revealed that the Swahili Language contains 44.3% of its words to day whose origin is Arabic. Nevertheless, this proportion, and even if it were more than the 44.3% does not mean at all that the Swahili Language is an Arabic language, or an Arabic dialect, or an Arabic pidgin. It remains, and will remain, on its own merit as a linguistic tool for communication, a <u>Bantu Language</u> spoken in the dominantly Bantu zones, South of the Sahara.

BIBLIOGRAPHY

1. Abdulaziz, M.H. Muyaka 19th Century Swahili, Popular Poetry, Nairobi Literature Bureau(1979).

2. Abdul-Noor, J. and Idriss, S. Al-Manhal (Francais - Arabe Dictionnaire) Beirut. (1977).

3. Al-Halugy, M. A Concise Dictionary of Swahili-Arabic and Arabic - Swahili (1987) Cairo.

4. Annandale, C. The Concise English Dictionary (Undated) Blackie and Son Limited London.

5. Anttila, R. An Introduction to historical and Comparative Linguistics, The Macmillan Company (1972), NEW YORK.

6. Ayers, O.M. English Words From Latin and Greek Elements. The University of Arizona Press TUCSON (1986).

7. Ba'albaki, M. AL-Maurid, A Modern English-Arabic Dictionary. Dar El-llm LilMalayin, Beirut (1984).

8. Batibo: H.M. An Introduction to the Study and application of Linguistic. Dar es Salaam (1984).

9. Johnson, F. A Standard Swahili-English Dictionary, Oxford University Press, Nairobi. Dar es Salaam (1939)

10. Journals (a) Journal of the Institute of Kiswahili Research, (Vol. 46/2 September 1976) Dar es Salaam.

(b) Journal of (BAKITA) Kiswahili National Council.

11. Kessel, L.V., Utenzi wa Rasi-LGHULI Tanzania Publishing House, Dar es Salaam (1979).

12. Krumm, B. Words of Oriental Origin In Swahili, The Sheldon Press (1940).

13. News Paper: (a) Daily News
(b) Uhuru, Mzalendo, Mfanyakazi.

14. Ohly, R. Primary Technical dictionary English-Swahili IPI, Dar es Salaam (1987).

15. Polome, E.C., Swahili Language Handbook, Centre of Applied Linguistics, Washinton (U.S.A.) (1967).

16. TUKI, Kamusi ya Kiswahili Sanifu, Oxford University Press (1981).

17. Weinreich, U., Language in Contact Mouton and Co. London (1964).

Marejeo ya Kiswahili

A.Kh. Hamed, Historia ya Kiswahili Taasisi, Zanzibar (Undated)

(١) أبوبكر محمّد السجستانى :

تفسير غريب القرآن ،مكتبة الجندى (مصر) (١٩٧٠م)

(٢) الياس أنطون الياس :

قاموس الياس العصرى (عربى — انجليزى) ، دار الجيل —بيروت (١٩٨٤م)

(٣) الياس أنطون الياس :

قاموس الجيب (عربى — انجليزى) ،المطبعة العصرية بمصر (ج٠ع٠م)

(٤) أبو محمّد القاسم بن على الحريرى :

درّة الغوّاص فى أوهام الخواص ،مكتبة المثنى — بغداد ٠

(٥) أبو هلال العسكرى :

الفروق فى اللّغة ،دار الآفاق الجديدة — بيروت ٠

(٦) مجلة الوعى الإسلامى :

الكويت ، العدد ٢٣٤ (مارس ١٩٨٤م)

(٧) مصطفى صادق الرافعى :

تاريخ آداب العرب ،دار الكتاب العربى بيروت ٠

(٨) محمّد التونجى :

عبقرية العرب فى لغتهم الجميلة — طرابلس الغرب (١٩٨٢م)

TRILINGUAL DICTIONARY

Signs and Abbreviations

[ ]**	The word is taken from this language e.g. [Persian]*, like sukari is taken from Persian.
____**	means this word is not used in Standard Arabic
*	not used in Arabic or used but not in that sense.
----	used in Swahili as well as in Arabic.
adj.	adjective
adv.	adverb
Ar.	Arabic
bot.	botanical term
conj.	conjuction
Eng.	English
esp.	especially
gramm	grammatical term
Greek	Greek
Hindi	Indian(Hind, Gujerati, etc.,
interj	interjection
lat.	latin
ling	linguistics
loc.Ar.	local Arabic
math	mathematics
N	noun
orig	originally
pl.	plural
pmb.	Pemba (Zanzibar)
prep.	preposition
rel.(Rel.)	religious
Russ	Russian
sing.	singular
snkt.	sanskrit
Spa	Spanish
tec. (tech.)	technical word.

Sw. Swahili Language(Kiswahili)

Turk. Turkish

Tz. Tanzania

usu. usually

V. Verb

ZNZ Zanzibar

Double Letters

Arabic Characters	Proposed
ذّ	d̲h̲
ضّ	ḍḍ
طّ	ṭṭ
ظّ	dḥ
وّ	w̲

Arabic Signs

Tablellum of Sounds and Signs

Arabic Characters	Proposed	I.P.A.*
أ	á	ʔ
ث	th	θ
ح	ḥ	ħ
خ	kh	X
ص	Ṣ	S̨
ض	ḍ	d̨
ط	ṭ	t̨
ظ	dḥ	ð̨
ع	ạ	ʕ
غ	gh	ɣ
ق	q	q
ـع	ā	ʔ

* Please see International Phonetic Alphabet (I.P.A. (Appendix A)).

INTRODUCTION

This Dictionary focusses on the Swahili words of Arabic origin and also the words which some people thought were Arabic words but really, were not.

No doubt that the Swahili language is a Bantu Language spoken by more than 80 million people, mainly in the following countries: Tanzania, Kenya, Uganda, Burundi, Rwanda, Zaire, Comoro Isles and Mozambique. In Tanzania alone Swahili language is spoken by almost everybody and it is a national and official language.

The Swahili Language was influenced by Arabic language by borrowing words. But it has its own words like kenda(tisa), fungate(saba), tandatu(sita), mfu(maiti), etc.

For some reasons Kiswahili used and it is still using Arabic in Religion Commerce and Administration. It is not only the Swahili language which was influenced by the Arabic language but also other vernacular languages in Tanzania. For example: Haya, Zigua, Nyamwezi, Sukuma etc. were influenced by borrowing some Arabic words through the Swahili language.

From the 17th century up to the 19th century, Swahili was written using Arabic characters but Taylor changed it in the 19th century. Today Arabic characters are still used by a few people like 1st year Students of the University of Dar es Salaam (Swahili Department).

Inspite of the close relationship between the Arabic and the Swahili languages, very little scientific research work has been done in this field. So I began to collect **some Swahili words of Arabic Origin** since January 1986.

I submitted my research at the University of Dar es Salaam when I went there for study. Dr. Nchimbi who was one of my close advisors, adviced me to prepare a dictionary of Swahili-Arabic-English by expanding the vocabulary of Swahili words of Arabic origin. After thinking for a while and after assuring me of his academic help and advice, finally I accepted to undertake the work. After few months I handed to him my first attempt - which he revised and made all the corrections.

Also Dr. Sengo, gave me guidance when he had sometime to spare.

The Dictionary contains current words, but words used in poetry, terminology, and technology have been left out (except very few words. (see Appendices A,B,C, etc.).

Finally, I am very gratefull to everyone who can give me his suggestion, information and guidance in this field, concerning either existing new words or the origin of these words.

IBRAHIM. BOSHA. AHMED

Dar es Salaam

13th June, 1990

UTANGULIZI

Kamusi hii inaangalia maneno ya Kiswahili yenye asili ya Kiarabu, aidha maneno ambayo baadhi ya watu wanadhani ni ya Kiarabu/kumbe kwa hakika hayakuwa hivyo.

Kwa hakika Kiswahili ni lugha ya Kibantu inayozungumzwa na watu zaidi ya milioni themanini (80) hasa katika nchi zifuatazo: Tanzania, Kenya, Uganda Burundi, Rwanda, Zaire, Visiwa vya Ngazija na Msumbiji. Katika Tanzania peke yake lugha hii inazungumzwa na karibu kila mtu na ni lugha ya Taifa na Rasmi.

Kiswahili kimeathiriwa na lugha ya Kiarabu kwa (njia ya mkopo) lakini lugha hii ina maneno yake ya asili badala ya maneno ya Kiarabu, Kwa mfano:- kenda (tisa), fungate (saba), tandatu (sita), mfu (maiti), nakadhalika. Kwa sababu kadhaa Kiswahili kilitumia na kinatumia maneno ya Kiarabu katika Dini, Biashara, na Utawala. Si Kiswahili pekee kilichoathiriwa na lugha ya Kiarabu tu, bali hata lugha nyingine zenyeji Tanzania. Kwa mfano: Kihaya, Kizigua, Kinyamwezi, Kisukuma ... ambazo ziliathiriwa kwa mkopo wa maneno kwa njia ya Kiswahili.

Kuanzia karne ya 17 hadi karne ya 19, Kiswahili kiliandikwa kwa kutumia hati za Kiarabu lakini Taylor alibadilisha hija hiyo mnamo karne ya 19. Hivi leo hati za Kiarabu bado zinatumiwa na baadhi ya watu kwa shughuli zao mbalimbali, kama wanafunzi wa mwaka wa kwanza wa idara ya Kiswahili, Chuo Kikuu cha Dar es Salaam, hususan kwa madhumuni ya utafiti. Pia watu wa kawaida wanaozijua hati hizo huzitumia kuandikiana barua na mawasiliano mengine.

Mbali na uhusiano uliopo baina ya Kiswahili na Kiarabu, kazi ndogo sana ya utafiti wa Kisayansi umefanywa katika uwanja huu, kwa hivyo nilianza kukusanya maneno kadhaa ya Kiswahili yenye asili ya Kiarabu (kamusi ya Kiswahili-Kiarabu) tangu Januari, 1986.

Niliwasilisha utafiti wangu Chuo Kikuu cha Dar es Salaam wakati nilipokuja kusomea (Isimu). Dr. A.S. Nchimbi alikuwa mmoja wa washauri wangu wa karibu na alinishauri nitayarishe kamusi ya (Kiswahili-Kiarabu-Kiingereza) kwa kupanua msamiati wa maneno ya Kiswahili yenye asili ya Kiarabu. Baada ya kufikiri kwa muda, na kuthibitisha msaada na ushauri wake wa kitaaluma, mwishowe nilikubali kufanya kazi hii, baada ya miezi michache nilikabidhi mswada wangu ambao aliupitia na kuufanyia masahihisho ya lazima.

Pia Dr. T.S.Y. Sengo amekuwa akinisaidia kwa ushauri wa kitaaluma.

Kamusi hii ina maneno ya kisasa lakini maneno yanayotumika katika ushairi, teknolojia, sayansi, uchumi na taaluma nyinginezo yameachwa (ila machache tu taz. nyongeza A,B,C).

Mwisho nitamshukuru kila mtu ambaye ataweza kunipa mapendekezo, taarifa na mwongozo kuhusu kazi hii, ama kwa maneno mageni ama asili ya maneno hayo.

(Wasalaam)

IBRAHIM BOSHA AHMED

DAR ES SALAAM

7 JUNI, 1990

بســـــــم اللـه الرحـمن الرحـيم

الحمد للـه رب العالمين و الصلاة و السلام على أشرف المرسلين وعلى الـه و صحبه و سلم •

مـقـدمـة

يتركز هذا المعجم فى بحث الكلمات السواحلية ذات الأصول العربية ، وأيضا الكلمات العربية التى يظن البعض انها عربية وهى ليست كذلك .

لا شك بأن السواحلية من لغات البانتو يتحدث بها أكثر من ثمانين مليون نسمة فى الاقطار التى تتحدث بها على وجه الخصوص هى تنزانيا ، أوغندا ، بوروندى ، رواندا ، زائير ، جزر القمر ، و موزمبيق ، فى تنزانيا السواحلية هى اللغة التى يتحدث بها الغالبية العظمى من السكان و هى اللغة القومية و الرسمية •

إن السواحلية تأثرت كثيرا بالعربية ولكنّ لها كلماتها الاصيلة الخاصة بها ، مثال ذلك : كلمة كندا " تسعة " (9) و فلقاتى " سبعة " (7) وتنداتو "ستة" 6 و مفو "ميت" (maiti) الخ • و يعزى ذلك التأثر لاسباب تتعلق بالدين و التجارة و النظم الادارية • ليست السواحلية (الساحلية) وحدها هى التى تأثرت بالعربية ، بل هناك لغات أخرى فى تنزانيا تأثرت بالعربية عن طريق السواحلية ، وعلى سبيل المثال : لغة هايا ، زيقوا ، منامويزى ، و سكوما •

فى الفترة ما بين القرن السابع عشر و التاسع عشر كانت السواحلية تكتب بالخط العربى بيد ان تيلور هو الذى أبدل التهجئة إلى الحروف اللاتينية) فى القرن التاسع عشر ، وإلى يومنا هذا ما زال الخط العربى مستعملا عند البعض فى مختلف الاغراض مثل دراسة الخط العربى ضمن منهج السنة الاولى ـ قسم اللغة السواحلية (جامعة دار السلام) بغرض البحث و البعض الاخر يستخدمه فى كتابة الرسائل و غيرها •

بالرغم من وجود علاقة بين السواحلية و العربية إلا أن الدراسات لم تكن وافية لذا قمت بمحاولة جمع بعض الكلمات السواحلية ذات الأصول العربية (مشروع معجم سواحلى ـ عربى) ابتداءا من يناير ١٩٨٦م •

أوصلت البحث الى جامعة دار السلام عندما التحقت بها لدراسة اللغويات وكان من ضمن المشرفين الذين أشرفوا على هذا البحث الدكتور التالى سعيد عمران بجعبى الذى أشار الى بجمع و تأليف معجم (سواحلى ـ عربى ـ انجليزى) بتوسيع مفردات

السَّواحِلِيَّةِ الَّتِى لَها جُذورٌ عَرَبِيَّةٌ • فَكَّرْتُ مَلِيًا وَاسْتَعَنْتُ بِاللّٰهِ أَوَّلاً ثُمَّ بِمُساعَدَةِ الدُّكْتُورِ المَذْكُورِ شَرَعْتُ فِى كِتابَةِ هَذا المُعْجَمِ وَبَعْدَ أَشْهُرٍ قَلائِلَ قُمْتُ بِتَسْلِيمِ المُسَوَّدَةِ لِلدُّكْتُورِ الَّذِى قامَ بِمُراجَعَتِها وَتَصْحِيحِها • كَما اسْتَفَدْتُ أَيْضاً مِنْ نَصائِحِ وَتَوْجِيهاتِ الدُّكْتُورِ تِقِسْ شَعْبانَ يُوسُفَ سِينْقُو •

إِنَّ هَذا المُعْجَمَ يَحْتَوِى عَلَى الكَلِماتِ المُتَداوَلَةِ حَدِيثاً • لَكِنَّ الكَلِماتِ المُسْتَخْدَمَةَ فِى مَجالِ الشِّعْرِ وَالمُصْطَلَحاتِ التَّقْنِيَّةِ وَالعِلْمِيَّةِ وَالاِقْتِصادِيَّةِ وَغَيْرَها تُرِكَتْ (عَدا القَلِيلِ مِنْها ـ انْظُرِ المُلْحَقَ الَّذِى بِآخِرِ المُعْجَمِ) •

وَفِى الخِتامِ أَمُدُّ يَدَ الشُّكْرِ لِكُلِّ مَنْ يُساهِمُ بِاقْتِراحاتِهِ وَنَصائِحِهِ فِيما يَتَعَلَّقُ بِتَزْوِيدِى بِكَلِماتٍ جَدِيدَةٍ أَوْ أُصولِ تِلْكَ الكَلِماتِ•

" كَما قالَ الشّاعِرُ :

لِى مَطْلَبٌ مِنْ كُلِّ قارِئٍ قَرَأَ * أَنْ يَسْتُرَ العَيْبَ الَّذِى فِيها يَرَى
مِنْ خَطَأٍ فِى السَّبْكِ وَالتَّعْبِيرِ * فَكُلُّنا مَظِنَّةُ التَّقْصِيرِ
وَلَيْسَ يَخْلُو أَحَدٌ مِنْ عَيْبٍ * ثُمَّ الدُّعاءُ لِى بِظَهْرِ الغَيْبِ

هَذا وَبِاللّٰهِ التَّوْفِيق • "

ابراهيم بوشة أحمد
دار السلام
السابع من يوليو ١٩٩٠م•

أُتَانْغُلِزِ

كَامُوسِ هِىِ اِنَاغُلِيَ مَنَ يَ كِسْوَاحِلِ يَنِيْ أَصْلِ يَ كِعَرَبُ . أَيِذَا مَنَ أَمْبَايَ بَعْذِ يَ وَتُ وَذَنِ نِ يَ كِعَرَبُ كُمْبِ كُوَ هَكِكَ هَتَكُوَ هِنْغِيِ .

كُوَ هَكِكَ كِسْوَاحِلِ نِ لُغَ يَ كِبَانْتُو اِيْنَيُوزُنْغُمْزُوَ نَ وَتُ زَاىِدِ يَ مِلْيُونِ ثَمَانِينِ (٨٠) هَسَ كَتِكَ نْچِ زِفُوَتَازَ: تَنْزَانِيَا ، كِنْيَ ، أُوغَنْدَا ، بُورُنْدِ ، رْوَانْدَا زَائِيرِ ، فِسِرَا فِيَا اَنْغَازِيجَا نَ مُسُمْبِيجِى . كَتِكَ تَنْزَانِيَا بِكِ يَكِ لُغَ هِىِ اِنَزُنْغُمْزَا نَ كِرِيبُ كِلَ مْتُ نَ لُغَ يَ كَاوَيْدَ نَ رَسْمِ .

كِسْوَاحِلِ كِمِعَثِرِيوَا نَ لُغَ يَ كِعَرَبُ كُوَ اَنْجِيَ يَ مْكُبَ ، لَكِنِ لُغَ هِدَانِ مَنَ يَكِ يَ أَصْلِ بَدَلَ يَ مَنَ يَ كِعَرَبُ كُوَ مْفَنُو : كِنْدَا "تِسَى" (tisa) ، فُنْتَاتِ "سَبَ" (saba) ، تَنْدَاتُو "سِتَ" (sita) ، مْفَ "مَيِتَ" (maiti) نَ كَذَالِكَ . كُوَ سَبَبُ كَذَا كِسْوَاحِلِ كِلِتُمِى نْ كِتُمِى مَنَ يَ كِعَرَبُ كَتِكَ دِينِ ، بِعَشْرَا نَ أُتَوَلَ . مِن كِسْوَاحِلِ رِمْكِس كِلِجَعَثِرِيوَا نَ لُغَ يَ كِعَرَبُ ، مِلِ لُغَ يَكِغِرِي زَنْچِ تَنْزَانِيَا . كُوَ مْفَنَ كِهَايَا ، كِزُقُوَا ، كِنْيَمْوِزِ ، كِسُكُومَا ... أَمْبَازِ زِلِعَثِرِيوَا كُوَ مْكُبَ وَ مَنَ كُوَ نْجِىَ يَ كِسْوَاحِلِ .

كُعَنْزِيَ كَرْنِ يَ ١٧ هَدِ كَرْنِ يَ ١٩ كِسْوَاحِلِ كِلِعَنْدِكُوَ كُوَ كُتُمِىَ هَتِ زَا كِعَرَبُ لَكِنِ تَاَبُلُور اَلْعَدِلِيش هِجَ هِيَ مْعَمَ كَرْنِ يَ ١٩ . مِقِ لِيَ هَتِ زَا كِعَرَبُ بَعْدَ زِلِتُمِيوَا نَ بَكْذِ يَ وَتُ كُوَ شُغُلِ مَالِ مَالِ كَمَا وَنَغُنْزِ وَ مْوَاك وَكُوَانْدَا وَاِدَاوَ يَ كِسْوَاحِلِ (چُوُ كِكُو چَ دَارِ السَّلَام) ، هُسُوسَنْ كُوَ مَذْمُونِ يَ أُتَامِتِ . رِيَ وَتُ وَ كَوَالِدَ وَيُوَزِجُوَا هَتِ هِزِ هُزِتُمِيَ كُعَنْدِكِيَانَا بُرُوَ نَ مُوسِلِغَنْ مِنْغِنِ .

مْهَالِ نَ اُهُسِيَانَ اَلِيبَ بَيْنَ يَ كِسْوَاحِلِ وَ كِعَرَبُ كَزِنْدَاغُ سَنَ يَ أُتَامِتِ وَكِسَيَنْسِ أُمِعَنِيوُ كَتِكَ أُونْجَا هُدُكُوَ هِغِيَ يِلِعَنْزَا كُكُسَنْدِ مَنَ كَذَا يَ كِسْوَاحِلِ يِنِيْ أَصْلِ يَ كِعَرَبُ (كَامُوسِ يَ كِسْوَاحِلِ – كِعَرَبُ) تَنْغُ جَنُوَارِ ١٩٨٦ يِلِيَسِلِيشَ أُتَامِتِ وَانْغُ چُوُ كِكُو چَ دَارِ السَّلَام وَكَتِ يَلِهَكُچَ كُسَمِيَ (اِسِمُ) . دُكْتَ آ . مَ نْجِمِى

ألكو ممو و وشاور وانغ وكيب النشاور نتيرش كاموس ى كمسواحل - كعرب - كِنقرزا ا كوكبِانو مسميات و مين ى كسواحل يني أصل ى كعرب . بعْد ى كفكر كومد ن كثبتيش مسائد ن أشاور واك وكتالم ، موشو تلكبال كفني كز هد ، بعْد ى ميز مجج بلمكبذ مسود وانغ أمباو الوه يتي ن كو فنيس مسمهش ى لزم . يبي دكت ت . س . ى . سينقو أمكو أكتسائدى كو أشاور و كتالم .

كاموس هد ان مين ى كساس لكن مين يبهتميك كتك أشائر ، تكنلوجيا ، سيس ، أجم ن تالم نيقنز بمججوا (إلا مجاج ت ، تزام نيقز أ ، ب ، س .) .

موش نتمشكر كل مت أمباى أتوز كيب مهندكز ، تاريف ن مونقز كمس كز هد ، أما كومين مقن أما أصل ى مين هي .

(والسلام)

ابراهيم بوشة أحمد

دار السلام

١٩٩٠ / ٦ / ٧

Swahili word	Transcription of Arabic word	Arabic word	Arabic word in Swahili sense	Swahili usage	Arabic usage.
abasodi (N)	ḥabba sawda:	الحَبَّةُ السَّوْدَاء	____	cummin (see habasodi)	____
abiri/a (V)	ạbar (a)	عَبَرَ	____	travel, cross.	____, traverse, to ford.
abiria (N)	ạ:bir	عَابِر	____	passenger, transit.	____, traversing, fording.
ada(N)(mila,desturi)	ạ:da	عَادَة	رُسُومٌ ضَرِيبَةٌ	fee, payment, customary, <u>gift</u>.**	custom, habit, practice, ordinary.
adabu (N)	ádab	أَدَب	____	politeness, courtesy, consideration, good manner.	____, culture, refinement, social graces
adesi (N) [Persian]*	ạdas	عَدَس	____	lentils (bot.)	____
adha (N)(udha,udhia)	ádha	أَذَى	____	trouble, discomfort.	injury, harm, damage, trouble annoyance, insult.
adhabu (N)	ạdha:b	عَذَاب	____	punishment, penalty, (2) pain, torment, pursuit, persecution, suffering.	____, castigation, agony, torture.
adhama (N)	adhama(t)	عَظَمَة	____	greatness, grandeur, dignity(2), fame(3)power, authority(4), pomp, splender.	majesty, proud-haughtiness, pride arrogance.
adhana (N)	ádha:n	أَذَان	____	call to prayer of the Muezzin.	____
adhibisha (V)	adhab (a)	عَذَّبَ	____	see adhabu.	____
adhimisha (V)	adhama	عَظَّمَ	____	see adhama.	magnify, to become great, large, grand, big, grand-

Swahili word	Transcription of Arabic word	Arabic word	Arabic word in Swahili sense	Swahili usage	Arabic usage.
					iose, agonizing, to aggrandize.
adhimisho (N)	taadhi:m	تَعْظِيم	——	celebration (solemnity) ceremony.	to be magnified aggrandizement, glorification, military salute.
adhini/ia (V)	ȧdhan (a)	أَذَّنَ	——	see adhana.	——
adhiri(V)/**ia/ika/isha/iwa/iana**(V) (aziri)	azzar (a)	عَزَّر	—— لَوَّم	to find fault with, reprove, criticize, degrade, defame, slander, humiliate.	——, to censure rebuke, restrain, reprimand, to re-refuse to have anything to do with.
adhuhuri (N)	adhuhr	الظُّهْر	——	midday, noon, times of prayer.	——
adia (N) (hedaya) (zawadi)	hadia	هَدِيّة	——	gift, present.	——
adibu (V) **ia/ika/isha.**	ȧddab (a)	أَدَّب	——	teach manners to.	——
adili (N)(ma-)(haki)	ạdl	عَدْل	——	justice, morality, ethics good - conduct, life, right, righteous.	——, straighten forwardness, uprightness, equitableness, honesty.
adili (V) **ia/ika/isha/iwa/iana.**	ạdal (a)	عَدَّل (ف)	——	teach righteous conduct to.	to straighten, to act justly, to adjust to modify, abandon to be equal to.
adilifu (adj.)	ạ:dil	عَادِل	——	upright, honourable, moral rightious, impartial.	——,

Swahili word	Transcription of Arabic word	Arabic word	Arabic word in Swahili sense	Swahili usage	Arabic usage.
adimika(V)**ia/isha/ iwa**	ạdim (a) (inạdam(a)	عَدِمَ (انْعَدَمَ)	——— نَدَر	be rare, unobtainable, very scarce.	to be deprived of to be lost, cease to be reduced to poverty.
adimu (adj.)(nadra) (chache)	ạdi:m	عَدِيم	نَادِر / غَيْرُ كافٍ خَالٍ / مُجَرَّد مِنْ	rare, scarce, insufficient, inadequate.	deprived of, lifeless, moneyless, non existent.
admeri (N)	ami:ral/ bahr	أَمِيرُ البَحْر	———	admiral [Ar.]*	———
adui (N) (ma-) (chuki) (hasimu)	ạdu:	عَدُوّ	———	enemy, opponent, bad.	———
afa (N) (ma-)	ảfa(t)	أَفة	———	misfortune, disaster, accident, danger.	———, blight, plight.
afadhali(adv.)(bora)	ảfdal	أفْضَل	———	better, particularly.	———, more excellent, preferable.
afadhali (adj.)	ảfdal	أَفْضَل	أَهْوَن	rather	———
afande (N)[Turk]*(1) (or, afandi)	ảfandi	أَفَنْدِى	——— سَيِّد	Sir, Master(used only by soldiers and police.)	———
afiki (V)**ia/ika/iwa**	wa:faq (a)	وَافَقَ (يُوَافِق)	———	to agree with, fit, accord to	———, to suit, fit, adapt, reconcile, accommodate
afikiana(N) (ma-) (mwafaka)	wifa:q	وِفَاق مُوَافَقَة	———	agreement, acccordance.	———, coincidence, chance, unanimity act justly, accident.
afiuni (N) [Hindi]*	ảfyun	أَفْيُون	———	opium	———

(1) From Latin (Afthenticus)

Swahili word	Transcription of Arabic word	Arabic word	Arabic word in Swahili sense	Swahili usage	Arabic usage.
afriti (N) (mjanja) (mwovu)	Ịfri:t	عِفْرِيت	شِرِّير / خَدَّاع مَاكِر	evilgenius, wicked.	___, sly, cunning, devil, mischievous malicious.
afu (V) (N)	ạfa: (N) (yaạfu)	عَفَا (يَعْفُو)	____	save, pardon, cure, free.	____, eliminate, to excuse, forgive protect, release.
afya (N) (uzima) (siha) (nguvu)	ạfia	عَافِيَة	____ صِحَّة قُوَّة	heal, health.	____, vigor, vitality, well being.
afyuni (N) (kileo) [hindi]*	àfyu:n	أَفْيُون	____	opium.	____
aghalabu (adj) (mara nyingi) (kwa kawaida) (kwa desturi)	àghlab	أَغْلَب	غَالِبًا / عَادَةً	usually, mostly, ordinary as a rule, majority, in most cases.	____, most probably, generally, in general.
ahadi (N) (mkataba)	ạhd	عَهْد	____	promise, obligation, convenant, contract, agreement, engagement.	____,acquaintance, knowledge, fulfillment, oath, liability, compact.
ahali (N) (rare) (jamaa) (kaumu) (familia)	àhl	أَهْل	____ زَوْجَة أُسْرَة / جَمَاعَة	wife, family, relatives, folk.	____, kinsfolk, kin.
ahasante (also ahasanta)	àhsanta	أَحْسَنْتَ	شُكْرًا	thank you, very much.	to do well, well done, bravo.
ahera(N)(rel)(akhera)	al-ãkhira (t)	الآخِرَة	____	hereafter, life to come, ressurrection day.	________
ahidi (V)**ia/ika/isha iwa/iana**	ạ:had (a)	عَاهَد	____,	to promise, vow, agree.	___, pledge, charge, authorize, obligate.
ahirisha/ika (chelewesha)	àkhar (a)	أَخَّر	____	postpone, put off, delay,	____

Swahili word	Transcription of Arabic word	Arabic word	Arabic word in Swahili sense	Swahili usage	Arabic usage.
ahsante(N) (ahsanta) (shukrani)	ȧhsanta	أحسنت	شكرا	see ahasante.	____
aibisha/ika/ (fedhe-heka(V)	ạ:b (a)	عاب	____	be disgraced, dishonoured be ashamed.	____, to mock at, find a fault, dishonour.
aibu (N) (dosari) (fedheha) (izara). (adv.)	ạib	عيب	____	fault, defecty, ashame, dishonour disgraceful.	___, fault, defect, blemish, vice, physical difect, foible, imperfection, weakness.
aidha (vilevile) (kadhalika) aidha	ȧiḍa (n)	أيضا	____	more over, futher more, thereupon.	____, also, too, again, besides.
aidha[Eng.]*(N.B.)	*	*	*	either (us. used as in English).	*
aina (N) (namna) (jinsi)	ạyna (t)	عينة	____	kind, sort, class	sample, specimen.
aini/ia/ika/isha/iwa (V) (onyesha)(panga) (dhihirisha)	ạyyan (a)	عين	____	distinguish, explain, define, classify.	_____, specify, designate, individualize, determine, assign, prescribe.
ajabu (N)(ma-)(mno) (sana) (ma-)	ạjab	عجب	____	marvel, be surprised, astonished amazed, extraordinary, many.	admire, concient, vanity, astonishmemt, wonder, amazement.
ajali (N) (tukio) (kifo) (bahati) **iwa/iana**	ȧjal	أجل		fate, end of time, chance accident.	____,period, term, deadline, instant of death, date, respite.
ajili(N) (sababu)	ȧjl	[illegible]		reason, cause, for, order	____

Swahili word	Transcription of Arabic word	Arabic word	Arabic word in Swahili sense	Swahili usage	Arabic usage.
(kisa) (maana)				to, sake.	
ajiri/ia/ika/isha/ iwa/iana (V)	ajjar (a)	أجَّر	——	engage for wages, hire	____, to reward, recompense, rent, lease.
ajmaina (adv.) (poet.) (wote) (rel.) (rare)	ȧjmaị:n(a)	أجْمَعِين	——	all, the whole, every.	____, entire.
ajuza (N) (ma-) (bikizee)	ạju:z	عَجُوز	للمرأة العجوز فقط	old woman (only).	for old woman and man (aju:z).
akali (N) (adv.) (kidogo) (uchache)	àqall	أقَلّ	——	few, very little, some.	less, smaller, lower, the least
akhera (N) (rel.)	al-ākhira (t)	الآخِرَة	——	see ahera.	________
akhi (N) (yakhe)	àkh	أخْ	صَدِيق	friend, common people, rabble.	brother, friend.
akiba (N)	ạqi:b	عَقِيب	تَوْفِير / ادّخَار	supply, reserve, savings.	following next, after that.
akida (N) (ma-) (mkubwa wa jeshi)	ạqi:d	عَقِيد	قَائِدُ الجَيْش	chief, leader (a military rank)	____, (colonel)
akidi (N) (ufungaji wa ndoa) (arusi) (nikah.)	ạqd	عَقْد (زواج)	——	celebration of a wedding, marriage.	____, contraction of marriage, marriage certificate.
akiki (N)	ạqi:qa (t)	عَقِيقَة	——	ceremony of babys first hair cut, the slaughtering of a goat for the first hair cut.	______
akili (N) (fahamu) (hekima) (ujuzi) (welekevu) (busara) (maarifa) (werevu) (uwezo) (ujanja) (hila), (shauri).	ạql	عَقْل	—— ذَكَاء فَهْم / حِكمَة ذَاكِرَة •	mind, intelligence, discretion, sence, thought, trick, intellect, ability, proficiency, competence, cleverness, judgement, reason, conscious-	____, memory, sane comprehension, insight, discernment, rationality.

Swahili word	Transcription of Arabic word	Arabic word	Arabic word in Swahili sense	Swahili usage	Arabic usage.
				ness, understanding.	
akthari (N) (wingi)	àkthar	أَكْثَر	____	a lot, many, much, great quantity.	___, more frequently, most.
ala (N)	ăla(t)	آلـة	____	case, instrument, tools, sheath, scabbard.	____
alaa (adv)	Allah	اللّٰـه	كَلِمَـةُ تَعَجُّـبٍ	a word used for exclamation.	____
alama (N) (dalili) (ishara) (athari) (maksi)	ạla:ma(t)	عَـلاَمَـة	____	sign, symbol, trace, indication, mark.	____ token, emblem, badge, symptom.
Alamina (N)	alạ:lami:n (a)	العَالَمِينَ	كَلِمَةُ دُعَـاءٍ	a word used to worship God.	world,universe.
alasiri (N) (wakati) (wakati wa sala)	alạṣr	العَصْـر	____	afternoon, times of prayer (mus).	____
alfajiri (N)	alfajr	الفَجْـر	____	dawn, daybreak, times of prayer (mus.)	____
alfeni (N) (rare)	alfain	أَلْفَيْن / أَلْفَـان	____	two thousand.	____
alhaji (N)	alḥaj	الحَاجّ	____	pilgrim (to Macca).	____
alhamdu (N)	alḥamd (u)	الحَمْـدُ	سُورَة الفَاتِحَة	the first sura in Quran	"praise be to God".
alhamdulillahi (N)	Alḥamdulilahi	الحَمْـدُ لِلّٰه	____	praise be to God, thank God.	____
alhamisi (N)	alkhami:s	الخَمِيس	____	Thursday.	____
aljebra (N)	al jabr	(عِلْمُ) الجَبْر	____	branch of mathemetics in which signs and letters are used to present quantities.	____,referred to Jabir ibn Hayyan.

Swahili word	Transcription of Arabic word	Arabic word	Arabic word in Swahili sense	Swahili usage	Arabic usage.
allah (N) (Mungu)	ʾAllah	اللّٰه		God (usually in Arabic formulas.	_____
almasi (N)	almas	المَاس	____	diamond.	_____
almurad (adj.)	almurad	المُرَاد	عَلَى ذَلِكَ / تَوّاً .	then, consequently, thereupon.	desire, to wish for.
ama (conj.) (au)	ȧmma:	أَمَّا	____	either, yet, however.	____, only, but, as to, as far as.
amali (N) (kazi) (matendo) (uchawi) (sihiri)	ạmal	عَمَل	_____	act, action, behaviour, activity, work.	deeds, action, work, business.
amana (N)	ȧmana(t)	أَمَانَة	_____	pledge, vow, trust.	faithfulness, honesty, condidence, faith.
amani (N)	ȧma:n	أَمَان	____	peace, security, safety.	_____
ambari (N)	ạmbar	عَنْبَر	____	ambergris.	_____
ambia (V) (eleza) (fahamisha) (simulia) (ardhia) **lia/lika/liza/iwa/iana**	ȧmbā	أَنْبَأَ	أَخْبَرَ / رَوَى	speak, say, inform, tell.	to inform, tell, bespeak.
amin (adv) (interj.) (kiitikio cha dua) (adv.)	ãmi:n	آمِين	حَقّاً ____	amen, so be it.	______
amina (interj.) (rel.) (also amin)	ãmina	آمِين	_____	see amin.	_____
amini (V) (sadiki) (kubali) (tegemea) **ia/ika/isha/iwa/iana**	ȧmin	آمَنَ / أَمِنَ	أَمَّنَ ____	beliave, trust, have faith in, put confidence in.	to assure, reassure.

Swahili word	Transcription of Arabic word	Arabic word	Arabic word in Swahili sense	Swahili usage	Arabic usage.
amini (N)	ȧmi:n	أَمِين	——	faithful, honest, trustworthy.	——
aminifu (adj.)	ȧmi:n	—— أَمِين	صَادِق / مُخْلِص .	faithful, devoted, reliable, trustworthy, honest.	——
aminisha (v) (kabidhi)**ia/ika/wa.**	amman(a)	أَمَّن	—— سَلَّمَ	to assure, reassure, deliver, trust, to trust one with, to hand over, consign.	——
(a) **amiri** (v) (anza) **ika/isha/iwa/** (maliki).	ạmmar	عَمَّر	—— بَدَأ	begin, start, something, begin a new village.	to be inhabited, to build, to repair, to populate
(b) **amiri**(N) (ma) (kiongozi) (rare)	ȧmi:r	أَمِير	——	a chief, a leader.	——
(c) **amiri jeshi**(N)	ȧmir/jaish	أمِير/الجَيش	القَائِد العَام/ الأعَلَى .	the first commander of military, supreme commander.	——
amirika (V) (kuwa imara)	ạmmar (a)	عَمَّر	قَوِيَ / صَلُبَ	be strong, be firm, be solid, to be established firmly.	see amiri(a).
amirisha (V) (stawisha)	(from)ȧmmar(or ạmmar)	عَمَّر أوْ أمَّر	عَمَّر	see amiri(a).	——
amirisho(N)	taạmi:r	تَعْمِير	—— بِدَايَة تَشْدِيد	see amir(a).	——
amri(N) (agizo) (uwezo) (nguvu).	ȧmr.	أَمْر	—— طَلَب	order, command, directive, authority, rule, mastery, power, responsibility	——
amu(N) (biniamu) (also ami)	ạmm.	عَمٌّ	——	uncle.	——

Swahili word	Transcription of Arabic word	Arabic word	Arabic word in Swahili sense	Swahili usage	Arabic usage.
amuru (V) (toa amri) (shurutisha) (lazimisha) (agiza) (amri sha) **ia/ika/isha/ iwa/iana.**	àmar (a)	أمَـر	____	order, command, prescribe decide.	____, instruct, charge, make anemir.
anasa (N) (starehe) (furaha) (utajiri) (raha) (ridhisha) (pendeza)	Ùns/ã:nasa (V)	أُنْس / آنَس	أَنْسٌ / سَعَادَةٌ	pleasure, joy, comfort, prosperity, luxery, <u>richness.</u>	to be pleased with sociability, geniality to percieve, see to become tame.
anwani (N)	ụnwan	عُـنْوَان / عُلْوَان	____	address of a letter.	address, title, epitome ,heading, model,sign.
Arabu (N)	ạrab	العَرَب	____	Arabs.	____
arabuni (N)	al ạrabia	(البِلاد) العَرَبِية	____	The Arab countries.	____
arbaini (adj.)	ȧrbai:n	أَرْبَعِـين	____	forty days (40).	____
ardhi(N) (nchi kavu) (udongo) (dunia)	ärd	أَرْض	____ العَالَم الكُرَة الأَرْضِيَة	land, earth, ground, soil world, globe.	____
ari (N) (hima)	ạ:r	عَـار	عَـار / هِمَّة / عَـزِيمَة / غَيْرَة	shame, disgrace, dishonour(2) will succeed, win, special effort, exerted to prevent being disgraced.	Disgrace, shame.
arifu (V) (sema) (eleza) **ia/ika/isha/ iwa/iana**	(ạraf(a) ạrraf(a)	(عَرَف) عَـرَّف	____ وَضَّح أَخْبَر	state, report, inform, tell, relate, say.	to know, define, introduce.
arifu (adj.)(enye maarifa)	ạ:rif	عَـارِف	____	well.informed, educated, proficient.	____
arobaini (adj.)(also arubaini)	årbai:n	أَرْبَعِين	____ أَرْبَعُون	forty.	____

Swahili word	Transcription of Arabic word	Arabic word	Arabic word in Swahili sense	Swahili usage	Arabic usage
arusi (N) (harusi)	ụrs	عُرْس	———	wedding, get married.	———, wedding feast.
asali(N)	ạsal	عَسَل	———	honey.	———
asante (adv.)	âḥsanta	أَحْسَنْتَ	شُكْراً	thank you very much.	to do well.
asharati (adj.)(also asherati)	muạ:shara	مُعَاشَرَة	زِنَا / فُسُوق فُجُور	dissipation, adultery, immorality, fornication.	society, companionship.
ashiki(N) (ma-)	ịshq/ạ:-shiq	عِشْقٌ (عَاشِق)	عِشْقٌ	love, passionate, desire, fondness.	———
ashiria (V) (dokeza kwa dalili au alama) **aka/wa/ana**.	âshar (a)	أَشَارَ	———	signal, inform, promptly, to make a sign to.	———
asi (V) (kosa kutii amri) (pinga) (hali fu) **ia/ika/isha/iwa iana**/.	ạsa:	عَصَى	——— / عَارَضَ خَالَفَ	to be disobedient, revolt, rebel.	———
asi (N) (mwasi)	ạsi (N)	عَاصٍ	——— مُتَمَرِّدٌ	disobedient, insurgent, rebel.	———
asili (N) (mzizi) (tabia ya mtu aliyezaliwa nayo) (kitu cha awali) (msingi) (sababu) (kiganyo katika hesabu)	âṣl	أَصْل	——— أَسَاس طَبِيعَة / جِبِلَّة أَصِيل المَقَامُ (فِي الحِسَاب)	root, beggining, source, foundation, basis, nature essence, originally, in in old time, origin, ancestor, root (math) denominator.	———
asilia (adj.)(-a mwanzo) a kweli) (safi) (bora)(asili)	âsi:l	أَصِيل	——— أَصْلِيٌّ أَوَّلِيّ / حَقِيقِيّ	original, genuine, real, true.	indigenous.
asilimia (%) (N)	aṣl/(fi-mia)	أَصْل / مِائَة	فِي المِائَة	percent, percentage, (%)	———

Swahili word	Transcription of Arabic word	Arabic word	Arabic word in Swahili sense	Swahili usage	Arabic usage.
asisi (V) (anzisha) **ia/ika/isha/iwa/**.	ȧssas (a)	أَسَّسَ	———	to find, establish, appoint.	———
askari (N) (mwanajeshi) (mlinzi) [Persian]	ąskari:	عَسْكَرِى	جُنْدِى ——— حَارِس / خَفِير	sodier, military man, guard.	———
askofu (N) (ma) (rel) (kasisi mkuu)	úsquf	أُسْقُف	———	bishop.	
asli (N)	ȧșl	أَصْل	———	see asili	———
asmini (N) (also asumini)	Yasmin.	اليَاسْمِين	———	Jasmine, jessamine	———
asubuhi (N) (mwanzo wa siku)	aṣṣubḥ (U)	الصُّبْح	الصَّبَاح ———	the morning, early in the morning.	———
athari (N) (alama) (kovu) (jeruhi) (kasoro) (dosari).	ȧthar	أَثَر	———	mark, spot, blemish, scratch, wound, scar, sore, abrasion, trace, fault, defect, mistake, ommission, deficiency influence.	———
athiri (V) (tia doa au dosari) (jeruhi) (shawishi) (vutia) **ia/ika/isha/iwa/iana/**.	ȧt͟har (a)	أَثَّر	———	damage, injure, destroy, disfigure, deface, attract, fascinate, to influence.	———
audhubillahi (conj.)	ȧụdhubilahi	أَعُوذُ بِاللّٰهِ	———	God forgive, God preserve me.	———
awali (N) (mwanzo) (chanzo) (kwanza).	ȧw͟al	أَوَّل	سَابِقًا ——— أَسَاس / أَصْل	beginning, start, inception, primary, at first, in the beginning.	first.
awamu (N) (enzi)	ȧąwa:m	أَعْوَام	عَهْد / زَمَن	during, time of, epoch.	years.
aya (N) (sehemu para)	ȃya(t)	آيَة	فَقْرَة ———	verse, (esp. of the Koran) <u>section,** part,** paragragh</u>.**	____, mark, sign, miracle, marvel, wonder.

Swahili word	Transcription of Arabic word	Arabic word	Arabic word in Swahili sense	Swahili usage	Arabic usage.
azima (N) (kusudio) (dhamiri) (nia)	ạzm	عَزْم	——— قَصْد نِيَّة	intention, purpose, resolution, motive.	____, firm will, determination, decision,
azimio (N)	ạzima (t)	عَزِيمَة	———	(1)see azima(2) proposal, scheme, project, plan, motion.	fixed resolution, incantation, spell resolve, decide, to do.
			B		
baa (N) (pia balaa) (shari) (msiba)	bala:ā	بَلَاء	———	evil, disaster, disturbance, calamity, trouble, catasrophe, pestilence, epidemic, person who does trouble or damage.	_____,tribulation, visitation, misfortune, affliction, trial.
baada (adv.)(kisha) (halafu) (mbele)	Baạd (u)	بَعْد	———	after, then, after that.	_____
baadaye(adv.)(halafu)	baạdaidhin	بَعْدَئِذٍ	——— فِيمَا بَعْد بَعْدَ ذَلِك	thereafter, afterwards, afterthen, next.	_____,thereupon.
baadhi (n)(sehemu) (upande)	baạd	بَعْض	———	part, section, quantity, some, partition.	_____
baasili (n) (also (bawasiri)	bawasi:r	بَوَاسِير	———	hemorhoids, piles.	_____
baathi (V) (fufua) (rel.)	baạth (a)	بَعَث	———	upright, place, set up, revive, to raise from death.	to rend, to commision, to omit, revive, to raise from dead.
badala (adv) (also (badili)	badal	بَدَل	———	substitute, replacement, instead of.	_____

Swahili word	Transcription of Arabic word	Arabic word	Arabic word in Swahili sense	Swahili usage	Arabic usage.
badhiri (V) **-ia/isha /iwa/-**	badhar (a)	بَذَّرَ	بَدَّدَ ——	embezzle, squander.	——
badhirifu (adv)	mubadhir	مُبَذِّر	——	wasteful, extravagant.	——
badili (V) **-ia/ika/ isha/iwa**	baddal (a)	بَدَّلَ	اِسْتَبْدَلَ ——	change, exchange.	——
badilifu (adj.) (danganyifu)	badal	بَدَل	اسْتِبْدَال تَبْدِيل / تَغْيِير	exchangeable, interchangeable, inconstant, changeable, whimsical, unstable.	——
badilika (N) (ma)	tabdi:l	تَبْدِيل	——	change, alteration, variation, transformation.	——
badilisha (V) ana.	taba:dal(a	تَبَادَل	——	see badili (V).	——
badilisho (a)	taba:dul	تَبَادُل	——	see badiliko.	——
bado (adv.)(si tayari)	baad	بَعْد	مَا زَالَ / لَيْسَ بَعْد .	not yet, still, soon, presently, after a while.	——
bahaimu (N) (ma.) (mpuuzi)	bahaim(pl)	بَهَائِم	بَلِيد / بَهِيمَة	livestock, cattle, silly, stupid.	——
bahari (N) (kitu kikubwa) (mtu mwenye ujuzi na elimu)	baḥr/baḥar	بَحْرٌ	مُحِيط —— عَالِمٌ / شَيْءٌ كَبِيرٌ .	sea, ocean, vast, immesurable,erudate, learned.	——
baharia (N) (mwanamaji)	baḥḥa:r	بَحَّار	——	sailor, seamen.	——
bahati (N) (nasaba) (neema) (jaha) [persian]*	bakht	بَخْت	——	luck, fortune, success.	——

Swahili word	Transcription of Arabic word	Arabic word	Arabic word in Swahili sense	Swahili usage	Arabic usage.
bahati nasibu (N)	bakht-naṣi:b	بَخْت نَصِيب	القِمَار / المَيْسِر .	sort of gambling.	*
bahatika (V) (pata bahati) iwa	(from) bakht	(مِنْ) بَخْت	سَعَدَ	be luck, be fortunate.	*
bahatisha (V) /**ishia** /**ishika.**	bakht (root)	(مِنْ) بَخْت	أَسْعَد	trust to luch.	*
bahatisho (N) (ma-) (kisio)	bakht	بَخْت	تَخْمِين ظَنّ /مُغَامَرَة	guess work, adventurism.	___
bahili (adj.)(enye choyo) (gumu)	bakhi:l	بَخِيل	___	miser, covetous person, avarice.	___
bahimu(N)(ma-)(rare)	bahima(t)	بَهِيمَة	___	see bahaimu.	___
baina (conj.)	baina	بَيْنَ	___	between, among.	___
baini (V) (dhihirisha) (eleza) (fafanua) (jua) (tambua) (fahamu)	bayyan (a)	بَيَّنَ	___	make clear, to distinguish, to know, to understand, recognise.	to appear, to explain, elucidate, demonstrate.
bainifu (kv.)	bayyin	بَيِّن	___	clear, obvious, plain.	___, evident, patent.
baki (V) (salia) **ia/ isha/iza/-iwa**	baqia	بَقِيَ	___	remain, be left over.	___
baki(N) (ma-)	baqi(n)	بَاقٍ	___	remainder, reduce, neutral, impartial, remnant.	___
balaa (N)	bala:a	بَلَاء	___	see baa (N).	___
balehe (V) (komaa) (pevuka)	balagh	بَلَغَ	___	reach puberty, reach the fruit of bearing stage.	___
balehe (N)	bulu:gh' ba:ligh	___ بُلُوغٌ بَالِغٌ	___	the age of puberty, puber/ maturity	___, /ripe.

Swahili word	Transcription of Arabic word	Arabic word	Arabic word in Swahili sense	Swahili usage	Arabic usage.
bali (conj.)(lakini)	bal	بَلْ	____	on the contrary, however, but.	____, yet.
balia (N)	balia	بَلِيَّة	____	see baa (N)	____
bamia (N)[Persian]*	ba:mia	بَـامِيَة	____	okra	____
bandari(N)[Persian]*	bandar	بَنْدَر	____	habour, port.	____
bangi (N)[Persian]*	banqu	البَنْقُـو	____	hashish, hemp.	____ (Loc. Ar.)
bara (N) (nchi kavu) (kontinenti)	bar	بَـرّ	____	land, mainland, interior, territory, <u>continent</u>.*	____
baraka (N)	baraka (t)	بَرَكَة	____	blessing, benefaction.	____
baraza (N) (halmashauri) (mkutano) (mahakama - korti)	baraza (a)	بَرَزَ (ف)	مَجْلِس / مَحْكَمَة اجْتِمَاع / صَالَة اسْتِقْبَال .	reception, entrance hall, court, committee,council, meeting.	to emerge, come, or issue forth, be prominent, project.
baridi (N) (upole) (utulivu) (utamu)	ba:rid	بَارِد	____	cold, frost, damp, refreshment, fever quietness, calmness, delicious, <u>delightful</u>.**	____, chilliness, allevlation,catrrh.
bariki(V) (rel) (neemisha)(tosha) **ia/iwa/iana.**	ba:rak (a)	بَارَكَ (يُبَارِكُ)	____ هَنَّأَ كفى	to bless, favour, prosper (for God).	____, to congratulate.
barikia (V) **sha/wa**	ba:rak (a)	بَارَكَ	____	see bariki.	____
baruti (N)[Turk.]*	ba:ru:d	بَارُود	____	gum powder.	____
bas (conj.) (basi)	bass	بَسّ	حَسَنًا	<u>well</u>**, <u>so</u>**, <u>and then</u>**, stop, <u>ok</u>**.	enough, only.
bas(i) (N)	*	*	*	bus.	*

Swahili word	Transcription of Arabic word	Arabic word	Arabic word in Swahili sense	Swahili usage	Arabic usage.
bashasha (N)(furaha) (mchangamfu) (mcheshi)	bashasha	بَشَاشَة	———	cheerful expression smilling	———
bashiri(V) **-ia/ika/ iwa/iana**	bashar (a)	بَشَّرَ	———	to announce, predict, bring news, convey.	———, to preach.
basi (conj.)	bass	بَسّ	———	see bas.	———
bata (N) (ma-)[persian]*	baṭṭa (t)	بَطَّة	———	duck.	———
batili (V) **-ia/ika/ isha/iwa/iana.**	àbṭal(a)	أَبْطَلَ (يُبْطِلُ)	——— أَلْغَى	revoke, declare invalid, cancel, annul.	———, abolish, to cease.
batili(N)(adj.)(sio haki)(mwongo)	ba:ṭil	بَاطِل	———	invalid, worthless, deceitful.	———, falsehood, lie.
batilifu (adj.)	ba:ṭil	بَاطِل	——— / كَاذِب / خَادِع / مُنَافِق	dishonest, insincere	bad, false, vein, useless, worthless
bawaba (N)	bawaba(t)	بَوَابَة	عُكْرَة / مِفْصَلَة	hinge, (of door).	gate.
bawasiri (N) (kitundu) (tuturi) (puri) (mjiko)	bawa:sir	بَوَاسِير	———	hemorrhoids, piles.	———
bayana (N)(ushahidi) (kizibiti)(dhahiri) (uwazi wazi)	bayan	بَيَان	——— بُرْهَان اِثْبَات.	proof, confirmation, clear, plain, obvious, legible.	———, exclamation declaration, proclamation, showing.
bayani (N)	baya:n	(عِلْمُ) البَيَان	———	elocution .	———
bedawi (N) (ZNZ)(ma)	badawi:	بَدَوِيّ	———	bedouin, wanderer, nomad, outcast	———
behewa (N)	bahwu (N)	بَهْو	مَقْصُورَةٌ فِى القِطَارِ.	compartment,(or carriage) of train,go-down.	Salon, hall.
bei (N) (kiasi) (kima) (thamani)	baią	بَيْع	———	price, value, cost, sale, selling.	———, hawking.

Swahili word	Transcription of Arabic word	Arabic word	Arabic word in Swahili sense	Swahili usage	Arabic usage.
bi (N) (ufupisho wa binti)	bint	بِنْت	——	abbreviation of the word "bint", it means girl.	*
bi (prep.)	bi	بِ (حَرْفُ جَرّ)	——	by, by means of, with, in at (e.g. binafsi)	——
biashara(N) (ununuzi na uuzaji)	baiạ/shira :ā	بَيْعٌ / شِرَاء	——	baia means sell and shira :a means to buy.	trade, commerce, merchandise.
bidaa (N) (Rel.)	bidạa (t)	بِدْعَة	——	heresy, novety.	——, creation, innovation.
bidhaa (N)	biḍa:aat	بِضَاعَة	——	merchandise, goods.	——
bidhaa (N) (rasili-mali)	biḍa:ạa(t)	بِضَاعَة	—— رأسمال	capital, fund.	——
bidii (N) (jitihada) (juhudi)	ibda:ạ badi:ị	إِبْدَاعٌ / بَدِيعٌ	——	effort, exertion, delige-nce, industry.	fashioning, crea-tion, marvelous.
bikari (N)	bika:r	بِيكَار	—— فَرْجَار بَرْجَل	compass for drawing, com-pass.	——
bikira (N)	bikra(t)	بِكْرَة / بَكَارَة	—— عَذْرَاء	virgin, maidenly, some-thing untouched.	——
bikira (N) (Mariamu)	bikra	" (مريم العذراء)	—— مَرْيَم العَذْرَاء	the Virgin Ma ry.	*
bila (interj.)(pasi-po) (pasi na)	bila	بِلَا	——	without, except.	——
bilashi (adv) (bure) (sababu)	bila/shayi (n)	بِلَا شَيْء	——	for nothing, gratuitously.	——
bilisi(N)	Ibli:s	إِبْلِيس	——	devel,an evil,spirit, satan, [Ar.]*	——
binadamu (N) (mtu) (mwanadamu)	ibni Adam	اِبْن آدَم (بَنُو/ بَنِي آدَم)	——	a human, being, fellow (son of Adam).	——, son of Adam.
binafsi (N) (adv)	bi/nafsi	بِنَفْسِى	——	by myself, personally, personality.	——

Swahili word	Transcription of Arabic word	Arabic word	Arabic word in Swahili sense	Swahili usage	Arabic usage.
binamu (N) (mtoto wa ami)	ibn amm	ابْنُ عَمٍّ	___	the son of cousin.	___
binti (N)	bint	بِنْت	___ فَتَاة	daughter, girl.	___
birika (N) (ma-)	ibri:q	إبْرِيق	___	kettle, tank**, cistern, vessel of water.	___, jug, tea-pot ewer, jug.
biringani (N) (ma-) [Persian]*	badhinja:n	بَاذِنْجَان	___	egg plant.	___
bismillahi (interj.)	bismilla: hi	باسْمِ اللَّهِ (بِسْمِ اللَّهِ)	___	in the name of Allah.	___
budi (N)	budd	بُدّ	___	wayout, escape, alternative	___
bughudha (N) (masengenyo) (kero) (chuki) (uhasama) (adawa)	bughḍ	بُغْض	___ بَغْضَاء	hate, abhori in sult, slander.	___, herted.
bunduki (N) [Hind. and Persian]*	bunduqiyya (t)	بُنْدُقِيَّة	___	gun, rifle, shot-gun, musket.	___
(a) **buni** (N) (mkahawa) (mbuni)	bunn	البُنّ	___	coffee-beans, coffee.	___
(b) **buni** (V) (jenga) **ia/ika/isha/iwa/iana** (rare)	bana:	بَنَى	___	put together, arrange, constract.	___, establish, erect.
(c) **buni** (V) (tunga) (zua)	bana:	بَنَى	___ [illegible] كتب رواية [illegible]	invent, write a fiction.	___
burudi (V) (tulia) (poa)	barad)a)	بَرَدَ (تبرّد)	___ [illegible]	refresh, confort, to cool chill.	___. alleviate, to soothe.
busara (N) (akili) (hekima)	baṣa:ra(t)	بَصَارَة	___	wisdom, discornment, skill plan, sharp, withedness.	___, perception, stratage.

Swahili word	Transcription of Arabic word	Arabic word	Arabic word in Swahili sense	Swahili usage	Arabic usage.
busati (N) (ma)	bisa:ṭ	بساط	—— سجادة	carpet, rug.	——
bustani (N) (ma-)[1] [Persian]*	busta:n	بستان	——	a garden.	——
busu (V) [Persian]*	ba:s(a)	باس (يبوس)	—— قبّل	to kiss.	——,[loc.Arabic].
busu (N) [Persian]*	bawsat	بوسة / بوس	—— التقبيل	kissing.	——,[loc. Arabic].
chai (N) [Persian, Hind]*	sha:i	شاى	CH ——	tea	——
chotara (N) (ma-) (suriama)(hafukasti)	shaṭr	شطر	——	half caste, half-breed person, hybird.	half, division, part, halving, portion,...etc.
dadisi (V)	dassa/ dassasa	دسّ/ دسّس	D ——	besiege with questions, pump, spy.	——, intrique or plot to slip, foist.
daftari (N) (ma-) [Pers., orig. Gr.]*	daftar	دفتر	——	ledger, account book, catalogue, note book, exercise book.	writting book, copy book, register, day-book letter book.
dai (V) **ia/ika/iwa/ iana**	iddaạa	ادّعى	—— زعم	demand, claim, sue, to accuse of.	——
dai (N) (ma-)	daạwa:	دعوى	—— ادّعاء زعم	demand, claim, case, pretence, pretension, accusation.	——

(1) bustani; bu: means fragrance, odour. stan: is a formative indicating places or countries where something is found in multitude cf. Hindustan, Baluchi-stan; bustan therefore means a place where much more odour is found. (Krumm: p.146).

Swahili word	Transcription of Arabic word	Arabic word	Arabic word in Swahili sense	Swahili usage	Arabic usage.
(a) **daima** (adv.) (maisha) (milele)	daːima (N)	دَائِمًا	___	constantly, always, continual.	___
(a) **daima** (adj) (-a kudumu)	daːim	دَائِم	___	permanent, constant, regular, perpetual.	___
dakika (N)	daquqa (t)	دَقِـيـقَـة	___	minute, a moment, at once immediately.	
dalali (N) (ma-)	dallal	دَلَّال	___	agent, broker, auctioner.	
dalili (ishara) (alama)	daliːl	دَلِيل	___	sign, mark, token, trace, vidence, signal, indication	___, guide, proof.
damma(N)(dhumma)	ḍamma(t)	الضَّمَّة	___	the vowel point damma in Arabic script.	___
damu(N)(ukoo)(nguvu) (hedhi)	dam	دَم	___	blood, menstruate, relatives force.**	
daraja (N) (ma-) (kantari) (kidato) (cheo) (hadhi) (ugazi)	daraja (t)	دَرَجَّة	___	step, stair, staircase, bridge, degree, rank, dignity, social, station.	___
daraka (N) (ma-)	idraːk	إِذرَاك	مَسْؤُلِيَّة	an arrangement, duty, responsibilities, obligation, appointment, liability.	to make good, put right, attainment comprehension
darasa (N) (ma-) (mafunzo)	dars(un)	دَرْس	فَصْل / مَدْرَسَة	class-room, school, academy instruction.	teaching study, obliteration.
dari (N)	daːr	دَار	سَقْف / دَوْر	upper floor, ceiling, roof, upper story.	house, home, residence, country.
dawa (N) (talasim) (hirizi) (uganga)	dawaːa	دَوَاء	___	medicine, medicament, insect killer.**	___, remedy, cure
dawati (N) (ma-) (jarari) (saraka) (kisanduku) (kidatu cha wino)	dawaːt	دَوَاة	مِحْبَرَة ___ خِزَانَة المَكْتَبِ إِطَالَة للقِرَاءَةِ / دُرْج	writting-desk, writting case, drawer.	___, inkstand drawer.

Swahili word	Transcription of Arabic word	Arabic word	Arabic word in Swahili sense	Swahili usage	Arabic usage.
deni (N) (ma-)	dain	دَيْنٌ	____, عَهْدٌ	loan, adept, money obligation.	____
desturi (N) (mazoea) (ada) (kawaida) (utamaduni) [Persian]*	dustu:r	دُسْتُور	____	custom,usage, regulation, practice routine, precedent.	____
dhahabu (N) (-yenye thamani)	dhahab	ذَهَبٌ	____	gold, value.	____
dhahalia (N)(daharia	da:khlia	دَاخْلِيَّة	____	board.	____
dhahania (N)	dhihn	ذِهْنٌ	مُجَرّد	abstract.	mind, intellect
dhahiri (adj.)(adv.) (isiyo siri)	dhahir	ظَاهِر	____	evident, plain, clear, exterior.	____
dhaifu (adj.) (-enye dhoofu) (-enye unyonge)	ḍai:f	ضَعِيف	____	weak, feeble, infirm, powerless, deficient, insignificance.	____
dhakari (N)(fikara) (uume) (mboo) (jengelele)	dhakar	ذَكَر	____	penis.	the male member, male.
dhalili (N)(adj.) (unyonge)(hafifu) (hakiri)(maskini) (dhaifu)	dhali:l	ذَلِيل	____	low, humbled, humiliated poor, abject, wretched.	____, cringing
dhalilisha (V) (hakilisha)	dhallal(a)	أَذَلَّ اذلَّل ا	____	to be low, to humble, cringe.	____
dhalimu (adj.) (ma-) (enye kudhulumu) (katili) (korofi) (mwonevu)	dha:lim	ظَالِم	____	unjest, oppressive, violent, fraudulent.	____

Swahili word	Transcription of Arabic word	Arabic word	Arabic word in Swahili sense	Swahili usage	Arabic usage.
dhamana (N)	ḍama:na(t)	ضَمانَة/ضَمان	____	surety, guarantee, warrant bail.	____, responsibility.
dhambi (N) (ma-) (makosa) (uhalifu) (hatia)	dhamb	ذَنْبٌ	____ إِثْمٌ	crime, religious offence, sin, guilt.	____, to do wrong.
dhamini (V) **ia/ika/isha/iwa**	ḍamin (a) ḍamman (a)	ضَمِنَ ضَمَّنَ	____	guarantee, become surety be sponsor, give bail.	____, to inclose, to include, comprise.
dhamira (N) (kibadala) (kiwakilishi)	ḍami:r	ضَمِير	____	real intention, secret thought, mind, resolution conscience. Pronoun (gram.)	____
dhamiria (V) (kusudia) (nuia)(fikiria) **sha/wa/ana.**	aḍmar (a)	أَضْمَر	____ نَوَى قَصَدَ.	to think of, to intend.	to conceal, hide, to emaciate.
dhamma (N) (dhumma)	ḍamma (t)	الضَّمَّة	____	the vowel point damma in Arabic script (U)	____
dhana (N) (wazo) (fikiria)	dh̲ann	ظَنٌّ	____	thought, idea, notion, suspicion.	____
dhani (V) (fikiria) **ia/ika/isha/iwa/iana**	dh̲ann(a)	ظَنَّ	____	to think, be of opinion, suppose,suspect.	____
dhara (N) (ma-) (maumivu) (hasara) (haribiko)	ḍarar/ḍur/ maḍarra(t)	ضَرَر/ ضُرّ مَضَرَّة	____	hurt, harm, violence, damage, injury.	____, adversity.
dharau (V) (dhalilisha) (puuza) **ulia/ulika/ulisha/uliwa/uliana.**	izdara:	اِزْدَرَى	____ حَقَّرَ	scorn, slight, despise, insult.	____

Swahili word	Transcription of Arabic word	Arabic word	Arabic word in Swahili sense	Swahili usage	Arabic usage.
dharau (N)	izdira:ã	اِزْدِرَاء	____	scorn, contempt, insult.	____
dharuba (N) (upepo) (tufani) (kimbunga)	ḍarba (t)	ضَرْبَة	____ خَبْطَة أعَاصِير	stroke, blow, <u>rush</u>, calamity.	____, knock, shock plague, blight, sunstroke.
dharura (N) (haja) (shida)	ḍaru:ra(t)	ضَرُورَة	____, اِضْطِرَاب	commotion, sudden, unexpected happenings.	____, necessity, need, necessarily.
dhati (N) (makini) (kusudi) (nafasi ya tatu) (asili) (tabia) (hali)	dha:t	ذَات	عَزْم / قَصْد عَقْد النِّيَّة.	intention, purpose, free will, resolve.	possessor, self, same.
dhibiti (V) (linda) (tunza) **ia/ika/iwa**	ḍabaṭ (a)	ضَبَطَ	صَانَ / حَرَسَ حَمَى	guard, protect against, manage.	to control, to seize, to detain, restrain, correct.
dhidi (adj) (-enye) kinyume)	ḍidd	ضِدّ	____	adversary, against, contrary to, contradiction, opposition.	____
dhifa (N)	ḍi:fa(t) ḍiya:fa(t)	ضِيفَة ضِيَافَة	____	entertainment, hospitable reception (official only).	____, accomodation.
dhihaka (N) (mzaha) (utani) (masihara) (ufyozi)	ḍaḥik	ضَحِكٌ	سُخْرِيَّة / مِزَاح اِحْتِقَار	mockery, ridicule, scorn.	____, joke, laughing, stock, fun, jest.
dhihaki (V) (chokozi) (cheka) (fyozi) **ia/ ika/isha/iwa/iana.**	ḍaḥik (a)	ضَحِكَ	سَخِرَ / مَزَحَ اِحْتَقَر	ridicule, mock, deride, makefan of, laugh at.	____, to laugh, to laugh at.

Swahili word	Transcription of Arabic word	Arabic word	Arabic word in Swahili sense	Swahili usage	Arabic usage.
dhihiri (V) (tokeza nje) (julikana) (fahamika) **ia/ika/ isha/iwa.**	dhahar (a)	ظَهَرَ	____	make clear, show, explain	____, to appear.
dhihirisho (N) (elezo) (ufunuo)	ḍha:hir	ظَاهِر	____ بَيِّنَة	clear, evidence, explain.	____
dhiki (N) (tabu) (mashaka) (udhia) (usumbufu)	ḍi:q	ضِيق	____	narrowness, confinement, distress	____
dhiki (V) (tia mashaka na tabuni) (udhi) **ia/ika/isha/ iwa/iana.**	ḍa:q (a)	ضَاقَ/ تضَايَقَ	____	press hard on, distress, to be annoyed, to narrow.	____
dhikiri (V) (Rel.) (sabihi) **ia/ika/isha /iwa.**	dhakar (a)	ذَكَرَ	____ سَبَّحَ	mention the name of God.	____
dhikiri (N) (Rel.) (also zikr)	dhikr	ذِكْرٌ	____	mentioning the name of God.	____
dhila (N) (usu - madhila) (tabu) (unyonge).	dhilla(t)/ dhull	ذِلَّة/ذُلٌّ مَذَلَّة	____	humiliation, law state, abasement.	____
dhima (N) (madaraka) (wadhifa)	dhimma (t)	ذِمَّة	مَسْئُولِيَّة/وَظِيفَة	responsibility, employment.	security, guarantee, obligation, conscience protection.
dhoofu (V) (fifia) (kuwa dhaifu) **ia/ika /isha.**	ḍauf (a)	ضَعُفَ	____	become weak, lose strength, to grow weak.	____

Swahili word	Transcription of Arabic word	Arabic word	Arabic word in Swahili sense	Swahili usage	Arabic usage.
dhoruba (N)(dharuba)	ḍarba (t)	ضَرْبَة"	عَاصِفَة شَدِيدَة" ، رِيَاح"	see dharuba.	____
dhuluma (N) (uonevu) (ukatili)	ḍhulm	ظُلْمٌ	____	injust, oppressive, fraudulent.	____, wrong, inequity.
dhulumu (V) (onea) (tesa) (nyang'anya haki au mali) **ia/ika/isha/iwa/iana.**	ḍhalam(a)	ظَلَم	____	defraud, oppress, treat unjustly.	____
dhumma (N) (aslo dhamma)	ḍamma(t)	الضَّمَّة	____	see dhamma.	____
dhuru (V) (haribu) (hasira) **ia/ika/isha/iwa/iana.**	aḍarr(a)	أَضَرَّ	____	to harm, injure, do harm to.	____
dia (N)	diyya(t)	دِيَّة	____	to atone for a murder.	____
dibaji (N) (utangulizi) [Persian]* (kitambaa cha hariri au sufu)	di:ba:ja (t)	دِيبَاجَة	____	introduction,preface,silk	____
	di:baj	دِيبَاج	____	silk.	____
dinari (N) [Latin - dinarius]*	di:na:r	دِينَار	____	gold coin.	____
dini (N)	di:n	دِين	____	religion,creed, worship.	____, piety, godliness.
dira (N)	da:i̱ra(t)	دَائِرَة	بُوصَلَة"	mariner's compass.	circle.
dirhamu (N) [Greek]*	dirham.	دِرْهَم	____	drachma.	____

Swahili word	Transcription of Arabic word	Arabic word	Arabic word in Swahili sense	Swahili usage	Arabic usage.
diriki (V) (kutana na) (kuta) **ia/ika/ isha/wa/iana.**	àdrak(a)	أَدْرَكَ	____	be able, be in time,reach attain arrange, manage, succeed.	____, catch, continue, get, arrive, overtake.
dirisha (N) (ma-) (mwangazo)[Persian]* (1)	diri:sha(t)	دِرِيشَة	شُبَّاك صَغِير	window.	____,(local Arabic)
diwani (N) (ma-) (1) [Persian]*	diwa:n	دِيوَان	____	cauncillor, public functionary magnate, a book of poetry.	____, divan, government.
diwania(N)(rare)	"	"	مَحْكَمَة أَهْلِيَّة	anative court.	board of adviser, council.
dola (N) (ma-) (taifa) (nchi)	dawla	دَوْلَة	____	government, authorities.	____
doria (N)	dawriyya (t)	دَوْرِيَّة	____	patrol.	____
dua (N) (Rel.)	duạ:ā	دُعَاء	____	make a request to God.	____
duara (N) (mviringo)	da:i̱ra	دَائِرَة	____	circle.	____
duati(N) (ma-)	duạ:(t) (pl.)	دُعَاة (ج)	دَاعِيَة	an Islamic Preacher, propagandist.	____
dudu (N)	du:d	دُودَة	____ جُرْثُومَة / مِيكْرُوب / حَشَرَة	microbe, germ, worm, insect and all small creeping flying creatures.	worms, maggot.
dufu (N)	duff	دُفّ	____	tambourine.	____
duka (N) [Persian]*	dukka:n	دُكَّان	____, مَتْجَر	shop, stall.	____
dumu (V) **-isha**/ (endelea kuishi) (fululiza) (baki)	da:m(a)	دَامَ	____, أَدَامَ, بَقِيَ.	continue, remain, endure, abide, last.	____
duni (adj.)(hafifu)	du:n	دُون	____	inferior, low, mean, abject, worthless, base.	__

(1)diwan = di meens"devil ",and a:n"(pl.)"of"devil"(in Persian Lanquage)

Swahili word	Transcription of Arabic word	Arabic word	Arabic word in Swahili sense	Swahili usage	Arabic usage.
dunia (N) (maisha) (ulimwengu)	dunya	دُنْيَا	—— العَالَم	world, universe, earth.	——
duri (N)	durra(r)	دُرَّة	——	pearl.	——
duru (V)	da:r(a)	دَارَ	——	surround, be round, go round.	——
durusu (V) (ZNZ)	daras(a)	درس	ذَاكِر / رَاجَعَ الدُّرُوس	to review.	to study, to learn.
eda (N)	ịdda(t)	E عِدَّة	——	time of customary ceremonial mourning or seclution from company of woman after a death or divorce.	——
edashara (N) (kumi na moja)	aḥdaashar	أَحَدَ عَشَرَ	——	(11) eleven, <u>eleventh</u>**.	——
elfu (N)	ạlf	أَلْف	——	a thousand (1000).	——
elimisha (V) (fundisha)	ạllam (a)	عَلَّم	—— دَرَّس	teach, educate, instruct impart knowledge to.	——
elimu (N)	ịlm	عِلْم		knowledge, wisdom, education.	——
enzi (N) (also ezi)	ịzz	عِزّ	——	power, might, dominion, rule.	——
esha (V) (Rel)	ịsha:ā	العِشَاء	——	time of prayer (for Muslims).	——

Swahili word	Transcription of Arabic word	Arabic word	Arabic word in Swahili sense	Swahili usage	Arabic usage.
Fa (V) (toka roho) (fariki)	wafa:(t) (tawa.ff.a:)	وَفَى / وَفَاة تَـوَفَّى	____	die, perish, cease to live, lose strength, come to an end.	____
fadhaa (N)	fazaạ	فَزَعٌ	____	dismay, confusion, perplexity, trouble, disquiet,bustle, agitation.	____, terror, fear, alarm.
fadhaika (V) **isha/**	faziạ	فَزِعَ	____	be troubled, disturbed, confused, to be frightened or terrified.	____, scare, startle.
fadhila (N)	faḍi:la(t)	فَضِيلَة	____	virtue, moral exellent advantage, kindness.	____,
fadhili (V) (kufanya hisani) **ia/ika/isha iwa/iana.**	faḍḍal(a)	فَضّل	____ أَكْرَم	to favour, do a kindness.	____
fadhili (N)(adj.) (wema)(ukarimu) (hisani) (shukurani) (zaidi ya) (bora) (kuliko)	fadl àfḍal ifḍa:l	فَضْل أفضَل / إِفْضَال	— إِحْسَانٌ	favour, kindness, benefit privilege, rather, better than.	____
fahali (N) (ma-) (ng'ombe dume) (mtu shujaa) (hodari)	faḥl	فَحْلٌ	____ شُجَاعٌ	bull, brave man.	____
fahamivu(adj.)(-enye akili) (-elevu)	fa:him	فَاهِـم	____	intelligent, acute, sagacious.	____
fahamu (V) (tambua) (maizi) (kuwa na tahadhari) (angalia) **ia/ika/isha/iwa/iana**	fahim(a)	فَهِـمَ	____, عَـرَف مَـيَّزَ	know, percieve,understand.	____

Swahili word	Transcription of Arabic word	Arabic word	Arabic word in Swahili sense	Swahili usage	Arabic usage.
fahamu (N) (akili)	fahm	فَهْم	ذَكَاء	mind, intellect.	____
faharasa (N)	fihris	فِهْرِس	____	index, table of contents.	____
fahari (N) (utukufu) (ukuu) (madaha) (makuu)	fakhr	فَخْر	____, تَفَاخُر تَبَاهٍ / مَظَمَة إِجْلَال	granduer, pomp, sublimity pride, display, show, ostentation.	____
faida (N) (manufaa) (nafuu) (neema)	fa:ida	فَائِدَة	____	profit, gain, advantage interest, benefit, good.	____
faidi (V) **ia/ika/ isha/iwa/iana.**	ȧfa:d(a)	أَفَادَ	____	benefit, get profit, prosper.	____
fakiri (N)(adj)(ma-) (masikini kabisa) (mhitaji) (mkata)	faqi:r	فَقِير	____	poor, needy.	____
falsafa (N) (elimu ya asili) (busara) (hekima) [mwendo wa maisha wa binadamu)[Greek]*	falsafa(t)	فَلْسَفَة	____	philosoghy. [Greek]*philosophia-philos, love, and sophia, wisdom.	____
fani (N) (kadiri) (stahili) (kiwango) (kiasi)	fann	فَنّ	____	valuable, prosperous, ant fitting, worthy, favorable, successful	____, variety, kind, science.
fanusi (N) (kandili) (taa ya mkono)(rare)	fanu:s	فَانُوس	____	lamp, lantern.	____ [Hindu]*
faradhi (N) (wajibu) (sharti) (lazima)	farḍ	فَرْضٌ	____	obligation, duty, a matter of neccessity.	____, supposition, ordinance.
faragha (N) (siri) (upweke) (wakati) (nafasi) (wasaa)	fara:gh	فَرَاغٌ	____ سِرٌّ اِنْفِرَادٌ	privacy, seclusion, secrecy, leisure, retirement.	emptiness, leisure time, vacation, vold, sparetime.
faraja (N) (utulizo) (raha) (furaha)	faraj	فَرَج	____	comfort, relief, cessation of pain, ease, consolation.	____, pleasure, happy ending.

Swahili word	Transcription of Arabic word	Arabic word	Arabic word in Swahili sense	Swahili usage	Arabic usage.
farakana (V) (tofautiana) (hitilafiana)	farraq(a)	فَرَّق	قَسَّم ——	be separated, be estranged.	____, to distribute, to frighten.
farakano (N) (ma-) (tofauti) (hitilafu)	furqa:n	فُرْقَان	تَقْسِيم / تَفْرِيق	separation, dividing off.	____, proof.
farasi (N)	faras	فَرَسٌ	____	horse.	____
faridhi (V) (lazimika) (shurutisha) **ia/ika/ish/iwa/iana.**	faraḍ(a)	فَرَضَ	____	to suppose, persume, to enact.	____, to appoint. to impose, decree enjoin.
fariji (V) (burudisha) (tuliza) **ia/ika /isha/iwa/iana.**	farraj(a)	فَرَّج	سَلَّى —— وَاسَى •	comfort, console, relieve, ease, bless.	___, to show, release, to separate
fariki (V) (kufa) (ondoka) (tenga) (acha) **ia/ika/isha/ iwa/iana.**	fa:raq(a)	فَارَق/فَرَّقَ	مَاتَ ——	die, decease, depart, <u>escape</u> **, divorse, leave.	____, part, separate, scatter, discriminate, divide.
fasaha (N) (also fasihi)	faṣa:ḥa(t)	فَصَاحَة	فَصِيح , ____	correct, pure, elegant, lucid.	eloquence, fluency purity of the language.
fasihi (adj.) (-enye lugha safi)	faṣi:ḥ	فَصِيح	____	see fasaha.	____
fasikhi (N)	fa:siq	فَاسِق	____	see fasiki.	____
fasiki (N) (ma-) (mzinifu) (mpotovu) (mwasherati)	fa:siq	فَاسِق	فَاجِر , ____	immoral, dissolute, impious, adulterer.	____, sinful.
(a)**fasili** (V) (eleza kwa urefu) **ia/ika/ isha/iwa/iana.**	faṣṣal(a)	فَصَّل	بَيَّنَ , ___	to make clear.	____
(b)**fasili** (V)(gawa maandiko kwa mafunguo) (rare)	faṣṣal(a)	فَصَّلَ	قَطَعَ (المَلَابِس)	cut, tailor(clothes), to divide into parts.	____

Swahili word	Transcription of Arabic word	Arabic word	Arabic word in Swahili sense	Swahili usage	Arabic usage.
(c) **fasili** (N) (ling.)	faṣl	فَصْل	تَعْرِيف / تَحْدِيد	definition of terms.	separation, class, section, part, chapter, final dicision.
(d) **fasili** (N)	faṣi:l	فَصِيل	____	shoot, sprout, descendant.	____
fasiri (V) (fafanua) **ia/ika/isha/iwa/iana**	fassar(a)	فَسَّر	____	explain, interpret, translate**.	____, expound, explicate.
fasiri (N) (tafsiri)	tafsi:r	تَفْسِير	____, تَرْجَمَة	explanation, exposition, interpretation, translation.**	____, elucidation.
fatiha (N) (Rel.) (Alhamdu)	Alfa:tiha (t)	الفَاتِحَة	____, الدُّعَاء	"opener", first sura in Koran, to require to God.	____
fatuwa (N) (Rel.) (also fatwa)	fatwa:	فَتْوَى	____	legal decision or opinion	____
fauka (N) (juu ya) (zaidi ya)	fauq(a)	فَوْقَ	____ عَلَاوَةً عَلَى	up, above.	____
fawidhi (V) **ia/ika/isha/iwa**	fawad(a)	فَوَّضَ	____	to authorise, to commit to, to discuss matter with.	____
fazaa (N) (hangaika) (wasiwasi) (fadhaa)	fazaạ	فَزَعٌ	____	difficulty, excitement, confusion	____
fazaika (V) (kosa makini) isha	faziạ(a)	فَزِعَ	____	be confused, terrified, to frighten.	____
fedha (N)	fiḍḍa (t)	فِضَّة	____ نُقُودٌ	silver, money, currency, coin.	____

Swahili word	Transcription of Arabic word	Arabic word	Arabic word in Swahili sense	Swahili usage	Arabic usage.
fedheha (N) (aibu) (soni) (haya)	faḍi:ḥa(t)	فَضِيحَة	___	disgrace, share, insult, scandal.	___
fedhehe (V) (aibisha) (tweza) **ea/eka/esha ewa/eana.**	faḍaḥ(a)	فَضَح	___	put someone to shame, disgrace, dishonor.	___
ferdausi (N) [Persian]*(pepo)	Firdaus	فِرْدَوْس	___	Paradise.	___
fetwa (N)	fatwa	فَتْوَى	___ حُكْم/رَأْيٌ	see fatuwa.	___
fetwa (V)	ȧfta:	أَفْتَى	___	to make legal decision or opinion.	___
fidia (V)	fada:	فَدَى	___	redeem, ransom, put up-bail, paya ransom, post bail.	___
fidia (N)	fidya	فِدْيَة	___	ransom, fine, redemption, consontion, compensation.	___
figili (N)	fujl	فُجْلٌ / فِجْلٌ	___	radish.	___
fikira (N) (mawazo) (maoni) (wasiwasi)	fikra (t)	فِكْرَةٌ	___	thought, idea, sudden, consideration	___
fikiri (V) (also tafakari) (dhani) **ia/ika/isha/iwa/iana.**	fakkar(a)	فَكَّرَ	___	to consider, think, reflect, examine, ponder,	___
fikra (N) (fikira)	fikra (t)	فِكْرَةٌ	___	see fikira.	___
filisi (V) **ia/ika/isha/iwa/iana.**	ȧflas(a) fallas(a)	أَفْلَسَ / فَلَّس	___	to declare bankrupt, make the highest bid, win all the money.	___
firauni (N)	firạun	فِرْعَوْن	___	pharaoh.	___

Swahili word	Transcription of Arabic word	Arabic word	Arabic word in Swahili sense	Swahili usage	Arabic usage.
firdausi (N) (also ferdausi)	firdaus	فِـرْدَوس	____	see ferdausi.	____
(a)**fisadi** (N) (ma-) (mpotevu)(mharibifu)	fa:sid	فَـاسِـد	____	corrupter, immoral person, seducer/libertine, spoilt.	____, rotten invalid, void, depraved.
(b)**fisadi**(N) (fitina) (ugonvi) (uharibifu)	fasa:d	فَسَـاد	____	corruption, depravity.	____, decomposition, invalidity.
fisidi (V) (fanya ugonvi) (fitini) **ia/ika/isha/iwa/iana**	fasad(a)	فَـسَدَ / أفْسَد	____	destroy, ruin, corrupt, rape.	____
fitina (N) (uadui) (chuki) (uchongezi)	fitna (t)	فِتْـنَة	____	discord, strife, intrigue, slander hatred, enmity.	____
fitini (V) (tia fitina) **ia/ika/isha/iana.**	fatan(a)	فَـتَن	____	discord, to slander one with, agitate do damage.	____
fitiri (N) (aslo fitri)	ifṭa:r	اِفْـطَار/ فِـطْر	____	evening meal after a day's fasting.	____
forodha (N) (ushuru) (bandari) (diko) (kikwezo)	farḍ	فَـرْضٌ	جَمَارِك (جُمْرُك)	custom house, custom.	supposition, notch incision.
fukara(**adj.**)	faqi:r	فَـقِـير	____	beggar, poor person.	____
fulani (N) (adj.)	fula:n	فُـلَان	____	such a one, any, so-and-so, somebody, a certain man.	____
fulusi (N) (fedha) (pesa) (senti)(rare)	fulu:s	فُـلُوس	____	money, cash, scales of fish.	____
furaha (N) (mchangamfu)	faraḥ	فَـرَح	____	gladness, joy, happiness, pleasure,gaienty,delight, enthusiasm.	____, wedding, marriage, ceremony.

Swahili word	Transcription of Arabic word	Arabic word	Arabic word in Swahili sense	Swahili usage	Arabic usage.
furahi (V) (ridhika) (starehe) **ia/ika/isha/iwa.**	fariḥ(a)	فَرِحَ	____	be glad, rejoice, to make glad, pleased.	____
furika (V) **ia/iwa.**	ȧfa:r(a)	أَفَارَ/ فَوَّرَ	فَرِقَ / فَاضَ	be full to the brim, flo-odtide.	to make water boil
furiko (N) (ma-) (gharika)	fawra:n	فَوَرَان	فَرِيقٌ /فَيَضَانٌ	flood, inundation.	see furika.
furkani (N) (Kurani)	furqa:n	فُرْقَان	____	Koran.	____
fursa (N) (nafasi) (wasaa)	furṣa(t)	فُرْصَة	____	incident, accident, oppo-rtunity, good occasion, chance.	____
fuska (N) (tabia mbaya)	fisq	فِسْق	____ , فُجُور	debauchery.	____
futari (N)	ifṭa:r	إِفْطَار	____	see fitiri.	____
futuru (V)	af ṭar(a)	أَفْطَرَ /يُفْطِرُ	____	eat the first meal after fasting.	____
		Gh			
ghadhabu (N) (hasira) (hamaki) (uchungu)	ghaḍab	غَضَبٌ	____	anger, rage, vexation, irritation.	____
ghadhibika (V) (ka-sirika)/**isha.**	ghaḍib (a)	غَضِبَ /يَغْضَبُ	____	to be angry.	____
ghafilika (V) (sahau)	ghafal (a)	غَفَلَ /تَغَفَّلَ	____	be forgetful, absentmin-ded, divert, neglect.	____, to fall asleep, to surpri-se, to omit.
ghafiri (V)	ghafar (a)	غَفَرَ	____	to pardon, forgive.	____
ghafla (N)	ghafla (t)	غَفْلَة	فَجْأَة	suddenness, unexpected, sudden death.	____, inadvertence inattention.
ghafula (N) (ghafla)	"			see ghafla(N).	____

Swahili word	Transcription of Arabic word	Arabic word	Arabic word in Swahili sense	Swahili usage	Arabic usage.
ghaibu (N)	ghayb	غَيْب	____	absence, lack, deficiency distance, remoteness, recite from memory.	____
ghairi (V)	ghayyar(a)	غَيَّرَ	____	to change, <u>surprise</u>, **dis-appoint	____, alter.
ghala (N) (stoo)	ghalla(t)	غَلَّة	____	storage place, store room	____, proceed, revenue, produce, yield, crops.
ghali (N) (bei kubwa) (isiyo rahisi)	gha:li	غَالِى /غَالٍ	____	scarce, rare, costly, expensive.	____, to exaggerate, go too far, dear.
gharama (N) (matumizi)	ghara:ma (t)	غَرَامَة	تَكْلُفَة	costs, expense, expenditure, payment, charges, fee.	to lose, to pay a fine.
gharika (N) (mafuriko_ (maangamizi)	ghari:q	غَرِيق	____ غَمْر	flood, inundation, deluge.	____
ghariki (V) (angamia) (jaa maji) **ia/isha.**	ghariq(a)	غَرِقَ	____	to sink, to be flooded, inundate.	____, to drown.
gharikisho (N) (ma-) (furiko la maji)	ghari:q/ ighra:q	غَرِيق / إِغْرَاق	____	a flood, inundation.	____
gharimu (V) **ia/ika/isha/iwa/iana.**	gharram(a)	غَرَّمَ	كَلَّفَ	spend money, incur expense.	to fine, to pay a fine.
ghasia (N) (machafuko) (matata) (fujo) (udhia) (kero) (usumbufu)	gha:ṣṣ	غَاصّ	فَوْضَى / ضَوْضَاء	confusion, complication, bustle, crowding.	full of, crowded with.
ghofiri (V) (samehe dhambi) **ia/ika/iwa.**	ghafar(a)	غَفَرَ	____	forgive, pardon, absolve.	____

Swahili word	Transcription of Arabic word	Arabic word	Arabic word in Swahili sense	Swahili usage	Arabic usage.
ghorofa (N)	ghurfa(t)	غُرْفَة	طَابِق / دَوْر / عِمَارَة .	flat, building, edifice, upper room.	room, chamber.
ghuna (N) (Ling.)	ghunna (t)	الغُنَّة	حَرفُ الجَهْر	a voiced sound.	singing chanting/ these letters(Y,R, M,L,W,N) in Tajweed of Koran are called ghunna(t).
ghuri (V) (danganya) (hadaa) **ia/ika/isha iwa/iana.**	gharr (a)	غَرَّ	____	cheat, deceive, beguile.	____, to allure, tempt.
		H			
haba (N) (kidogo) (chache)	ḥabba (t)	حَبَّة	قَلِيل	very few in number, a little.	seed, grain, berry a little, pill, pimple.
habari (N) (also with kh=khabani)	khabar	خَبَر	____	news, message, information, report.	____, rumours, predicate of a sentence.
haba Soda (N) (abasodi usu.heard)	alḥabba(t) assawda:ā	الحَبَّةُ السَّوْدَاء	____	cumin, or cummin haba means"grain" (Ar.)and sawdaa means "black" a kind of a native medicine.	____
haba sodi (N)	"	"	____	see haba soda.	____
habeshi (N) (also mhabeshi)	ḥabashy	حَبَشِي	____	an Ethiopian man (Abyssinian).	____
habithi (N) (ma-) (mtu mwovu) (fisadi) (mtu mjanja) (also with kh)	khabi:th	خَبِيث	____	a cruel, malicious, bad, wicked, offensive, evil person.	____, noxious, harmful, vicious.

Swahili word	Transcription of Arabic word	Arabic word	Arabic word in Swahili sense	Swahili usage	Arabic usage.
hadaa (V) (danganya) (punja) **ia/ika/isha/wa/ana.**	khadaạ(a)	خدع	____	to deceive, cheat.	____, dupe, mislead.
hadaa (N),(adj.) (hila) (udanganyifu)	khidaạ (t)	خُدْعَة خِداع	____, حِيلَة	trick, ruse, stratagem, deceit.	____, duplicity, deception, fetch.
hadhara (N)	ḥaḍara (t)	الحَضَرَة	____	infront of, in the presence of.	____
hadhari (V) (tahadhari)	ḥadẖar(a)	حَذَّر	____	avoid, exercise care, be cautious, or careful, warn.	____
hadhari (N) (uangalifu)	ḥadhar	حَذَر / حَذْر	____	caution, care, prudence.	___, watchfulness.
hadhi (N) (cheo) (utukufu) (heshima)	ḥadẖ	حَظّ	____ بَخْت	luck, forture, position of respect, honour, comfortable circumstances.	____, delight, pleasure.
hadhiri (V) **ia/ika/isha/iwa.**	ḥadẖar (a)	حَذّر	____	see hadhari(V).	____
hadhirina (N) (watu walio hudhuria)	ḥaḏiri:n	الحاضرين	____ الحَاضِرون	attendants.	____
hadi (N) (conj.) (mpaka) (hata)(sana) (kwa kweli) (mwisho) (upeo) (ukomo)	ḥadd	حَدّ	____	until, up to, as far as, as much as.	____, limit(end), boundary, edge, border, frontier definition.
hadia (N) (hidaya) (zawadi) (utungo)	hadiyya(t)	هَدِيّة	____	present, offering.	____
hadimu (N) (ma-) (mtumishi)	kha:dim	خَادِم	____	servant, attendant	____

Swahili word	Transcription of Arabic word	Arabic word	Arabic word in Swahili sense	Swahili usage	Arabic usage.
(a)**hadithi** (N)(kisa) (hikaya) (ngano)	ḥadi:th	حَدِيث	____, حِكَايَة	story narrative, tale, history, report, fiction, legend, account.	____, recent, speech, conversation, new.
(b)**hadithi** (N)	ḥadi:th	حَدِيثُ الرَّسُولِ	____	says of the Prophet Muhammad (S.A.W.).	____
(c)**hadithi** (V) (simulia)/**ia.**	ḥaddath(a)	حَدَّثَ	____, حَكَى / رَوَى	narrate, describe, talk about, recount.	____
hafifisha (V) (punguza thamani) (dunisha) (also with kh)	khaffaf(a)	خَفَّفَ	____	reduce, to make light of, insignificance.	____
hafifisho (N) (upunguzo wa thamani)	takhfi:f	تَخْفِيفُ	____	tightening.	____
hafifu (adj.)(udogo) (duni) (dhaifu) (unyonge) (yenye uzani udogo) (kh)	k hafi:f	خَفِيف	____	light, trifling, insignificant.	____
hafla (N) (sherehe) (karamu)	ḥafla(t)	حَفْلَة	____	meeting, assembly.	____
hai (N) (isiyokufa)	ḥayy(un)	حَيٌّ	____	alive, living, animate, existance.	____, quarter (of a city)
haiba (N) (tabia nzuri) (sura nzuri) (uzuri) (urembo) (uvutio wa heshima)	hayba(t)	هَيْبَة	هُدُوء / رَزَانَة سِيمَاء	beauty of countenance, appearance.	fear, awe, respect
haidhuru (conj.) (usifikiri)(si neno)	la/yaḍurr	لِمَنْ الفِعْلِ يَضُرّ	لَا يَضُرُّ	never mind, it does not matter.	from verb dhuru (see).

Swahili word	Transcription of Arabic word	Arabic word	Arabic word in Swahili sense	Swahili usage	Arabic usage.
haini (V)(asi)(saliti) (toa) (danganya)	kha:n(a)	خَانَ (يَخُون)	—	betray, deceive, to be dishonest.	—
haini (N) (ma-) (mwasi) (msaliti) (mtoro)(mdanganyifu) (also with kh)	kha:i̲n	خَائن	—	traitor,betrayer, deceiver renegade.	—
(a)**haja** (N) (maombi) (mahitaji)	ḥa:ja(t)	حَاجَة	—	need, want, necessity, object, cause, reason, engagement, call for nature.	—
(b)**haja** (N) (choo)	"	"	مِرْحَاض	priry, water closet, cespit.	*
(c)**haja kubwa** (N) (mavi)	"	"	غَائط / بِرَاز	excrement, stool.	—
(d)**haja ndogo** (N) (mkojo)	"	"	بَوْل	urine.	*
haji (N) (ma-) (also Alhaji) (Rel.)	ḥa:jj	حَاجّ	—	a pilgrim (to Macca).	—
haki (N) (uwajibiko) (uadilifu) (sahihi) (mali)	ḥaqq	حَقّ	—	right, correct, true, real, lawfulness, justice	—
hakika (N) (kweli) (ukweli) (yakini)	ḥaqi:qa(t)	حَقِيقَة	—	truth, reality, infact, certainty, essential, genuineness.	—
hakiki (V)(peleleza) (chunguza) **ia/ika/isha/iwa/iana.**	ḥaqqaq(a)	حَقَّقَ	—	investigate, make sure, prove.	—
hakikisho (N) (ushahidi) (uthibitisho).	taḥqi:q	تَحْقِيق	—	verification, Realisation investigation.	—

Swahili word	Transcription of Arabic word	Arabic word	Arabic word in Swahili sense	Swahili usage	Arabic usage.
hakimu (N) (ma-) (jaji)(kadhi)	ḥa:kim	حاكم	___ قَاضٍ	judge, ruler, chief.	___, governor.
halafu (adv.) (baa-daye) (kisha)	khalaf	خَلَفٌ (بَدَل)	بَعدئذ / بَعْدَ ذَلِكَ	afterwards, later, presently, in future.	substitute, successor, created beings.
halaiki (N) (wingi) (umati) (gwaride) (also with kh)	khala:i̱q	خَلَائق	خَلْقٌ كَثِير / حَشْد	large gathering, crowd.	created beings.
halali (adj.)(haki)	ḥala:l	حَلَال	___	lawfulness, legitimate, licit.	___
halalika (V) (ruhu-sika) (idhinika)	uḥilla(la-hu) ḥall(a)	أُحِلَّ لَهُ حَلَّ	___,	to be lawful, to be fall.	___, to unbind, to descend, to solve.
halalisha (V) (ruhu-sisha) (idhinisha)	aḥall(a)	أحلّ / (يُحِلُّ)	___	permit, legalize, cause to be allowed.	___
hali (Conj.)	ḥa:l	حَالٌ	___	state, condition, situation.	___
halifa (N)(also kha-lifa)(kiongozi wa tarika za dini)(kh)	khali:fa (t)	خَلِيفَة	___	caliph, successor.	___
(a) **halifu** (V) (ka-taa kutii)	kha:laf(a)	خَالَف	___ عَصَ	be contrary to, disobey, infringe.	___, disagree with.
(b) **halifu** (V) (pin-ga) **ia/ika/isha/iana**	kha:laf(a)	خَالَفَ	___, نَقَض	to break, violate.	___
(c) **halifu** (V) (ri-thisha) (achia)	khallaf(a)	خَلَّفَ	___	to leave behind, bequeath	___

Swahili word	Transcription of Arabic word	Arabic word	Arabic word in Swahili sense	Swahili usage	Arabic usage.
(a) **halisi** (adj.) (kweli kweli)(thabiti)	kha:liṣ	خَالِصٌ	حَقِيقَةٌ/ صَحِيح / أصِيل حَقِيقِىّ	real, true, exact, precise, genuine, accurate.	clear(pure), unmixed, free (at liberty).
(b) **halisi** (adv.)	kha:liṣ	خَالِصٌ	حَقِيقَةً	see halisi (a).	____
halizeti (N) (also halzeti) (mafuta ya halzeti)(alizeti)	azzait	الزَّيْت	زَيْتُ الزَّيْتُون	olive oil, sunflower.	oil.
halmashauri (N) (ma=(pl.)and shauri)	áhlashu: ra:	أَهْلُ الشُّورَى	لَجْنَة / مَجْلِسٌ اسْتِشَارِىّ	adivisory body, commitee.	____
halua (ji) (ZNZ)	ḥalwa:	حَلْوَى	____	common sweet meat [Turkish delight].	sweat meat.
halwaridi(N)(waridi) (uturi)	al-ward	الوَرْد	عِطْر/ طِيب عَبِير / شَذَا	perfume. attar.(Ar.)*.	roses,blossoms; flowers.
hama (V)(hajiri) **ia/ ika/isha/wa/ana.**	ḥa:m(a)	حَامَ (ف)	هَاجَر / هَجَّرَ	immigrate, remove (from) flit.	to hover, glide, swarm.
hamaki (V) (ghadhibika) (kasirika) (chukia)	ḥamu q(a)t	حَمُقَ	____	be siezed with sudden temper.	____, to be foolish.
hamaki (N)	ḥama:q(t) ḥumq	حَمَاقَة حُمْقٌ	____	burst of temper, act heedlessly, rash.	____
hamasa (N) (bidii) (kani)	ḥama:sa(t)	حَمَاسَةٌ حَمَاس	____	enthusiasm.	____
hamasisha (V)	ḥammas(a)	حَمَّس	____	to excite, stir up, to enthuse.	____
hamdulillahi(N)	Al-ḥamdulillahi	الحَمْدُ للّهِ	____	to praise God.	____

Swahili word	Transcription of Arabic word	Arabic word	Arabic word in Swahili sense	Swahili usage	Arabic usage.
hami (V) (linda) (tunza) (hifadhi) (saidia) (tetea) **ia/ika/iwa/iana**	ḥa:ma:	حَامَى (ف)	____	to defend, protect, show favour.	____, to advocate.
hamira (N)	khami:ra (t)	خَمِيرَة	____	yeast, barm	____, leaven, ferment.
hamisha (V) (zuia) **ia/ika/wa/ana.**	ḥa:ma	حَامَ	هَجَّرَ	expel, resettle.	see hama (V).
hamsa (N) (tano)	khamsa(t)	خَمْسَةٌ	____ خَمْسٌ	five.	____
hamsini (N) (makumi matano) (50)	khamsi:n	خَمْسِينَ	____ خَمْسُونَ	fifty (50).	____
hamu (N) (uchu) (shauku)	hamm	هَمٌّ	____ رَغْبَةٌ تَوْقٌ/ تَلَهُّف	desire (urgent),wish, anxiety.	anxeity,care.
handaki (N) (ma-) (shimo) (mtaro) [Persian]*	khandaq	خَنْدَق	____	trench, channel, ditch.	____
hani (V) (taazii) **ia/ika/iwa/iana.**	hannaȧ	هَنَّأَ	عَزَّى/تَعْزِيَة	condole, comfort, show sympathy, console.	to congratulate.
hanithi (N) (msenge) (shoga) (mpumbavu) (kh)	khanith/ mukhannath	خَنِثٌ مُخَنَّثٌ	____	pervert, homosexual, impotent man, shameful,effeminate,hermaphrodite.	
hara (V) (endesha/ (tumbo) **ia/ika/isha/ wa.**	harr(a)	هَرَّ/سَلَحَ (ف) (تَغَوَّطَ)	أَسْهَلَ/تَغَوَّطَ	purge, have diarrhea, evacuate.	____
haradali (N)	khardal	خَرْدَل	____	mustard.	____
harafa (N)	khura:fa (t)	خُرَافَة	____	fable, superstition, legend	____, fairytale.
haraka (N) (adj.) (adv.) (hima) (upesi)	ḥaraka (t)	حَرَكَة	سُرْعَة عَجَلَة	haste, speed, hurry, excitement, rapidity.	movement, motion.

Swahili word	Transcription of Arabic word	Arabic word	Arabic word in Swahili sense	Swahili usage	Arabic usage.
harakati (N) (bidii) (juhudi) (jitihada)	ḥaraka:t	حَرَكَات	____ ، (التَحْرِير)	liberation.	____
harakisha (V) **ia/ika /wa/ana**	ḥarrak(a)	حَرَّكَ (فِ)	أَلَحَّ / حَثَّ اسْتَعْجَلَ (أَمْرًا)	urge, press, hurry.	to move/stir/slide to incite, to vocalize.
(a) **haram** (N)	haram	هَرَم	____	pyramids.	____
(b) **haram** (N) (Rel.) (eneo la Alkaaba)	ḥaram	حَرَم	____	sacred area of Alkaaba	____, sacred, prohibited,santuary, shrine.
haramia (N) (ma-) (mwizi wa baharini) (jambazi) (mnyang'a-nyi)	ḥara:mia (harami)	حَرَامية (جَمْع) حَرَامِي (مفرد)	لحَرَامِي قاطِعُ طَرِيق لِص / نَهَابٌ • (مِنَ الحَرَام)	robber, bandit, pirate, outlow.	____, malefactors, thief,(loc.Arabic) from (hara:m)see. (haramu).
haramu (N) (isio haki) (isio halali) (mwana haramu)	ḥara:m	حَرَام	____	forbidden, prohibition, avoidance, unlawful, illegitimate.	____
(a) **harara** (N)(moto) (hari) (jasho)(joto)	ḥara:ra(t)	حَرَارَة	____	warmth, temperature, heat fever, inflammation.	____
(b) **harara**(N) (hamaki)(mori)(ghadhabu)	"	"	غَيْرة	anger, rage, fury, exaperation.	zeal, ardour, passion, enthusiasm.
(b) **harara** (N) (pele ndogo ndogo)	ḥara:ra(t)	"	طَفْحٌ جِلْدِى	rash, itch, eruption, scabies, ache.	____, (loc.Arabic)
haribifu (adj.) (-enye kuharibu)	mukharrib	مُخَرِّب	____	destructive, pernicious, ruiner.	___, destroyer.
haribifu (adj.) (potovu) (bathirifu)	mukharrib	"	مُبَذِّر	extravagant, wasteful.	____
haribivu (adj.)(also haribifu)	kha:rib/ mukharrib	خَارِب / مُخْرِب مُخَرِّب	____	see (haribifu).	____
haribu (V) **ia/ika/ iwa/**	kharrab(a) /kharab(a)	خَرَّب / خَرِبَ	____	destroy, ruin, damage, damolize.	____,demolish devastate.

Swahili word	Transcription of Arabic word	Arabic word	Arabic word in Swahili sense	Swahili usage	Arabic usage.
harimisha (V)(batilisha) (vunja) (tengua) **ia/ika.**	ḥarram(a)	حَرَّم	____	to forbid, interdict.	____
hariri (N)	ḥari:r	حَرِير	____	silk.	____
hariri (v) **ia/ika/isha/iwa.**	ḥarrar(a)	حَرَّر	____	to revise, to edit.	____, to liberate to adjust.
harisha (V)(see hara) **ia/ika/wa/ana.**	harr(a)	هَرَّ	____	see (hara)	____
harisho (N) (ma-) (ugonjwa wa kuhara)	hura:r	هُرَار (البِرَاز) (سَلَحٌ)	إِسْهَال	diarrhea, laxative (-strong).	____
(a) **harufu** (N) (see herufu)	ḥarf	حَرْف	____	letter (of the alphabet).	____
(b) **harufu** (N)(mnukio) (also arufu)	ạrf	عَرْف	رَائِحَة	smell, aroma, scent, an odour of any kind.	perfume, aroma, scent.
(a) **harusi** (N) (ndoa) (ni-kahi) (uozi) (akidi)	al-urs al-ụrs	عُرْس (العُرْس	____	wedding, matrimony, marriage.	______,
(b) **harusi** (N) (bwana harusi)	ạru:s	العَرُوس (الزَّوْج)	____	bridegroom.	____
(c) **harusi** (N) (bibi harusi)	"	العَرُوس (الزَّوْجَة)	____	bride.	____
(d) **harusi** (N) (sherehe ya kuoana)	Ụrs	العُرْس (عُرْس	حَفْلَة الزِّفَاف	wedding ceremony and festivity.	see harusi(a).
(e) **harusi** (N) (furaha)	"	العُرْس (عُرْس)	الفَرَح / السَّعَادَة	delight, pleasure, gaiety,	____

Swahili word	Transcription of Arabic word	Arabic word	Arabic word in Swahili sense	Swahili usage	Arabic usage.
hasa (adj.) (conj.) (also hassa) (kh)	kha:ṣṣ kha:ṣṣa(t)	خَاصّ خَاصَّة	____	just, specially, exactly, <u>completely</u>,** <u>very much</u>,** <u>wholly</u>.**	____, particularly, properly.
hasa (V)(rare)(tec.) (also hasi) (kh)	khasa:	خَصَى	____	eunuch, to castrate.	____
(a) **hasada** (N) (uji wa unga wa mtama) (rare)	aṣi:da (t)	عَصِيدَة	____, ثَرِيد	porridge, <u>a native paste</u>.**	____
(b) **hasada** (N) (also husuda)	ḥasad	حَسَد	____	envy, grudge, be jealous of.	____
hasama (N) (also uhasama)	khiṣa:m/ khuṣu:ma	خِصَام خُصُومَة	____	dispute, controversy.	____
hasara (N) (uharibifu) (maangamizi katika bahari)(upotevu)	khasa:ra (t)/ khusra:n	خَسَارَة خُسْرَان	____	loss, damage, injury.	____
hasha (int.)(hapana) (la) (siyo)	ḥa:sh(a)	حَاشَ	____	by no means!, certainly not!, impossible, God forbid.	____
hashakum (adv.)	ḥasha:kum	حَاشَاكُم	____	a word used before mentioning something not usually mentioned, e.g. shameful.	without offence to you.
hasharati(N) (asherati) (ma-)	muaashara (t)	مُعَاشَرَة	انْغِمَاسٌ فِي المَلَذَّات	dissipation, profligacy, fornication, debauchery.	____, society, companionship.
hasi (V) **ia/ika/isha /wa/ana.**	khaṣṣa:	خَصَّى	____	castrate, geld.	____
hasibu (V) **ia/ika/ isha/wa/ana**	ḥa:sab(a)	حَاسَب	____	count, calculate, reckon-up, consider.	____

Swahili word	Transcription of Arabic word	Arabic word	Arabic word in Swahili sense	Swahili usage	Arabic usage.
hasidi (N) (ma-)	ḥasu:d	حَسُود / حَاسِد	____	envious, malevolent, a jealous person, enemy, spiteful person.	____
hasidi (N) **ia/ika/isha/iwa/iana**	ḥasad (a)	حَسَد	____	to envy, grudge.	____
hasira (N) (ghadhabu) (hamaki) (uchukivu) (uchungu) (ukali) (ghaidhi) (kani)	ḥasra (t)	حَسْرَة	____	passion, wrath, anger, affliction.	grief, sorrow.
hata (conj.) (adv.) (sivyo) (kabisa) (mpaka)	ḥatta:	حَتَّى	____ أَبَدًا	until, up to, even, as far as, till, so that.	____
hatari (N) (also with Kh)	khaṭar	خَطَر	____	danger, risk, hazard, peril, jeopardy.	____
hatarisha (V)	kha:ṭar(a)	خَاطَرَ	____ جَازَفَ	put in danger, risk, imperil, endanger.	____
hati (N) (maandishi rasmi) (mwandiko) (waraka) (barua) (kh)	khaṭṭ	خَطّ	____	<u>memorandum</u>,** document, writting, <u>written note</u>.**	____, line, streak, stripe, handwriting, script, penmanship.
hatia (N) (kosa) (taksiri) (dhambi) (uovu)	khaṭiyya (t)	خَطِيَّة / خَطِيئَة	____, ذَنْب	fault, transgression, crime, guilt, blame, sin.	____
hatibu (N) (ma-) (mfawidhi) (kh)	khaṭi:b	خَطِيب	____	speaker, preacher.	____
hatima (N) (mwisho)	kha:tima (t)	خَاتِمَة	____	end, conclusion.	____
hatimaye (adj.) (mwishoni)	fi-alkhita:m	فِي الخِتَام خِتَامًا	____	finally, in conclusion, at last.	____

Swahili word	Transcription of Arabic word	Arabic word	Arabic word in Swahili sense	Swahili usage	Arabic usage.
hatirisha (V) (jusurisha) (hatarisha)	kha:ṭar(a)	خَاطَر	——— مُعَرِّض للخَطَر جَازَف	see hatarisha.	———
hatua (N) (maendeleo) (nafasi) (faragha) (kh)	khatwa(t)	خَطْوة	———	step, footstep, page, stride, opportunity, progress.	———
hawala (N) (hundi) (cheki)	ḥawa:la (t)	حَوَالة	——— تَحْوِيله/ أَمْر	order of cheque or draft, money-order, exchange.	———,
hawara (N) (kimada)	ḥaw ra:ā	حَوْرَاء	مُومِس/ زَانيَة	paramour, adulter, adultress, prostitute.	a girl who has eyes with a marked contrast of white and deep-black.
hawili (V) (hamisha) **ia/ika/isha/iwa**	ḥawal (a)	حَوَّل	———, تَقَلَّ غَيَّر.	to change, transfer.	———
hawilisho (N) (ma-)	taḥwi:l	تَحْوِيل	———	change, transfer, removal.	———
haya (N) (fedheha) (soni)	ḥaya:ā	حَيَاء	——— خَجَل	modesty, bashfulness, coyness, shame, disgrace, humility, respect, reverence.	———
(a) **hayati** (N) (marehemu)	ḥaya:t	حَيَاة	المَرْحُوم	departed, deceased (pertaining to life time).	life, existence.
(b) **hayati** (N) (uhai)	ḥaya:t	"	———	life, the condition of being alive.	———, existence.
hayawani (N) (mnyama) (asiyetumia akili)	ḥaywan	حَيْوَان	——— بَلِيد	brute, beast, a silly person.	———
hazina(N) (dafina) (kh)	khazi:na (t)	خَزِينَة	———, كَنْز خِزَانَة / المَالِيَّة وِزَارَة المَالِيَّة	treasure, privy purse, treasury.	———, cashbox (safe), exchange.

Swahili word	Transcription of Arabic word	Arabic word	Arabic word in Swahili sense	Swahili usage	Arabic usage.
hazini (V) (tunza fedha) **ia/ika/isha/iwa**	khazan(a)	خَزَن / خَزَّن	——— إِدَّخَر	to store, hoard	———
heba (N) (also haiba)	haiba	هَيْبَة	—— هَيْبَة/رَزَانَة	see haiba	———
hebu (int.) (also ebu)	habb(a)	هَبَّ	——	well then!, come then! come now.	to begin or commence, to do, to arise, arise, get up.
hedashara (N) (kumi na moja)	iḥdashara (t)	أَحَدَ عَشَر إِحْدَى عَشَر	———	eleven, eleventh.	eleven.
hedaya(N) (also hidaya)	hidiyya(t)	هَدِيَّة		gift, present.	———.
hedhi (N) (mwezi wa damu)	ḥaiḍ	حَيْض	——	menses, menstruation.	———
hedhi tamati(N) (tec.)	ḥaiḍa(t) tamat	حَيْضَة تَامَّة	الحَيْضَة الأَخِيرَة	last monthly period.	———
hekaya (N) (also hikaya)	ḥika:ya(t)	حِكَايَة	———	narrative, story, tale, wonder, miracle.	———
hekima (N)	ḥikma(t)	حِكْمَة	———	wisdom, knowledge, philosophy, judgement.	———, medicine.
hema (N)	khaima(t)	خَيْمَة	———	a tent.	———
(a) **heri** (N) (neema) (baraka) (bahati) (ustawi) (kh)	khair	خَيْر	———	good, success, happiness, advantage, goodfortune, blessedness.	———
(b) **heri** (adv.) (afadhali) (bora)	khair	خَيْر	——— أَفْضَل	better, rather than.	———
herufi (N)(mwandiko) (also harufi)	ḥarf	حَرْف	———	a letter(of the alphabet).	———

Swahili word	Transcription of Arabic word	Arabic word	Arabic word in Swahili sense	Swahili usage	Arabic usage.
hesabati	ḥisa:ba:t	حِسَابَات	—— رِيَاضِيَات	see hisabati.	——
(a) **hesabu** (V) (kadiria) (dhania) (fikiria) **ia/ika/isha/iwa.**	ḥa:sab(a) ḥasab	حَاسَبَ حَسَبَ	—— قَدَّرَ خَمَّنَ	count, calculate, estimate, appraise, consider, reckon up.	——
(b) **hesabu** (N) (jumla) (idadi) (mapato) (matumizi) (also hisabu)	ḥisa:b	حِسَاب	——	arithmetic, mathematic, bill, sum, number, account rate, credit, numeration.	——
(c) **hesabu** (N) Rel.) (also hisabu)	ḥisa:b	(يَوْمُ) الحِسَاب	يَوْمُ القِيَامَة	judgement-day, resurrection-day.	——
heshima(N) (utukufu) (cheo) (haya) (daraja) (also hishima) (adabu)	ḥishma(t)	حِشْمَة	—— اِحْتِرَام	honour, respect, courtesy, esteem, modesty, bashfulness, reverence.	____, diffidence, timidity, shame.
heshimu (V) (tukuza) **ia/ika/iwa/iana.**	taḥashsham (a)	تَحَشَّمَ / اِحْتَشَمَ	——	to respect, to honour, to be bashful or modest.	____, to shame, shy.
hewa (N) (upepo) (anga)	hawa:ā	الهَوَاء	—— الطَّقْس	air, atmosphere, climate, weather.	____, wind, draft.
hiana (N) (unyimaji) (uchoyo) (udhalimu) (kh)	khiya:na (t)	خِيَانَة	——	deceit, treachery, betrayer, renagade, faithless, dishonesty treason.	____, falseness.
hiari (N) (chagua) (penda) (kh) (ridhia) **ia/ika/isha/iwa.**	khayyar(a)	خَيَّرَ (فِ)	——	choose, select, prefer.	——
hiari (N) (uchaguzi) (ridhaa) (pendo) (also hitiari, ihtiari) (kh)	khiya:r	خِيَار	—— اِخْتِيَار	choice, selection, wish, will, pleasure, judgement discretion.	____, option.
hiba(N)(zawadi)(tunzo) (hidaya)	hiba(t)	هِبَة	—— عَطَاء	present, gift, donation, grant.	——

Swahili word	Transcription of Arabic word	Arabic word	Arabic word in Swahili sense	Swahili usage	Arabic usage.
hidaya (N) (zawadi) (aṭia) (tunzo)	hadiyya(t)	هَدِيَّة	———	see hedaya.	———
hifadhi (V) (linda) (tunza) (hami) (weka moyoni) **ia/ika /isha/iwa**	ḥafidh (a)	حَفِظَ	———	to keep, preserve, guard, save.	———, to keep in mind, to memorize.
hifadhi (N)(ulinzi)	ḥifdh	حِفْظٌ/حِفَاظٌ	——— حِمَايَة	gaurding, protection, keeping.	———
hija (N)(ibada ya kuhiji)	ḥajj	الحَجُّ / الحِجُّ	———	a pilgrimage to Macca.	———
hijabu (N) (kinga ya mwili)	ḥija:b	الحِجَابُ	———	neuralgia, swelling of glands in the neck.	———, veil.
hiji(V) **ia/ika/isha/ iwa.**	ḥajj(a)	حَجَّ (يحجّ)	———	go on the pilgrimage to (Macca).	———
hikaya (N) (also hekaya)	ḥikaya(t)	حِكَايَة	———	see hekaya.	———
hikima (N) (also hekima)	ḥikma(t)	حِكْمَة	———	see hekima.	———
hila(N) (hadaa) (udanganyifu) (ujanja) (werevu)	ḥi:la(t)	حِيلَة	———	trick, expedient, contrivance, strategem, deceit, cunning.	———
hiliki(V)(angamia) (potea) (haribika) **ia/ika/isha/iwa.**	halak(a)	هَلَك	———	be destroyed, to perish, be lost, die.	———
hima(N)(adv.)(bidii) (ari)(nguvu)	himma (t)	هِمَّة	———	haste, hurry, energy, stamina, quickly, persistently.	ambition, endeavour, intention, resolution, energy ardour, zeal.

Swahili word	Transcription of Arabic word	Arabic word	Arabic word in Swahili sense	Swahili usage	Arabic usage.
himaya (N) (ulinzi) (utunzo)	ḥima:ya(t)	حِمَايَة	———	protection, guardianship.	———
himidi (V) (shukuru) (sifu) (tukuza)	ḥamid(a)	حَمِدَ (ف)	———	to praise God.	———. to thank.
himili (V) (stahamili) (vumilia)	taḥmmal(a)	تَحَمَّلَ	———	see stahamili.	———
himiza (V) (harakisha) **ia/ika/wa/ana**	hamm(a)	هَمَّ / أَهَمَّ	اسْتَحَثَّ اسْتَعْجَلَ أَمْرًا	urge, hasten, cause to be done quickly.	to begin, take care of, take interest in, to mind.
hina(N)	ḥinna:ā	الحِنَّاء / حِنَّة	———	henna[Ar.]**	———
hini (V) (nyima) (fanyia hiana) **ia/ika/isha/iwa/iana**	kha:n(a)	خَانَ (ف)	———	to be dishonest, unfaithful, to betray, deny oneself, withhold.	———
hinikiza (V)	ḥaniq (a)	حَنِقَ / أَحْنَقَ	تَدَاخَلَ أَثْنَاءَ الكَلَامِ / اعْتَرَضَ	interrupt some one speaking.	to enrage, to be enraged.
hirimia (V) (dhamiria) (nia) (kusudia)	harram(a)	هَرَّمَ (فرم)	نَوَى / قَرَّرَ	intend, decide, purpose.	to mince, to chop.
hirizi (N) (kinga) (azima)	ḥirz	حِرْزٌ	———	amulet, talisman.	———
(a) **hisa** (N) (fungu) (sehemu) (kiwango)	ḥiṣṣa(t)	حِصَّة	———	part, share, portion.	———
(b) **hisa** (N) (katika hesabu)	"	"	خَارِجُ القِسْمَة (فِي الرِّيَاضِيَات)	in arithmetic, quotient.	*
hisabati (N) (also hesabati)	ḥisa:ba:t	حِسَابَات	عِلْمُ الحِسَاب	arithmetic, computation.	(pl. of hisab) which see.
hisabu(N)	ḥisa:b	حِسَاب	———	see hesabu(N).	———
hisabu (V)	ḥa:sab(a)	حَسَبَ / حَاسَبَ	———	see hesabu(V).	———

Swahili word	Transcription of Arabic word	Arabic word	Arabic word in Swahili sense	Swahili usage	Arabic usage.
hisani(N) (wema) (fadhili) (also ehsani, ihsani)	iḥsa:n	إِحْسَان	——	kindness, favour, benevolence, preference, benefaction.	——
hishima (N) (heshima)	ḥishma(t)	حِشْمَة	——	see heshima.	——
hishimu(V) (heshimu)	taḥasham (a)	تَحَشَّم/اِحْتَشَمَ	——	see heshimu.	——
hisi (V) (jua moyoni) (dhania) **ia/ika/isha/iwa.**	ḥass(a)	حَسَّ/ أَحَسَّ	——	feel, perceive, recognize, sense.	——
hisi(N) (mapenzi) (also hisia)	ḥiss	الحِسُّ	——	feeling, sense.	——
hitaji (V) (kuwa na haja) (taka) **ia/ika/isha/iwa/iana.**	iḥta:j(a)	اِحْتَاجَ	——	want, desire, need, lack, require.	——
hitilafiana (V) (tofautiana) (kosa kusikilizana) **ika/isha/iwa**	kha:laf(a) Ikhtalaf (a)	خَالَف / اِخْتَلَف	——	be different, disagree, contradict, distinguish, differentiate, differ.	——
hitilafu (N) (tofauti) (kasoro) (ila) (dosari) (pungufu).	ikhtilaf khilaf	اِخْتِلَاف خِلَاف	——	distinct, disagreement, difference, exception, defect, fault, contradiction.	——
hitima(N) (Rel.)	khatma(t)	خَتْمَة	——	reading of entire Koran, funeral sermon, feast of a funeral service.	——
hitimu (V) (fikia mwisho) (maliza) **ia/ika/isha/iwa.**	khatam(a)	خَتَمَ	—— أَكْمَلَ أنْهى / تَخَرَّجَ	end, stop, conclude, finish, complete.	——, to stamp.

Swahili word	Transcription of Arabic word	Arabic word	Arabic word in Swahili sense	Swahili usage	Arabic usage.
hiyana (N)	Khiya:na (t)	خِيَانَة	____	see hiana.	____
hizaya (N) (laana) (kh) (aibu) (fedheha)		خِزْيٌ	____	disgrace, dishonor, curse, misfortune.	____, shame, bashfulness.
hizi (V) (also stihizai) **ia/ika/isha** (hizaya.)	khaziya	خَزِيَ	____	abuse, insult, disgrace, curse, execrate.	to abash, confuse, to put to shame, vile, to disgrace
hodari (N) (adj.) (shujaa)	ḥa:ḍir Al-badi:ha(t)	حَاضِرُ البَدِيهَةِ	ذَكِيٌّ / شَاطِر	active, firm, strong, stable, solid, brave, earness.	improvised, intuitive.
hodhi (N) (birika)	ḥauḍ	حَوْضٌ	____ , صِهْرِيج	tank, large vessel for holding water boiler.	basin, tank, reservoir.
(a) **hofu** (V) (ogopa) (chelea)(kh) **ia/ika/isha/iwa/iana**	khawaf(a)	خَوَّفَ/ أَخَافَ	____	feel fear, awe, fear for frighten.	____
hofu(N) (woga) (tisha)	khawf	خَوْفٌ	____	fear, apprehension, awe.	____
hoja(N) (kweli) (wazo) (fikira) (swali) (also huja)	ḥujja(t)	حُجَّةٌ	____ حِجَاجٌ جِدَالٌ	request, argument, proof, pretext.	____
hojaji (N) (ma-)	ḥija:j	حِجَاج /مُحَاجّة	الاسْتِفْتَاء	quiestionnaire.	argument, dispute.
hoji (V) **ika/ika/isha/iwa/iana.**	ḥa:jj(a)	حَاجَّ	____ , جَادَل	to argue, dispute or reason with.	____
homa (N)	ḥumma:	حُمَّى	____	fever, any sickness with high temperature.	____
hotuba (N) (khotuba)	khuṭba (t)	خُطْبَة	____	speech, asermon address, homily.	

Swahili word	Transcription of Arabic word	Arabic word	Arabic word in Swahili sense	Swahili usage	Arabic usage.
hubiri(V) (simulia) **ia/ika**	akhbar(a)	أَخْبَر	___, وَعَظ	preach, announce, report, inform.	to tell, inform.
hudhuria (V) (fika) **ka/sha/wa.**	ḥaḍar(a)	حَضَر	___, وَصَل	to come, be present, to attend.	___, arrive.
hudhurio(N) (ma-)	ḥuḍu:r	الحُضُور	___	attendance, presence.	___, coming.
huduma(N) (utumishi) (msaada)	khidma(t)	خِدْمَة	___	service, employment, attendance	___
huduma(V) (tumikia) **ia/ika/isha/iwa/iana**	khadam(a)	خَدَم	___	serve, employ, attend (on, to)	___
huja(N) (hoja)	ḥujja(t)	حُجَّة	___	see hoja	___
hujaji(N) (ma-) (Rel.) (sing.)	ḥujja:j	حُجّاج	حَاجّ	pilgrim (Islamic Rel.)	pilgrims.
hujuma(N) (shambulio) (vamia)	hajma(t) huju:m	هَجْمَة هُجُوم	___	an attack, an assault.	___
hujumu(V) (vamia) (fisidi) (haribu) (haribu) (vuruga) **ia/ika/isha/iwa/iana**	hajam(a)	هَجَم	___	to attack, assail, rush upon.	___, to raid a place.
(a) **hukumu**(V) (tawala) (amuru) **ia/isha/iwa/iana.**	ḥakam(a)	حَكَم	___	to govern, rule, to command, to judge, decide, pass sentence.	___
(b) **hukumu**(N) (amri)	ḥukm.	حُكْمٌ	___	rule, government, judgement, sentence.	___, authority, decision.
humusi(N) (ma-) (sehemu ya moja ya tano) (kh)	khums	خُمْسٌ	___	fifthpart ($^1/_5$).	___

Swahili word	Transcription of Arabic word	Arabic word	Arabic word in Swahili sense	Swahili usage	Arabic usage.
hurulaini(N)(ma-) (wanawake wazuri wa peponi) (also huruleini)	ḥurulạyn	حُوْرُالعَيْن	___	nymph (Islamic Rel.).	___
huruma(N) (imani) (rehema) (upole)	ḥurma(t)	حُرْمَة	شَفَقَة / رَحْمَة	sympathy, mercy, pity, compassion.	sacredness, forbidingness.
hurumia(V) (fanya huruma) **ika/iwa/iana**	ḥarram(a)	حَرَّمَ	شَفِقَ / رَحِمَ	have pity, have mercy on.	for bidden, deprivation.
husika(V) **ia/isha/iwa/iana.**	ikhtaṣṣ(a)	خَصَّ / إِخْتَصَّ	خَصَّصَ لِ ___	assign, give a share, belong to.	___, to a single out.
husisho(N) (ma-)	khaṣṣ(a)	خَصَّ	حَرْفُ الجَرّ	preposition.	to belong to.
husuda(N) (jicho baya)	ḥasad	حَسَدٌ	___	envy, grudge, jealousy, spitefulness.	___
husudi(V) **ia/ika/isha/iwa/iana.**	ḥasad(a)	حَسَدَ (ه)	___	envy, grudge, be jealous of.	___
husuma(N) (ugomvi) (vita) (shonde) (nunia)	khuṣu:ma (t)	خُصُومَة	___	dispute, controversy, violence, sulkiness.	___
(a) **hususa**(adv.) (hasa) (halisi) (maalum)	khuṣu:ṣan khuṣu:ṣi:	خُصُوصًا خُصُوصِيّ	___ خِصِّيصًا / بِخَاصَّة	particularly, specially, exactly.	___
(b) **hususa** (adj.)	"	"	خَاصّ ___	particular, special, exact.	___
hususan(adv.)(adj.) **(khususan)**	khuṣuṣan	"	___	see hususa(a,b).	___
hutuba(N) (khutuba)	khuṭba(t)	خُطْبَة	___	see hotuba.	___

Swahili word	Transcription of Arabic word	Arabic word	Arabic word in Swahili sense	Swahili usage	Arabic usage.
hutubu(V) (hubiri) **ia/ika/isha/iwa/iana** (khutubu)	khaṭab(a)	خَطَبَ	____	see hubiri.	____
huzuni(N) (majonzi) (msiba)	ḥuzn	حُزْن	____	grief, sorrow, sadness, mourning, distress, calamity, disaster.	____
huzunika(V) (sikitika) (ona haya au aibu)/**isha**.	ḥazin(a)	حَزِن (ف)	____	to sadden, grieve, to mourn.	____
		I			
ibada(N) (Rel.) (mazoea)	ịba:da(t)	عِبَادَة	____	worship, adoration, habit.	____
ibadhi(N) (Rel.)	iba:ḍiyya (t)	الإبَاضِيّة	____	ibadism (sect of the ibadites.).	____
ibara(N) (kifungu cha maneno)	ịba:ra(t)	عِبَارَة	____	phrase.	____, explanation, diction, style, which means.
ibilisi(N) (ma-) (shetani) (mjanja) (mkorofi)	ibli:s	إبْلِيس	____, شِرِّير	the devil, satan, evil-minded fiend, brutal, malgnant.	____
ibra(N) (mafundisho) (maonyo)	ịbra(t)	عِبْرَة	____ عِظَة	warning.	____
idadi(N) (hesabu) (namba)	ạdad	عَدَد	إحْصَاء / ____، تَعْدَاد .	computation, counting, reckoning, enumeration, quantity, amount.	number, enumeration.
idara(N) (shirika) (ofisi) etc.	ida:ra(t)	إدَارَة	____, مَصْلَحَة	administration, department, division.	____, management.

Swahili word	Transcription of Arabic word	Arabic word	Arabic word in Swahili sense	Swahili usage	Arabic usage.
idhaa(N) (matangazo, stesheni ya redio)	idha:ạa(t)	إِذَاعَة	___	broadcasting.	___
(a) **idhini**(N) (ruhusa) (kibali)	idhn	إِذْنٌ	___	leave, permission, sanction, authorization.	___
(b) **idhini**(V) (ruhusu) (kubali) (ridhia) **ia/ika/isha/iwa**	ȧdhin(a)	أَذِنَ	___	allow, permit, sanction, authorize, assent.	___
I(d)di(N)	ị:d	العِيْدُ	___	Islamic festival, feast.	___
I(d)dil Fitiri(N) (Idi ndogo)	ị:d al-fiṭr	عِيدُ الفِطْرِ	___	the festival at the end of the fast of Ramadhan, lesser Bairam.	___
I(d)dd-Al-haji(N) (Idi kubwa)	ị:d-Al-ḥajj.	عِيْدُ الأَضْحَى، عِيدٌ الحَجِّ		the festival in commemoration of Islamic journey to Macca, greater Bairam.	___
I(d)di-mbarak(N)	ị:d Mubarak	عِيدٌ مُبَارَكٌ	___	the blessed Idi.	___
Ihramu(N) (Rel.)	iḥra:m	إِحْرَام	___	special clothes worn by Muslims for doing pelgrimage.	___
ihsani(N) (also hisani)	iḥsa:n	إِحْصَان	___	see hisani.	___
ihtilafu(N) (also hitilafu)	ikhtila:f	إِخْتِلَاف	___	see hitilafu.	___
Ijumaa(N) (Rel.)	jumạa(t)	الجُمُعَة	___، يَوْمٌ/صَلَاةُ	Friday, prayer of Friday.	___
ikama(N) (Rel.)	iqa:ma(t)	إِقَامَة	___	performing of religious service.	___, residence, raising, establishing,sojourn.

Swahili word	Transcription of Arabic word	Arabic word	Arabic word in Swahili sense	Swahili usage	Arabic usage.
ikhlasi(N) (ukweli) (usafi wa nia) (uaminifu)	ikhla:ṣ	إِخْلَاصٌ	____ صِدْقٌ	sincerity, faithfulness.	____, candor, fidelity.
ikirahi(N) (also karaha)	ikra:h	إِكْرَاهٌ	____	being offended, disgust, aversion, compulsion, insult, hatred, abhorrence, provocation.	___, hate, dislike repugnance, louthing, detestation reluctance.
ikrahi(N) (also ikirahi)	ikra:h	"	____	see ikirahi.	____
ikrari(N)(ukubalifu)	iq ra:r	إِقْرَار	____	confession, acknowledgement, admission.	____
iktisadi(N) (also kitisadi) (uchumi)	iqtiṣa:d	إِقْتِصَاد	____	economy, thirift.	____
(a) **ila** (N) (hitilafu) (walakini)(aibu) (kasoro)	i̥lla(t)	عِلَّةٌ	____ نَقِيصَة	defect, blemish, drawback stain, disgrace.	____
(b)**ila**(conj.) (lakini) (isipokuwa)	illa(t)	إِلَّا	____ سوى عدا	except, but, unless.	____, save.
ilani(N) (tangazo)	iạla:n	إِعْلَان	____	notice, proclamation, announcement.	____, declaration, advertisement.
ili (conj.) (kwa sababu, ajili ya)	i̥lla(t)	عِلَّةٌ	____ لِأَجْلِ بِسَبَب	that, in order that.	cause, reason, disease, illness.
ilimuradi(adv.) (conj.) (bora) (hata) (also muradi)	al-murad	المُرَاد	____	desire, purpose.	___, intention, wish.
ilimu(N)(also elimu) (ZNZ)	i̥lm	عِلْمٌ	____	see elimu.	____
ilmu(N)	i̥lm	عِلْمٌ	____	see elimu.	____

Swahili word	Transcription of Arabic word	Arabic word	Arabic word in Swahili sense	Swahili usage	Arabic usage.
ima(conj.) (au)	imma:	إِمَّا	___, أَوْ	or, either,"this or that"	___
imamu(N) (au)	ima:m	إِمَامٌ	___,	one who conducts the prayers in mosque.	___, leader, chief.
imani(N) (itikadi) (huruma)	i:ma:n	إِيمَانٌ	___, إِعْتِقَاد شَفَقَةٌ	faith, trust, belief, confidence, honesty, uprightness, kindliness.**	___
imara(N), (adj.) (madhubuti)(thabiti) (ukweli)	ịma:ra(t)	عِمَارَة	قُوَّةٌ / ثَبَاتٌ	firmness, strength, hardness, solidity, stability compactness.	building, edifice.
imarisha(V) (fanya imara)	ạmmar(a)	عَمَّر	قَوِيَ / ثَبَتَ	establish, make firm, strong, solid.	to inhabit, to build, construct, repair.
Imla(N)	imla:ā	إِمْلاَء	___	dictation.	___
Inadi(N) (kishindo) (rare)	ịna:d	عِنَاد	مُعَانَدَة ___ مُشَاكَسَة / سُوءُ طَبْع .	provocation, perversity, wilfulness, meanness of spirit, obstinacy.	___, pertinacity, opposition, resistance, stubbornness.
Injili(N)	Inji:l	الإِنْجِيل	___	the New Testament.	___
insha(N)	insha:ā	الإِنْشَاء	___	composition, an essay.	___, creating, originating, treatise.
irabu(N) (vokali)	iạra:b	الإِعْرَاب	حَرْفُ عِلَّةٍ / لِين .	a vowel letter.	parsing(gr.), expression.
isha(N) (Rel.) (wakati) (sala)	ịsha:ā	العِشَاء	___	a prayer or period of time after sunset.	___
ishara(N) (alama) (dalili_	isha:ra(t)	إِشَارَةٌ	___	a sign, mark, signal, indication, token, fact.	___

Swahili word	Transcription of Arabic word	Arabic word	Arabic word in Swahili sense	Swahili usage	Arabic usage.
ishara ya msalaba(N)	isha:ra(t) aṣṣali:b	إِشَارَةُ الصَّلِيب	الصَّلِيب	cross.	____
ishi(V) (dumu) (kaa) **ia/ika/iwa**	ạ:sh(a)	عَاشَ (يَعِيشُ)	____	to live, exist, continue, endure, remain, last.	____
ishirini(N)	ịshri:n	عِشْرِين	____	twenty (20), twenth.	____
isimu(N) (Ling.) (jina) (sayansi ya lugha)	ism.	إِسْمٌ	مَادَّةُ اللُّغَوِيَّات	linguistics, essence, name.	noun(gr.) substansive, name.
Islamu(N) (Rel.)	Isla:m	الإِسْلَام	____	faith, religious, proclaimed by the prophet Muhammad, all muslims.	____
Ismailia(N)	ismaị:lia	الإِسْمَاعِيلِيَّة	____	a shia sect.	____
Israfili(N) (Rel.)	Isra:fi:L	إِسْرَافِيل	____	the angel who blows on the last Day. (Mus.)	____
israfu	isra:f	إِسْرَاف	____,	extravagance, prodigality.	____, immoderateness.
istakabadhi(N)	qabaḍ(a)	قَبَضَ / اسْتِقْبَاض	____, (إِيصَال)	a reçeipt.	to recieve money.
istilahi(V) (maneno ya kitaaluma)	iṣṭila:ḥ	اصْطِلَاحٌ	____, مُصْطَلَح	terminology, term.	____, idiomatic.
istihadha(N) (tec.)	istiḥa:ḍa (t)	الاسْتِحَاضَة	____	break-through bleeding.	____
istiskaa(N)	istisqa:ā	الاسْتِسْقَاء	صَلَاةُ ____	Islamic prayer for rain, dropsy.	____
istiwai(N) (ikweta) (rare)	istiwa:ā	(خَطُّ الاسْتِوَاء)	____	equator.	____

Swahili word	Transcription of Arabic word	Arabic word	Arabic word in Swahili sense	Swahili usage	Arabic usage.
ithibati(N) (uhaki-kisho) (ushahidi)	ithba:t	إثبات	____	evidence, proof, confirmation.	____, establishment, assertion.
itifaki(N) (maafiki-ano)	ittifa:q	إتّفاق	____	agreement, concord, harmony.	____
ituri(N) (manukato) (marashi) (uturi)	ụṭu:r(pl.)	عُطور	____	perfume.	____
izraili(N)	ịzra:ịː:L	عِزْرائيل	____	the angel of death(mus.).	____
		J			
ja(V) (fika) (hudhu-ria) (tokea)	ja:ā	جاءَ	____	come, arrive, happen,** turn out,** result**(of event).	____, commit, receive, to do, to bring.
jaalia(V) (saidia) (wezesha) (also jalia)	jaạl(a)	جَعَلَ	____	grant, enable, give power (esp.) of God's favour and help.	God willing, make, to do, to put, render.
jabali(N) (ma-)	jabal	جَبَل	____	rocky hill or mountain, rock.	____
jabari(N) (ma-) (shujaa) (mjeuri)	jabba:r	جَبّار	____	a brave, proud person, a violent person.	____
jadi(N) (nasaba) (ukoo) (kizazi) (asili)	jadd	جَدّ		an ancestor, lineage, origin, descent, genealogy.	grand-father.
jadili(V) **ia/ika/iwa /iana.**	ja:dal(a)	جادَلَ	____	argue, ask, inquire,cross question.	____, to dispute.

Swahili word	Transcription of Arabic word	Arabic word	Arabic word in Swahili sense	Swahili usage	Arabic usage.
jaha(N) (heshima) (cheo kikubwa) (utukufu) (bahati)	ja:h	جَاه	_____	honour, prosperity, glory.	_____, dignity.
jahanamu(N) (jahim) (Rel.)	jahannam	جَهَنَّم	_____	Hell, Gehenna.	
jahara(adj.) (wazi wazi)	jahar	جَهْرٌ	_____	open, to raise the voice, public.	_____
jahazi(N) (ma-) (chombo) (meli)	jiha:z	جِهَازٌ	مَرْكَب / سَفِينَة	ship, dhow.	outfit, equipment.
jahili(adj.) (asiyena huruma) (mkatili) (mjinga) (mpumbavu)	jaħil	جَاهِلٌ	_____	ignorant, cruel, merciless, foolish.	_____
jahimu(N) (jahanam) (Rel.)	jaḥi:m	جَحِيمٌ	_____	Hell.	_____
jalada(N) (ma-) (funiko la kitabu)	jila:d	جِلَادٌ	_____ غِلَافٌ	cover of a book, binding.	_____
jalada(N) (faili)	jila:d	جِلَادٌ	مَلَفّ	file.	binding.
jali(V) (heshimu) (tii) (stahi) **ia/ika/isha/iwa/iana**	jaạl(a)	جَعَل	_____	see jaali.	_____
jalidi(V) **ia/ika/isha/iwa**	jallad(a)/ jalad(a)	جَلَّدَ / جَلَدَ	_____ , فَلَّف	bind a book,/whip, scourge.	_____
jamaa(N) (ndugu)	jama:ạa(t)	جَمَاعَة	_____ , عَشِيرَة	family, society, company, meeting, gathering, assembly.	_____, party.
jamala(N)(adabu) (madaha)(fadhili) (also tajamala)(V)	jama:l	جَمَال	_____ , حُسن / مَلَاحة / ظرف	courtesy, grace, manners, kindness,elegance,complaisance,affability,decorum, propriety, beauty, behaviour, gracious.	beauty, prettiness.
jamhuri(N)	jam huria	جَمْهُورِيَّة	_____	republic.	_____

Swahili word	Transcription of Arabic word	Arabic word	Arabic word in Swahili sense	Swahili usage	Arabic usage.
(a) **jamii**(V) (rare) isha.	jamaạ(a)	جَمَعَ	____	collect together.	____, to campile, to add up, to join.
(b) **jamii**(V) (tomba) **ia/ika/isha/iwa/iana**	ja:ma ạ(a)	جَامَعَ	____ اِتَّصَلَ جِنْسِيًّا.	have sexual intercourse.	____
(c) **jamii**(N)	jamạ	جَمْعٌ	____	gathering or collecting of.	____,
(d) **jamii** (adv.) (pamoja)	jami:ạan	جَمِيعاً	____	all together.	____
janaa(N) (aibu) (fedheha) (haya)	juna:ḥ	جُنَاح	____ عَيْب فَضِيحَة	shame, disgrace.	offence, guilt, sin.
janaba(N) (unajisi) (uchafu)	jana:ba(t)	جَنَابَة	____	defilement, pollution.	____
janna(N)(pepo)(Rel.) (poet.)	janna(t)	جَنَّة	____	paradise.	____
jaraha(N)	jira:ḥ	جِرَاح	____	wound, cut, sore, ulcer.	____
jaribio(N) (ma-)	tajruba(t)	تَجْرُبَة	____, تَجْرِيبٌ	a trial, trouble, temptation.	____, experience.
jaribu(V) (pima) (kadiria) **ia/ika/isha/iwa/iana.**	jarrab(a)	جَرَّبَ	____	try, test, attempt, tempt prove.	____
jarida(N) (ma-)	jari:da(t)	جَرِيدَة	مَجَلَّة	journal.	____, newspaper. palm-leaf stalk.
jasho(N) (tabu) (nguvu) (mvuke)	jaăsh	جَأْشٌ	عَرَق	perpiration, sweat, sultriness.	emotion, agitation.
jasi(N)	jaṣṣ/jiṣṣ	جَصٌّ/ جِصٌّ	____	gypsum.	____, plaster of Paris.

Swahili word	Transcription of Arabic word	Arabic word	Arabic word in Swahili sense	Swahili usage	Arabic usage.
jasiri(V) (thubutu) **ia/ika/isha**.	jassar(a)	جَسَّر	____	dare, embolden, risk, venture.	____
jasiri(adj.)(hodari) (shujaa)	jasu:r	جَسُور	____	bold, courageous, daring, brave, andacious.	____
jasusi(adj.) (ma-) (mpelelezi)	ja:su:s	جَاسُوس	____	spy, sly, betrayer.	____
jauri(N)(also jeuri)	jaur	جَوْر	____,	violence, oppression, injustice.	____
jawabu(N) (ma-) (also jibu)	jawa:b	جَوَاب	____	answer, reply, matter, affair, reponse.	____, message.
jazi(V) (Rel.) (thawabu) **ia/ika/iwa**	ja:za:	جَازَى	____	reward, grant a favour to, supply.	____
jedhamu(N) (ukoma)	jidha:m	جِذَام	____	leprosy, <u>elephantiasis</u>**	____
jedwali(N) (ya hesabu) (tebo)	jadwal	جَدْوَل	____	a table, timetable, schedule.	____, list.
jehannamu(N) (Rel.)	jahannam.	جَهَنَّم	____	see jahanamu.	____
jeraha(N) (ma-) (kidonda) (athari)	jira:ḥa(t)	جِرَاح / جِرَاحَة	____	see jaraha.	____
jeruhi(V) (umiza) **ia/ika/isha/iwa/iana**	jaraḥ(a)	جَرَح	____	wound, hurt.	____
jeshi(N) (ma-) (jumla ya askari)	jaysh	جَيْش	____	army, troops.	____
jeuri (N) (-nye kiburi) (uchokozi)	jawr	جَوْر	____	see jauri.	____
jezra(N) (kisiwa) (rare)	jazi:ra(t)	جَزِيرَة	____	island, isle.	____

Swahili word	Transcription of Arabic word	Arabic word	Arabic word in Swahili sense	Swahili usage	Arabic usage.
jezra Alkhadra (N) (Pemba)	jazi:ra(t) Alkhaḍra:ā	الجزيرة الخضراء	Proper name	Pemba(Zanzibar).	the green island.
jibini (N) (chizi)	jubn	جُبْنٌ	___	cheese.	___
Jibril(N) (Rel.)	jibri:L	جِبْرِيل	___	Gabriel.	___
jibu(V) **ia/ika/isha /iza/iana.**	åja:b(a)	أَجَـاب	___	to answer, reply, respond retort.	___
jihadi(N)	jiha:d	جِهَادٌ	___	jihad[Ar]* religious war by Muslims against unbelievers.	___
jihirisha(V) (rare) (ZNZ)	jahar(a)	جَهَـر	___	to declare, openly.	___, announce.
jinai(N) (kosa la uhalifu)	jinaya(t)	جِنَايَة	___	crime, criminal case.	___
jini(N) (ma-) (habithi)	jinn	جِـنّ / جن	___ خَبِيث	jinn,[Ar],* afairy, a spirit, weekedness.	___
(1) **jinsi**(N)[orig.skt.]* (namna) (njia)(aina) (mwendo)[lat.genus]*	jins	جِنْس	___	sort, kind, method, class, procedure.	___,race, genus, sex, gender (gr.).
Jinsia(N)	jinsi yya(t)	الجِنْسِيَّة	جِنْس	gender.	nationality.
jirani(N) (ma-)	jira:n (Pl.)	جيران (جمع)	جَارٌ	neighbour, anything near.	___
jirim(N) (ma-) (ZNZ)	jirm	جِـرْم	___	bulk, body.	___
ji **saidia**(V)	sa:ạd(a)	سَـاعَـدَ	سَـاعَدَ (نَفْسَهُ)	self help, (one self).	*
ji **sifu**(V)	waṣaf(a)	وَصَـفَ	وَصَفَ (نَفْسَهُ)	brag, boast(one self).	*

(1)genus(N) [Latin]* 1. birth, descent, origin, family; (a) ....,noble birth; (b) people, nation, tribe; (c) race ..., (d) Posterity, desendant 2. gender; 3. kind, class ..., (a) order, division; (b) ... character, fashion, manner, way, style ..., shorter Latin Dictionary (p.146)Berlin(1966).

Swahili word	Transcription of Arabic word	Arabic word	Arabic word in Swahili sense	Swahili usage	Arabic usage.
jitahidi(V) (jaribu sana)	ijitahad (a)	اجتهد (جهد)	____	to make effort, strain, try hard, exert, strive, endeavour	____
jitihadi(N)	ijtiha:d	اجتهاد	____	diligence, assiduity, exertion, effort, endeavour.	____
jiuzulu(V)	iạtazal(a)	اعتزل	____, استقال	resign, abdicate, retire.	____
johari(N) (kito) [Persian]*	jawhar	جوهر	____	jewel, gem, precious stone, nature, essence, element.	____
jozi(N)	joz	جوز (زوج)	____	a pair, brace, couple of anything.	____,(local Arabic)
juha(N) (ma-) (mpumbavu)	juḥḥa(t)	جحا	الساذج / المغفل	an idiot, ignoramus, simpleton.	an intelligent character.
juhudi(N) (bidii) (nguvu)	juhd	جهد	____	effort, ardour, strain, zeal, agony.	____
juma(N) (wiki)	juma̤ a(t)	جمعة	____, أسبوع	week, Friday.	____
jumla(N) (adv.)	jumla(t)	جملة	____	total, the sum, amount, quantity, a lot, altogether, wholesale.	____, sentence, phrase, several, many.
jumlisha(V)	jamal(a)	جمل (ف)	____	tot up, add together, sum up.	____, to speak generally.
jumuia(N) (ushirika) (chama)	jama̤iyya (t)	جمعية	____	a society, association, community.	____
juruhi(V) **ia/ika/isha/iwa/iana.**	juru:h jurḥ	(pl.) جروح (sing.) جرح	جرح	see jeruhi(V).	Pl. (in Arabic) of wound.

Swahili word	Transcription of Arabic word	Arabic word	Arabic word in Swahili sense	Swahili usage	Arabic usage.
juzu(V) (pasa) (faa) (husu) **ia/ika/**	ja:z(a)	جَازَ/ يَجُوز	———	be allowable, be permissible, be fitting for, be suitable, to allow.	———
(a) **juzuu**(N) (Rel.)	juzū(n)	جُزْءٌ	———	the thirtieth chapter of holly Koran.	———
(b) **juzuu**(N)	"	"	مُجَلَّد / قِسْمٌ	division, section, volume.	———, part, portion.
		K			
kababu(N)[Persian]*	kaba:b	كَبَاب	———	kebab.	———, grilled or roasted meat.
kabaila(N) (ma-) (mkuu)	qaba:i̲l	قَبَائِلُ	شَهِيرٌ مَشْهُورٌ	a man of high birth, an important man, exploiter.	tribes.
kabaili(N) (ma-) (also kabaila)	"		"	see kabaila.	———
kabidhi(V) (pokea) (chukua) **ia/ika/isha /iwa/iana.**	qabaḍ(a)	قَبَضَ	——— اسْتَلَمَ	receive, seize, hold, keep, deliver.	———
kabidhi(N) (bahili) (rare)	qa:biḍ	قَابِضٌ	——— بَخِيلٌ شَحِيح	miser, grasping, parsimonious.	———
kabila(N)	qabi:la(a)	قَبِيلَة	———, جِنْسِيَّة	tribe, nationality**.	———
kabili(V) (pambana na) (kuwa dhidi ya) **ia/ika/isha/iwa/iana**	qa:bal(a)	قَابَلَ	———, وَاجَه	be opposite to, be in front of, face, correspond to, confront, defy.	———, to encounter, meet.
kabla(conj.)	qabl(a)	قَبْلَ	———	before, previously.	———, formerly.
kaburi(N) (ma-)	qabr	قَبْرٌ	———	grave, tomb, cemetery, interment.	———

Swahili word	Transcription of Arabic word	Arabic word	Arabic word in Swahili sense	Swahili usage	Arabic usage.
kadamnasi(adv.) (mbele) (hadhara)	qidda:m anna:s	قَدّامُ النّاسِ	_____	before people, in public.	_____
kadari(ji) (Rel.) (majaaliwa)	qadar	قَدَرٌ	_____	destiny, fate, predestination.	_____
kadha (adv.)	kadha	كَذَا	_____	thus, so, like this,	----
kadha(N) (adj.) (Rel.)	qaḍa:ā	قَضَاء	_____	excution, paying a dept, accomplishment.	_____
kadhaa(adj.) (-a idadi maalum)	kadha	كَذَا	_____	a certain number.	_____
kadhalika(conj.) (vilevile)	kadhalik (a)	كَذَلِكَ	_____	so, thus, like this.	_____, like wise, also.
kadha wa kadha(adj.) (hivyo)	kadha wa kadha	كَذَا وَكَذَا	_____	so and so, et cetera.	_____
kadhi(N) (hakimu) (mwamuzi) (jaji)	qa:ḍi(n)	قَاضٍ	_____	an Islamic judge.	judge.
kadhi (Mkuu)(N)	qa:ḍi(n)	"	رئيسُ القضاء	a principal Islamic judge.	*
kadhibisha(V) (also kidhibisha) (rare)	kadh̲ab(a)	كَذَّبَ	_____ أَنْكَرَ	refute, deny, give the lie to.	_____
kadiri(V) **ia/ika/isha/iwa/iana**	qaddar(a)	قَدَّرَ	_____	estimate, reckon, judge, appreciate.	_____
kadiri(N),(adj.) (uwezo) (nguvu) (kiasi) (eneo) (jinsi) (thamani)	qadr	قَدْرٌ	_____ تَقْدِيرٌ مِقْدَارٌ	amount, measure, rank, immoderation.	_____
kadiria(V) (kisia) **(pima)**	qaddar(a)	قَدَّرَ	_____	see kadiri(V).	_____

Swahili word	Transcription of Arabic word	Arabic word	Arabic word in Swahili sense	Swahili usage	Arabic usage.
kadirifu (adj.) (angalifu)	muqaddir	مُقَدِّر	____	valuer, estimator, careful.	____
kadirio(N) (ma-)	taqdi:r	تَقْدِير	تَخْمِين قوض	valuation, moderation, estimation.	____, supposition, hypothesis.
kafani(N) (sanda) (rare)	kafan	كَفَن	____	shroud, winding, sheet.	____
kafara(N)	kaffa:ra (t)	كَفَّارَة	____	sin offering, expiation, a charm.	____, atonement (sin).
kafiri(N) (ma_)	ka:fir	كَافِرٌ	____	infidel, pagan, unbeliever, athiest, one who is not a muslim.	
kafuri(N) (namna ya miti) [Sanskrit]*	ka:fu:r	كَافُورٌ	____	camphor.	____
kahawa(N)		قَهْوَةٌ	____	coffee.	____
kahini(N) (ma-) (Rel.) (kuhani) (mchawi) (dhalimu) (mdanganyifu) (laghai)	ka:hin	كَاهِنٌ	عَرَّاف , ____	priest(in jewish dispensation) soothsayer, deceiver, swindler.	
kaidi(V) (bishi) (kosa kutii) **ia/ika/ isha.**	ka:d(a) ka:yad(a)	كَاد / كَايد	مَايَدَ	be obstinate,rebel,contradict,refuse to obey.	to deceive, beguile.
kaidi(adj.)(bishi) (shupavu)	kaid	كَيْدٌ	عَبِيدٌ	obstinate, refractory, disobedient.	slyness, cunning, deceit, ruse, artifice.
kaifa haluka(N) (greeting)	kayf(a) haluk(a)	كَيْف حَالُك	____	how are you.	
kaimati(N)	luq aima:t	لُقَيْمَاتٌ	____ ,	dumpling, fritter.	____
kaimu(N) (ma-) (naibu) (msimamizi)	qa:im	قَائِمٌ	____	deputy, in the place of, on behalf of, acting of, superintendant, agent, guardin.	____

Swahili word	Transcription of Arabic word	Arabic word	Arabic word in Swahili sense	Swahili usage	Arabic usage.
kaimu(N) (mganga)	"	قَائِمٌ	الذي يطرد الأرواح الشريرة بالرقى	one who exercizes spirits	*
kalamu(N)	qalam	قَلَمٌ	____	pen, pencil.	____
kalbi(N) (ZNZ) (ma-)	qa:lib	قَالِبٌ	قَالِبُ الاسْمَنْت	a mould of cement put in well after digging.	mould, form, boot-lost.
kalifisha(V) (also kalifu) **ia/ika/iwa**	kallaf(a)	كَلَّفَ	____	to take the trouble to do discomfort, course annoyance to, trouble.	____, to impose a task upon.
kalifu(V) (lazimisha) (sumbua) (taabisha)	takallaf (a)	تَكَلَّفَ	____	see kalifisha(V).	____
kalima(N) (neno) (rare)	kalima(t)	كَلِمَةٌ	____	word (see mkalimani).	____
kama(conj.) (ikiwa) (kuliko)	kama:	كَمَا	____	as, such as, like, just as, as if, as it is, as through.	____
kamari(N)	qima:r	قِمَار	____ المَيْسِر	gambling, playing for a money stake.	____
kamili(adj.) (timilifu) (halisi)	ka:mil	كَامِل	____	complete, perfect, entire, whole.	____, full, total, plenary.
kamili(V) (timiza) (maliza) **ika/isha**	kammal(a)	أكْمَلَ / كَمَّل	____	complete, finish, bring to perfection.	____
kamilio(N) (ma-) (kusudio kubwa)	takmi:l/ ikma:l.	تكْميل /إكْمَال	مَقْصَدٌ عَظِيمٌ	intention, purpose.	completion.
Kamilifu (adj)	kamil	كَامِل	____	perfect, smart, complete.	----
kamusi(N)	qa:mu:s	قَامُوسٌ	____ مُعْجَمٌ	lexicon, dictionary.	
kandili(N) (fanusi) (taa ya mkono)	qindi:l	قِنْدِيلٌ	____ شَمْعَةٌ شَمْعَدَانٌ	lantern.	____, candle-stick lamp.

Swahili word	Transcription of Arabic word	Arabic word	Arabic word in Swahili sense	Swahili usage	Arabic usage.
kanisa(N) (ma-) (Rel.) (jumuia ya wakristo)[Gr.]* [orig. Aramaic.]*	kani:sa(t)	كَنِيسَةٌ	____	church, chapel.	____, synagogue.
kanuni(N) (desturi) (utaratibu) (sheria) (amri)	qa:nu:n	قَانُونٌ	____	rule, regulation, law, a canon [Gr.]*.	____,
karabai(N)[Persian]*	ka:hraba:	كَهْرَبَاء	مِصْبَاحٌ (لَمْبَة)	a pressure lamp, an acetylene lamp.	electric.
karadha(N) (mkopo)	qarḍ	قَرْضٌ	____	advance, credit, a loan money. (without interest)	____
karafuu(N) [Gr.]*	qaranful	قَرَنْفُل	____	cloves.	____
karaha(N) (maudhi) (uchafu)	kara:ha(t)	كَرَاهَةٌ	____	hatred, aversion, disgust	_ ____
karama(N)	kara:ma(t)	كَرَامَةٌ	____	honour, consideration, talent, privilege, (especially from God).	
karamu(N)	karam	كَرَمٌ	____	a feast, banquet, a festive entertainment.	liberality, generosity,
karatasi(N) [orig. Gr.]*	qirṭa:s	قِرْطَاسٌ	____	paper, sheet of paper.	____
karibia(V) (sogea) (jongea) **isha/iwa/iana.**	taqarrab (a)	تَقَرَّبَ/ قَارَبَ	____, قَرَّبَ	come in, approach, go near to, move close, bring near.	____
karibiano(N) (msogeleano)	taqa:rub qara:ba(t)	تَقَارُبٌ قَرَابَةٌ	____	closing together, coming nearer to each other, relationship, kinsman.	____
karibisha(V) (kirimu) (pumzisha) **ia/ika/wa/ana.**	qarrab(a)	قَرَّبَ	رَحَّبَ بِ	welcome, invite to a meal.	____

Swahili word	Transcription of Arabic word	Arabic word	Arabic word in Swahili sense	Swahili usage	Arabic usage.
(a) **karibu** (adv.)	qari:b(an) (taqri:b an)	قريبٌ / تقريبًا	قريبًا ——	presently, lately, nearly almost, about.	——
(b) **karibu**(N)	"	قريب	——	near, kinsman.	——
(c) **karibu** (conj.) (kwa heri) (kwa heshima)	"	"	مع السلامة وداعًا	goodbye.	*
karibuni(adv.)	"	"	توًّا / قريبًا	see karibu(a).	*
karidhi(V) (kopesha fedha) **ia/ika/isha/iwa/iana.**	qaraḍ(a)	أقرض	——	borrow, lend, advance.	——
karimu(adj.)	kari:m	كريمٌ	سخيٌّ —— جواد	liberal, geneous, openhanded.	——
karimu(N) (ma-)	kari:m	كريمٌ	مضيافٌ ——	hospitable, generous, kindman.	——
kariri (v) **ia/ika/isha.**	**karrar (a)**	كرّر	——	repeat, <u>Memorize</u> **	——,rectify, reiterate
karne(N) (miaka mia moja)	qarn	قرنٌ	مائة عام ——	a century.	——, horn, age, generation.
kasarobo(adj.)(also kasorobo)	kasr/ruba	كسرٌ/ ربعٌ	إلّا ربعًا	quarter to.	*
kashifa(N) (also kashfa)	kashf	كشفٌ / مكاشفة	طعنٌ —— قذفٌ	slander, libel, false statement	----, disclosure.
kashifu(V) (fungua) (weka wazi) (aibisha) (singizia) **ia/ika.**	kashaf(a)	كشف	قذف / طعن	libel, slander, reveal secrets.	——
kasi (adv.) (bidii) (mbio sana)	qaṣa:	قصى / أقصى	جدًّا / كثيرًا	much, very much, very, with energy.	to send far away, extreme, uttermost.

Swahili word	Transcription of Arabic word	Arabic word	Arabic word in Swahili sense	Swahili usage	Arabic usage.
kasida(N) (Rel.) (vipokeo)	qaṣi:da(t)	قَصِيدَة	قَصِيدَةٌ دِينِيَّة	a religious poem.	poem.
kasirika(V) (ghadhibika) **ia/wa**.	inkasar(a)	اِنْكَسَرَ / أَوْ مِنَ الفِعْلِ قَصَرا	غَضِبَ/ اِغْتَاظَ	be angry, be vexed, cause to be angry, vex, provoke.	to be broken, defeated, routed.
kasirisha(V) (chukiza)	kasar(a)	كَسَرَ/كَسَّرَ	أَغَاظَ/اغْضَبَ	see kasirika(V).	to defeat, violate, break.
kasisi(N) (ma-) (padre) (Rel.)	qissi:s	قِسِّيسٌ لقَسٌّ)	____	a priest, clergyman	____
kasoro(N) (dosari) (upungufu)	kasar	كَسْرٌ أَوْ مِنْ قَسرا	عَيْب	defeat, blemish.	see kasirika(V).
kaṣoro(adj.)	maksu:r	مَكْسُورا أَوْ مَقصورا	مُعَاب	see kasoro(N).	defeated, routed.
kaṣoro(adv.) (ila) (isipokuwa)	kasr	كَسْر	إلاَ	less by, short by, less.	____
kasorobo(adj.)	kasr/ruba	كَسْرٌ/رُبْعٌ	إلاَ رُبْعاً	see kasarobo.	____
kasra(N)(also kisra)	kasra(t)	الكَسْرَة	____	a defeat, a rout.	____
kasri(N)	qaṣr	قَصْرٌ	____	palace, castle.	____
(1) **kata**(V)	qaṭaạ(a)	قَطَعَ	____	cut, cut off, cut up divide, decide, to cut to pieces, reduce/interrupt.	____
(2) **kata**(N)	muqa:ṭaạa(t) (t)	مُقَاطَعَة	دَائِرَةٌ لِمِنْ مَدِينَة/ حَيٌّ	ward.	region, district, province.
(3) **kata**(N)*	*	*	*	scoop.	*
kataa(V) (zuia) (nyima) **lia/lika/za/liwa/ana**.	qa:ṭaạ(a)	قَاطَعَ	رَفَضَ	refuse, reject, decline.	devidedly, final decision, prevent.
katabahu(N)	katabahu	كَتَبَهُ	____	he wrote it, written by.	____
katani(N) (also kitani)	katta:n	كَتَّان	____	flax.	____

Swahili word	Transcription of Arabic word	Arabic word	Arabic word in Swahili sense	Swahili usage	Arabic usage.
kataza(V) (ma-)	qaṭaạ(a)	قَاطَعَ	رَفَضَ	see kataa.	—
katazo(N) (ma-)	qaṭạ	قَطْعٌ/ مُقَاطَعَةٌ	رَفْضٌ	see kataa.	—
katiba(N)	muka:taba(t)	مُكَاتَبَةٌ	دُسْتُورٌ	ordinance, custom, natural, constitution.	correspondence, exchange of letters.
katibu (N) (ma-) (mwandishi)	ka:tib	كَاتِبٌ	— (اسِكْرتِير) أَمِينُ السِّرِّ	clerk, a writer, amannensis, secretary.	—
katibu (<u>mkuu</u>)(N)	"	كَاتِب (أَوَّل)	وَكِيلُ وِزَارَةٍ	principle secretary.	*
katibu mahsusi (N) (tec.)	"	كَاتِبٌ خَاصٌّ	— شَخْصِي	personal secretary.	*
katibu muhtasi(N) (tec.)	"	كَاتِبٌ مُخْتَصٌّ	— / خُصُوصِيٌّ خَاصّ	private secretary.	*
katibu shakhsiya(N) (tec.)	"	كَاتِبٌ (شَخْصِي)	— / شَخْصِي خَاصّ	personal secretary.	*
katili(N) (dhalimu) (also mkatili)	qa:til	قَاتِل	— قَاسٍ مُجْرِمٌ / ظَالِمٌ	cruel, murderous, bloodthirsty.	—
katu(conj.) (hata kidogo) (asilani) (abadani)	qaṭṭ	قَطّ	—,	never, not even a little, not at all.	—, only.
kauli(N) (ahadi) (maelezo) (usemi) (maoni) (hisia)	qaul	قَوْلٌ	رِوَايَة / وَصْفٌ عَهْدٌ	expression, advice, account, promise.	saying, statement.
kawafi (N) (poet.)	qawa:fi:	قَوَافِ (قَوَافِي)	قَافِيَةٌ	rhyme.	—
kawaida(N)	qawa:iḍ	قَوَاعِد	— قَاعِدَة	custom, regulation, rule, system.	base, basis, foundation rule, regulation, model.

Swahili word	Transcription of Arabic word	Arabic word	Arabic word in Swahili sense	Swahili usage	Arabic usage.
khabari(N)	khabar	خَبَرٌ	——	see habari.	——
khalaiki(N) (rare)	khala:iq	خَلَائِق	حَشْدٌ / جَمْعٌ كَثِيرٌ	see halaiki.	——
khaini(N) (rare)	kha:in	خَائِن	——	see haini.	——
khedaa(N)	khida:ạ	خِدَاعٌ	——	see hadaa(V), deceit.	——
kheri(N)	khair	خَيْرٌ	——	see heri.	——
khiari(N)	khiya:r	خِيَارٌ	——	see hiari.	——
kiarabu(N)	Ạrabia	عَرَبِيَّة	اللُّغَةُ العَرَبِيَّةُ الأَمْرُ مَا يَتَعَلَّقُ بِالعَرَب	Arabic language.	——
kiarifu(N)	taạri:f	تَعْرِيفٌ	خَبَرٌ ـ جُمْلَة خَبَرِيَّة	predicate of a sentence (ling.).	definition.
kiasi(N) (wastani) (kadiri) (bei)	qiya:s	قِيَاسٌ	——	amount, a meature, quantity moderation, numerator(Arith.).	——, comparison, rule syllogism.
kiaskofu(N)	ụsqufiyya(t)	الأُسْقُفِيَّة	——	bishopric.	——
kibali(N) (ruhusa) (idhini)	qabu:l	قَبُولٌ	إِقَامَة ـ أَذَن	acceptance, assent, consent, sanction, approval, favour, residence.	——, reception.
kibaraka(N) (vi-) (karagosi)	baraka (root)	(مِنَ البَرَكَة)	عَمِيلٌ / جَاسُوسٌ	stooge, spy, agent.	blessing.
kibilisi(N)	ibli:sy	إِبْلِيسٌ	الشَّيْطَنَة	satanic, devilish.	——
kiberiti(N) (also kibiriti)	kibri:t	كِبْرِيت	——	matches, sulphur, a firework.	——
kibla(N) (Rel.)	qibla(t)	قِبْلَة	——	kibla, the direction of kaaba(for praying), north**.	——

Swahili word	Transcription of Arabic word	Arabic word	Arabic word in Swahili sense	Swahili usage	Arabic usage.
kibti(N) (rare)	qibṭ	قِبْطِيٌّ	الأَقْبَاط ———	copts, a copt.	———
kiburi(N) (majivuno) (ndweo)	kibr	كِبْرٌ / تَكَبُّرٌ	———	pride, haughtiness, conceit arrogance, haughtiness.	———, presumption.
kiburudishaji(N) (vi-)	buru:da(t)	بُرُودَةٌ/ تَبْرِيدٌ	انْتِعَاشٌ	refreshment, relief, recreation.	coldness, coolness/cooling.
kiburudisho(N) (vi-) (kinywaji)	"	"	شَرَابٌ/ مَشْرُوبٌ	something to drink, beverage.	coldness, coolness/cooling.
kidhi(V) (timiza) (tosheleza) **ia/ika/isha/wa.**	qaḍa:	قَضَى	كَفَى ، ———	satisfy, grant, to finish.	———, end, to sentence, to execute, to judge, die.
kifaranga(N) (Vi-) (mtoto wa ndege au kuku)	farkh (fira:kh)	فَرْخٌ	فِرَاخٌ ، ———	chick.	———
kifo(N) (vi-)(mauti)	wafa:	وَفَاةٌ	المَوْت ، ———	death, act of dying, decease.	*
kiharusi(N) (faliji)	ụrs/ạru:s	العرس / العَرُوس	فَالِج	apoplexy, palsy, paralysis.	see harusi.
kihusishi(N)	khuṣu:ṣ	خُصُوص	حَرْفُ الجَرِّ	preposition, see hususa(n).	*
kiislamu(N)	Isla:m	الأسْلَام	إِسْلَامِيٌّ	Islamic, see Islam .	*
kijamaa(N)	jama:ạ(t)	جَمَاعَةٌ	اشْتِرَاكِيَّة	socialism, see jamaa.	*
kijini(N)	jinny	الجِنُّ	جِنِّيٌّ	satanic, develish, see jini.	*
kikafiri(N)	kufry	الكُفْر (كُفْرِيٌّ)	مُتَعَلِّقٌ بِالكُفْر	something pertaining to infidelity.	*

Swahili word	Transcription of Arabic word	Arabic word	Arabic word in Swahili sense	Swahili usage	Arabic usage.
kikamilifu(N) (vi-)	kamil(an)	كَامِلاً	———	completly. see kamili.	*
kikanisa(N)	kanisa(t) (root)	كَنِيسَة / كَنَس	كَنَسِيّ	something pertaining to church. see kanisa.	*
kila(adv.) (adj.)	kull	كُلّ	———	every, each, everyone.	———
kima(N) (bei) (thamani) (kadiri)	qi:ma(t)	قِيمَة / قَامَة	——— سِعْر	price, worth, foot rule, measure, value.	———
kima(N) (not Arabic)	*	*	*	a kind of monkey.	*
kima(N) [Persian, Hind]*	*	*	*	minced meat.	*
kimataifa(N)	ṭa_ifa (t)	(مِنْ طَائِفَة)	عَالَمِيًّا / دَوْلِيًّا	international. see taifa.	people class, sect, faction communion, party, denomination.
(a)**kimu**(V) (Rel.) **ia/ika/isha/iwa**	ȧqa:m(a)	أَقَامَ	أَقَامَ الصَّلَاةَ	to perform religious service, begin prayers.	———
(b)**kimu**(V) (lisha) (lea) (tunza) (weka) **ia/ika/isha/iwa/iana**	qa:m	قَامَ	عَالَ / رَعَى مَوَّنَ	to support one's family, maintain, supply with food.	———
kinai(V) **ia/ika/isha /iwa.**	qana ạ	قَنِعَ	———	to be satisfied or content with.	———, to be convinced, or persuaded.
(a)**kinaya**(N)	qana:ạa(t)	قَنَاعَةُ	———	independence, self-content, selfish isolation, isolence, conceit.	contentment, moderation, satisfaction, temperance.

Swahili word	Transcription of Arabic word	Arabic word	Arabic word in Swahili sense	Swahili usage	Arabic usage.
(a) **kinaya**(N)(inadi) (stihizai) (kifani)	kina:ya(t)	كِنَايَة	سَبّ / سِبَابٌ	curse, disgrace, wilfulness, provocation, perversity.	motonymy, indirect expression, allusion.
kinubi(N)	nubiyy	نُوبِيّ / نُوبِيَّة	اللُّغَةُ النُّوبِيَّة مَا يَتَعَلَّقُ بِالنُّوبَةِ	Nubian language, a Nubian Sudanese.	Nubia, Nubian, black.
kirahi(N) (also ikrahi, karaha)	ikra:h	إِكْرَاه	———	see karaha.	———
kiraia(adv.)	raịyya(t) (root)	(مِنْ الرَّعِيَّة)	مَا يَتَعَلَّقُ بِالرَّعِيَّة	as/like a citizen, civil rights.	———
kiraka(N) , (adv.)	ruqạa(t)	رُقْعَة (صَغِيرَة)	———	spot of colour, patch, mend spotted, speckled.	a patch, label, to patch, to resow.
kiri(V) **ia/ika/isha/iwa/iana.**	ȧqarra	أَقَرَّ	———	to recognize, accept, acknowledge, confirm, ratify, approve, grant, confess, admit, assent, aver.	———
kirihi(V)	kariha	كَرِهَ	———	see karaha.	———
kirimu(V) **ia/ika/isha/iwa**	ȧkram(a)	أَكْرَمَ	———	be hospitable, to honour, to be kind, be generous.	———
kiroho (adj.)	ru:h(root)	(مِنْ الرُّوح)	رُوحِيًّا ———	spiritual.	———
kirumi(N)	Ru:m	الرُّوم	لُغَةُ الرُّومِ أَوْ مَا يَتَعَلَّقُ بِالرُّوم	Latin language, Roman, Latin.	———
Kirusi(N)	Ru:s	الرُّوس	اللُّغَةُ الرُّوسِيَّة أَوْ مَا يَتَعَلَّقُ بِالرُّوسِ	Russian language, Russian.	———

Swahili word	Transcription of Arabic word	Arabic word	Arabic word in Swahili sense	Swahili usage	Arabic usage.
kisa(N) (masimulizi) (sababu) (jambo) (tukio)	qiṣṣa(t)	قِصَّة	——	story, tale, narrative, report, explanation,** cause,** reason,** matter,** affair,** business** complaint,** charge,** history.	——, forelock.
kisahani(N)	saḥn	صَحْنٌ	—— (صَغِيرٌ)	a small dish, or plate, a soucer.	see sahani.
kisamaki(N)	samak	سَمَك	سَمَكَةٌ (صَغِيرَةٌ)	a small fish.	see samaki.
kisanamu(N) (dimin of sanamu)	ṣanam	صَنَمٌ	—— (صَغِيرٌ)	picture, postcard, a small object.	see sanamu.
kisanduku(N) (vi-) (dimin of sanduku)	ṣandu:q	صَنْدُوق	—— (صَغِيرٌ)	a small box, casket.	see sanduku.
kisasi(N) (vi-)	qiṣa:ṣ	قِصَاصٌ	——	revenge, relation, vengeance, compensation, indemnification.	——, punishment.
kisheria(N)	shariyyan	شَرْعِيًّا	——	legal, see sheria.	——
kishetani	shayṭa:niyy	شَيْطَانِي	——	see shetani.	——
kisukari(N)	sukkary	سُكَّرِيٌّ	——	diabetes.	——
kiswahili(N)	sawahilia	سَوَاحِلِيَّة	اللُّغَةُ السَاحِلِيَّة (سَوَاحِلِيَّة)	swahili language.	——
kitabu(N) (vi-) (msahafu) (chuo)	kita:b	كِتَابٌ	——	a book, koran.	——
kithiri (V) (ongezeka) (zidi) **ia/ika/isha/iwa**	kathur (a)	كَثُرَ	——	to be much or many, increase, to do more, cause to do much.	——
kitini (V) (dimin of matini)	matn	مَتْنٌ	مَتْنٌ (صَغِيرٌ)	see matini.	——

Swahili word	Transcription of Arabic word	Arabic word	Arabic word in Swahili sense	Swahili usage	Arabic usage.
kiwakilishi (N) (vi)	wakkal(a)	وكّـل (ف)	اِسْمُ المَوْصُول	a ralative pronoun.	to appoint as agent.
kofi(N) (ma-)	kaffa(t)	كَـفّة	___ الضَّرْبُ بالكـفة	flat of the hand, a blow with the open hand, box on the ear, slap.	___
kofia(N)	ku:fiya(t)	كُـوفِيَة	___	cap, a kind of tarboash.	silk head wrapper.
kohl(N) (also kohli)	kuḥl	كُـحْل	___	antimony used for beautifying the eyes.	___
kubali(V) (ridhika) (kiri) (ruhusa) **ia/ika/isha/iwa/iana**	qabil(a)	قَـبِلَ (ف)	___	accept, assent, acknowlege, agree.	___
kudura(N) (uwezo) (Rel.)	qudra(t)	قُـدْرَة (الهية)	___	power, strength, might (only for God).	___
kufuli(N) (ma-) (kitasa)	qufl	قُـفْل	___	padlock.	___
kufuru(V) (Rel.) **ia/ika/isha/iwa**	kafar(a)	كَـفَر	___	to be irreligious, be an infidel, not to believe, to blaspheme God, curse, revile.	___, to cover, hide, to expiate.
kuhani(N) (ma-) (also kahini)	ka:hin	كـاهِن	___	see kahini.	___
kulateni(N) (Rel.)	qullatain	قُـلَّتَيْن	___	tank of water in a mosque commonly containing about (50) gallons.	two jugs, two pitcher, two water coolers.
kunradhi(conj.)	kunra:di (n)	كُـنْ راضٍ	___	be contenting, satisfied, willing, be pleasant, pardon me, excuse me.	___

Swahili word	Transcription of Arabic word	Arabic word	Arabic word in Swahili sense	Swahili usage	Arabic usage.
kura(N)	quraa(t)	القُرْعَة	الاقْتِراع	voting, balloting, lots, chance, a vote, fate.	____, conscription recruitment,
kurani(N)	qurã:n	قُرْآن	____	the Holy book of Islam.	____
kurasa(N)	kurasa(t)	كَرّاسة	صَفْحَة صفحات ـ جمع	page, a paper, sheet, leaflet.	book, copybook, pamphlet.
kurub(adv.) (ZNZ)	qurb	قُرْب	مَرْحَبًا	wellcome! enter.	nearness, closeness.
kurubia(V)	taqarrab	تَقَرَّبَ	____	to approach, go near to, come near, approximate, be near, enter.	____
kusudi(N) (adv.) (shauri) (azimio)	qasd	قَصْد	____	purpose, intention, object, aim, end.	____
kusudia(V) (nuia) (azimia) (dhamiria)	qasad	قَصَدَ	____	purpose, intend, aim at, design.	____
		L			
la!(conj.) (hasha) (siyo) (hakuna) (hapana)	la	لاَ	____	not, no, not so, by no means.	____
(a) **laana**(N)	laana(t)	لَعْنَة	____	curse, execration, imprecation, oath.	____
(b) **laana**(N)(shonga)	lia:n laana(t)	لِعَان لَعْنَة	____	oath of condemnation, sworn allegation of adulry committed by either husband or wife.	____

Swahili word	Transcription of Arabic word	Arabic word	Arabic word in Swahili sense	Swahili usage	Arabic usage.
laani(V) **ia/ika/isha /iwa/iana**	laạn(a)	لَعَنَ (ف)	____	curses, damn, swear at, execrate.	____
laanifu(adj.) (-nye sifa ya kulaanika)	la ị:n	لَعِين / مَلْعُون	____	cursed, accursed, damned.	____
laasiri(N) (also alasiri	alạṣr	العَصْر	____	see alasiri.	
labda (adv.) (huenda) (yawezekana)	la/budda	لَابُدَّ	رُبَّمَا يُمْكِن	probably, perhaps, possibly, no doubt.	no escape, by all means.
labeka! (intej.) (abee) (bee) (beka) (naam)	labbaika	لَبَّيْكَ	____	at your service!, yes, sir (naam)!.	____, here!, am!
ladha(N) (also laza, ludha)	ladha(t)	لَذَّة	____ طَعْم	ador, fragrance, aroma, to find it whether pleasant or unpleasant.	delight, pleasure.
lafidhi(N) (also lafudhi, lafuzi)	lafdḥ	لَفْظٌ	____	pronunciation, accent, style, manner of speaking, excuse, evasion.	____, term, phonetic, word, expression, articulation.
lafudhi(N)	"	"	____	see lafidhi.	____
lafuzi(N)	"	"	____	see lafidhi.	____,
laghai(V) (shawishi kwa hila) (nyenga)	laghwu(n)	لَغَا/ لَغْوٌ (يَلْغُو)	خَدَعَ	deceive, cheat, beguile, confuse.	nonsense, faulty language.
laghai(N) (also mlaghai) (mjanja) (mwelevu)	"	لَغْوٌ	خَدَّاعٌ	sly, false, deceitful, dishonest.	foolish talk, mall, nonsense.
lahaja(N)	lahja(t)	لَهْجَة	____	dialect.	____, accent, tone, vernacular.

Swahili word	Transcription of Arabic word	Arabic word	Arabic word in Swahili sense	Swahili usage	Arabic usage.
(a) **laini**(N) (teke-teke) (-ororo) (isiyo ngumu)	li:n	لِين / لُيُونَة	——	softness, tenderness,	____, lenity.
(b) **laini** (adj.) (-pole, -taratibu)	layyi:n	لَيِّن	——	soft, tender, flexible, supple, thin, delicate, fine, smooth, pliable, gentle, good-nature.	____
lainifu(N) (adj.)	"	"	——	see laini(b).	____
lainika(V) (kuwa laini)	la:n(a)	لاَنَ (ف)	——	be soft, delicate, smooth be gentle.	____
lainisha(V)	layyan(a)	لَيَّنَ / ألاَنَ (ف)	——	to soften, smothen, alleviate, ease.	____
laiti(interj.)	layt	لَيْت	——	would that, if only, oh that.	____
lakabu(N) (jina la kupanga)	laqab	لَقَب	——	surname.	___, epithet, title of honour.
laki(N) [Persian, Hind.]*	lakk	اللَّكّ	——	hundred thousand.	ten million.
laki(V) **ia/iwa/iana**	la:qa:	لاَقَى	____, اِسْتَقْبَلَ	to meat, welcome, to receive.	____
lakini(V) (Rel.)	laqqan(a)	لَقَّنَ	——	to dictate a muslim (shahada) during his death.	___, to instruct, teach, to promt.
lakini(conj.)	la:kin	لَكِن	——	but, however, yet, nevertheless.	____

Swahili word	Transcription of Arabic word	Arabic word	Arabic word in Swahili sense	Swahili usage	Arabic usage.
laumu(V)	lawam(a)	لَـوَمَ	____	criticise, blame, accuse, reproach, up braid, reprove.	____, centure.
lawama(N) (ma-) (maonyo)	lawm	لَـوْمٌ	____	reproach, charge, blame, guilt, reproof, criticism responsibility.	___, censure, rebuke.
lawiti(N) (fira) **ia/ika/isha/iwa/iana**	la:ṭ(a)	لاَطَ	____	commit, practice sodomy.	____
lazima(N) (adv.) (hapana budi) (sharti)	la:zim	لاَزِم	____	necessity, obligation, responsibility, bail, need, surety, necessarily.	____
lazimu(V) (shurutisha) **ika/isha**	alzam(a)	أَلْزَمَ	____	to oblige,be responsible, compel force.	____
lilahi/lillahi(adv.) (Rel.) (kwa kusudia Allah.)	lilla:hi	لِـلّٰهِ	______	to do something for Allah.	_____
liwali(N) (ma-) (also luwali, wali) (rare)	Alwa:li	الـوَالِي	____	administrative official, headman.	ruler, governor.
lozi(N) (mlozi)	lawz	الـلَّوز	____	almond.	____
lugha(N)	lugha(t)	لُـغَة	____	language, dialect, speech.	____
lujna(N) (ZNZ)(also lujuna)	lajna (t)	لَجْنَة	____	commitee, council.	___, commission, board.
lukuki(N)	luku:k	لُـكُوك	____	countless number, myriad.	___, see(laki).
lulu(N)	lūlū	اللُّؤْلُـؤْ	___	pearl.	_____

Swahili word	Transcription of Arabic word	Arabic word	Arabic word in Swahili sense	Swahili usage	Arabic usage.
maabara(N) (lebu)	maạbara(t)	مَعْبَر/ مَعْبَرَة	مَعْمَل / مُخْتَبَر	laboratory.	lobby, traverse, crossing point, ford.
maabudu(N) (rare) (Rel.)	maạbu:d	مَعْبُود	———	worship, object of worship.	———
maadamu(conj.) (madhali) (kama)	ma/da:m(a)	مَا / دَام	———	when, since, if, while because, seeing that, as long as, as, in as much as.	____, continue, to last.
maadhimisho(N)	taạḍhi:m	تَعْظِيم	احْتِفَال بِـ ——— تمجيد	see adhimisho.	aggrandizement, glorification, exaltation, military salute.
maadhura(N)	maạdhira (t)	مَعْذِرَة	اِعْتِذَار	absence with apology.	___, excuse, plea.
maadili(N) (pl. of adili)	ạdl/ạda:la (t)	العَدْل/ العَدَالَة	سُلُوك تَصَرُّف ، ___	conduct, good, righteous, life, see adili(N).	___, fairness, impartiality, probity, honesty, decency, equitableness, integrity.
maafa(N) (pl. afa) (balaa) (msiba) (ajali) (masaibu) (kisirani) (nuksi)	ã:fa (t)	آفَة	كَارِثَة ، ___	see afa(N).	———
maafikiano(N) (mapatano) (mwafaka)	wifa:q/ muwa:faqa (t)	وِفَاق / مُوَافَقَة	———	see afikiano(N).	agreement, conformance, correspondence, fitness, approval, authorization, sanction, consent, analogy, suitability, assent.

Swahili word	Transcription of Arabic word	Arabic word	Arabic word in Swahili sense	Swahili usage	Arabic usage.
maalum(u) (adj.) (hakika) (halisi) (mahususi) (maarufu) (hasa)	maạlu:m	مَعْلُوم	____	known, proper, peculiar, recognized special.	____, determined, of course, certainly, sure.
maamuma(N) (Rel.) (mfuasi)	maạmu:m	مَأْمُوم	____	Muslim or Muslims who follow imam (prayer leader in a mosque or another place)	____
maana(N) (sababu) (sababu) (kisa) (kusudio) (lengo) (heshima) (akili) (busara)	maạna:	مَعْنَى	____	meaning, impose, intention, sense, often, cause, reason, sake, consideration.	____, signification idea, thought, notion, concept.
maanisha(V)	ạna:/yaạni:	عَنَى / يَعْنِي	____	to mean, that is to say, to concern.	____, take care of.
maarifa(N) (hekima) (elimu) (ujuzi)	maạrifa(t)	مَعْرِفَة	____	knowledge, intelligence, news, plan, information.	____, love, skill, experience, congnition, realization.
maarufu(adj.)	maạru:f	مَعْرُوف	____	well-known, famous, imformed, celebrated, known, recognized.	____, beneficial, convertional, kindness.
maasi(N) (uhalifu) (ukaidi)	maạ:ṣi(n)	مَعَاصٍ (مَعَاصِي)	____ مَعْصِيَة مُخَالَفَة	disobedience, insubordination, revolt, rebelion, mutiny, insurrection, sin.	____, refractoriness,
maasia(N) (madhambi) (Rel.)	maạṣiya(t)	مَعْصِيَة	____	s. maasi(N).	____
maasumu(N)	maạṣu:m	مَعْصُوم	____	inviolable, sacrosanct, sinless.	____, impeccant.

Swahili word	Transcription of Arabic word	Arabic word	Arabic word in Swahili sense	Swahili usage	Arabic usage.
maazimio(N) (pl. azimio)	aẓm	عَـزْمٌ	——	see azimio(N).	___, determination, decision, firm well, resolution.
mabruki(adj.) (-enye baraka)	mabru:k	مَـبْرُوك	——, مُبَارَك	blessed, fortunate, lucky auspicious.	____
maburudisho(N)	mubarrid	مُـبَرِّد	انْتِعَاش / استجمام	refreshment, relief, recreation.	____
mada(N) (muktadha)	ma:dda(t)	مَـادَّة	——	subject, article, topic.	____, material, element.
madaha(N) (maringo)	mad'ḥ(un) madi:ḥ.	مَـدْحٌ / مَـدِيحٌ	اخْتِيَال / عُجْبٌ	airs, fascinating manner, graces, gait, swagger.	praise, eulogy, laudation, approbation.
madai(N)	iddia:ā	اِدِّعَـاء	——	legal process, claim, suit, prosecution, accusation, allegation.	____, arrogation, assumption.
madaraka(N) (wadhifa)	idra:k	ادْرَاك	مَسْؤُولِيَّة / وَظِيفَة	arrangement, obligation, appointment, liability, duty, undertaking.	achievement, attainment, accomplishment, awareness, perception, consciousness.
madhali(conj.) (maadamu)	ma:za:l(a)	مَـا زَالَ	——	see maadamu.	still, (not) yet.
madhara(N) (also dhara)	maḍarra (t)	مَـضَرَّة	——	violence, harm, hurt.	____
madhehebu(N) (kanuni) (kawaida) (desturi)	madhhab	مَـذْهَب	——	sect, party, denomination ideas, customs, usages, tenets, persuation.	____

Swahili word	Transcription of Arabic word	Arabic word	Arabic word in Swahili sense	Swahili usage	Arabic usage.
madhii(N)	madhiyy (un)	مَذِيّ	____	the clear viscid discharge of the male organ when sexually excited	___
madhila(N) (mateso) (unyonge) (tabu)	madhilla (t)	مَذِلَّة	___	lowness, abasement, humbleness.	submissiveness.
madhubuti(N) (imara)	maḍbu:ṭ	مَضْبُوط	____ قَوِيّ	accurate, strong, firm, solid precise.	__, correct, exact
madhumuni(N) (makusudi) (maazimio)	maḍmu:n	مَضْمُون	____	purpose, intention.	___, guaranteed, ensured.
madini(N)	maạdin	مَعْدِن	____ مَعَادِن	mine, metal, lode, mineral.	___, treasure-trove.
madrasa(N) (Rel.)	madrasa(t)	مَدْرَسَة	____, خَلْوَة	Islamic school, Koranic school.	school.
maduati(N) (sing. duati)	duạ:t(pl.) da:ịya (sing)	دُعَاة (دَاعِيَة)	دَاعِيَة	preacher, propagandist (Islamic).	_____
mafahali(N) (sing. fahali)	faḥl	فَحْل	فُحُول	see fahali.	____
magharibi(N)	maghrib	المَغْرِب	___, الغَرْب	time of sunset, evening prayers, the west.	____
maghufira(N) (Rel.)	maghfira (t)	مَغْفِرَة	____	forgiveness, pardonable.	___, remission.
mahaba(N) (mapenzi) (rare)	maḥabba(t)	مَحَبَّة	____	love, liking, affection.	____, attachment.
mahabusi(N)	maḥbu:s	مَحْبُوس	____ مُنْتَظَر	a prisoner awaiting trial.	___, prisoner, convict.

Swahili word	Transcription of Arabic word	Arabic word	Arabic word in Swahili sense	Swahili usage	Arabic usage.
mahafala(N)	maḥfil	مَحْفِل	احْتِفَال	celebration, ceremony, festival.	assembly, congregation, meeting, party, gathering.
mahakama(N) (korti)	maḥkama(t)	مَحْكَمَة	___	court, tribunal, place of judgement.	___
mahala(N) (also mahali)	maḥall	مَحَلّ	___	place, situation, position, region, district, space, room, interval.	___
mahali(N) (nafasi) (badala)	maḥall	"	___	see mahala.	___
mahamumu(N) (poet.)	maḥmu:m	مَحْمُوم	___	fevered, one who is affected with fever.	___, feverish.
mahari(N)	mahr	مَهْر	___	dowery, bridal money, a marriage settlement.	___, dot.
mahashumu(N), (heshima)	muḥtasham	مُحْتَشَم	مُحْتَرَم	respected person, an honoured.	___
mahiri(N) (adj.) (mwenye busara) (rare)	ma:hir	مَاهِر	___	clever, skilful, artful, tactful.	----, proficient.
mahitaji(N) (haja)	iḥtiya:j	احْتِيَاج	___	need, want, requirement, necessity.	___
mahtuti(adj.) (also (mahututi)	munḥaṭṭ	مُنْحَطّ/ مَحْطُوط	مُحْتَضَر مُشْرِف عَلَى المَوْت	dying, in the throes of death, very serious, difficult(in illness).	fallen, lower, lower grade, low-level.
mahususi(adj.) (halisi)	makhṣu:ṣ	مَخْصُوص	___	special, particular, exact.	___

Swahili word	Transcription of Arabic word	Arabic word	Arabic word in Swahili sense	Swahili usage	Arabic usage.
maisha (N)	maị.sha(t)	مَعِيشَة	___	life, way of life, continence.	___
maiti(N)	may t	مَيْتٌ	___	a dead person/body, lifeless, corpse.	___
maizi(V) (jua) (fahamu) (tambua) (elewa)	mayyaz(a)	مَيَّزَ	___	recognize, know, understand.	differ, distinguish, prefer.
majaribio(N)	tajruba(t)	تَجْرُبَة / تَجْرِيب	___	see jaribio or jaribu.	___
majeruhi(N)	majru:ḥ	مَجْرُوح	___	a wounded person(s).	___
majira(N)	majra:	مَجْرَى (المَاءِ)	فَصْلُ الأَمْطَارِ	season, period, time.	water, course, flood of water, stream.
majlisi(N) (poet.)	majlis	مَجْلِس	___	council, party, committe,	___, board, meeting.
majununi(N) (punguani) (kichaa) (mwendawazimu)	majnu:n	مَجْنُون	___	madman, <u>jester</u>,** <u>buffon</u>,** foolish.	___, crazy, possessed.
majusi(N)	maju:sy	مَجُوسِي	___	astrologer, magi, magus, magian.	___
maka(N)	makka(t)	مَكَّة		Macca(Mecca).	___
makadirio(N)	taqdi:r	تَقْدِيرٌ	___, تَخْمِينٌ	estimation, assessment, valuation.	___, appreciation.
makala(N)	maqa:la(t)	مَقَالَةٌ	___,	article, treatise, piece of writing.	___
makalbi(N) (also makalibu) (ZNZ)(also tec.)	qa:lib	(قَالِبٌ) قَوَالِب (ج)	___	pl. of kalbi see it.	___

Swahili word	Transcription of Arabic word	Arabic word	Arabic word in Swahili sense	Swahili usage	Arabic usage.
makamu(N)	maqa:m	مَقَام	كَهْلٌ	a middle-aged person, state things	rank, standing, situation, position, place.
makasi(N) (also mkasi)	miqaṣṣ	مِقَصّ	———	scissors, a pair of scissors.	———
makbadhi(N) (aina ya viatu) (ZNZ)	maqbiḍ maqbaḍ	مَقْبِض/ مِقْبَض	نَوْعٌ مِنْ الأَحْذِيَة	a kind of shoes.	habdle, knob, grip.
makini(N) (utulivu)	ma:kin maki:n	مَاكِنٌ مَكِينٌ	قَوِيٌّ/ (ثَابِتٌ) (راسخ)	strong, firm, calm, solid gentle, well behaved, diginity, composed.	___, unshakable.
makisio(N) (pl. of kisio)	qiya:s	قِيَاسٌ	تَقْدِيرٌ ———	approximation, estimation, a guess at.	———
maksai(N) (also mahsai) (kuhasiwa)	mukhaṣṣa khasiyy (un)	مُخَصّ خَصِيّ	———	a castrated animal, bullok eunuch geld.	———
maktaba(N)	maktaba(t)	مَكْتَبَة	———	library.	____, booshop.
makubadhi(N) (also makbadhi)	maqbiḍ	مَقْبِضٌ / مِقْبَض	نُوْعٌ مِنْ الأَحْذِيَة	see makbadhi.	———
makubaliano(N)	qabu:l	قَبُول	———	acceptance, favour, assent, sanction.	____, wellcome, admission, approval, concurrence.
makubazi(N)	maqbiḍ	مقبض مقبض	نوع من الأحذية	see makbadhi.	———
makusudi(adv.) (madhumuni) (azma)(lengo)	maqṣu:d	مقصود ،	قصدا ——— ———	intentionally, purposely, on purpose.	intentional, aimed at.
makusudio(N)	maqṣad	مَقْصَد	———	purpose, intention, object, goal, end.	___, resolution, sense.

Swahili word	Transcription of Arabic word	Arabic word	Arabic word in Swahili sense	Swahili usage	Arabic usage.
malaika(N) (mtoto mchanga)	mala:i̱ka (t)	مَــلَائِكَة (جَمْعٌ)	___ ، مَلَكٌ طِفْلٌ رَضِيعٌ	angel, a baby**.	___
mali(N)	ma:l	مَــالٌ	___ ثَرْوَةٌ	property, estate, wealth, riches, goods, money, possession.	___
malkia(N)	malika(t)	مَلِكَةٌ	___	queen.	___
maluuni(N)	malụ:n	مَلْعُون	___	see laani.	___
mamlaka(N)	mamlaka(t)	مَمْلَكَة	سُلْطَة / نُفُوذٌ مَسْئُولِيَةٌ مِلْكِيَه	power, authority, rule, dominion, right of ownership **, possession.**	___, kingdom, state, empire, sovereignity.
mamluki(N)	mamlu:k	مَمْلُوك	مُرْتَزَق	mercenary.	owned, belonging, in possesion, slave.
manii(N) (shahawa)	maniyy(un)	مَنِيّ	___	emen.	___
mantiki(N)	manṭiq	مَنْطِقٌ	___	logic.	___
manufaa(N) (faida)	manfaa̦(t)	مَنْفَعَة	___ ، فَائِدَةٌ	provision, usefulness, use, profit.	___, benefit, advantage, gain.
mara(N) (safari) (zamu)	marra(t)	مَرَّة	___ فِي الحَالِ	time, turn, once, at once, occasionally, immediately.**	___
maradhi(N) (ugonjwa) (uwele)	marad̲	مَرَضٌ	___	illness, sickness, disease.	___
marahaba(interj.)	marḫaba(n)	مَرْحَبًا	___	a salute used to respond a younger person.	wellcome!
marahamu(N)	marham	مَرْهَم	___	ointment, glue, plaster	___
marasharasha(N) (marashi)	rash	رَشٌّ / رَشَاش	___	sprinkling, watering, showers (perfume only).	___, (in general).
mardudi(N)	mardu:d	مَرْدُود	___ رَفْضٌ / نَبْذٌ	rejection, repudiation, second time to do a thing.	___
marejeo(N) (pl.)	marjaa̦	مَرْجَع	___	reference(s).	___

Swahili word	Transcription of Arabic word	Arabic word	Arabic word in Swahili sense	Swahili usage	Arabic usage.
marekebisho(N)	tarki:b	تَرْكِيب	____,	fitting in, fastening, making preparation.	____, construction.
maridhia(N) (mpole) (rare)	marḍiyy (un)	مَرْضِيٌّ	____	gentle, kind, mild, meek.	____
marmari (N) (marumaru)	marmar	مرمر	____	marble.	____
marudio(N) (marejeo)	tardad	تَرْدَاد / (تَكْرَار)	إِعَادَة / إِرْجَاع	correction, a return, discipline, recompence.	____
marudufu(N) (mara mbili)	mura:dif mardu:f	مُرَادِفٌ مَرْدُوفٌ	____	double, synonym.	____
masahaba(N) (pl. of sahaba)	ṣaḥa:ba(t)	(pl.) الصَّحَابَة	____ صَحَابِي	the companions of the prophet Muhammad. (S.A.W.).	
masaibu(N) (maafa)	maṣa:ib	مَصَائِب (جَمْعًا مُصِيبَة)	كَارِثَة / نَكْبَة ____ بَلْوَى	calamity, affliction.	____
masalkheri(conj.)	masa:ā-al-khair.	مَسَاءُ الخَيْر	____	good evening.	____
masarifu(N) (rare)	maṣa:rif	(pl.) مَصَارِيف	____ مَصْرُوف	money spent, pocket money.	____
mashairi(N)	shiaṛ	شِعْر	____	poem, poetry, song, verse.	____
mashaka(N)	mashaqqa (t)	مَشَقَّة	____	difficulty, distress, trouble, hardship.	____, toil, labor.
mashariki(N) (matlai) (macheo) (uche wa jua)	masha:riq mashriq	مَشَارِق مَشْرِق	____ الشَّرْق	the East, eatern, oriental.	____
mashuhuri(N)	mashhu:r	مَشْهُور	____	famous, well-known, renowned.	____, celebrated, notorious, ill-reputed.
masihara(N) (utani) (dhihaka) (mzaha)	maskhara (t)	مَسْخَرَة	____	play, light matter, jest, droll, laughingstock.	____, ridiculous.

Swahili word	Transcription of Arabic word	Arabic word	Arabic word in Swahili sense	Swahili usage	Arabic usage.
masihiya(N) (Rel.)	masi:ḥ (i:y)	المَسِيح / مَسِيحِيّ	___,	a christian, christ, Jesus.	___
masijala(N)	tasji:l	تَسْجِيل	___, (مَكْتَب)	see masjala.	
masilaha(N) (also masilahi)	maslaḥa(t)	مَصْلَحَة	___, فَائِدَة, نَفْعٌ.	benefit, welfare, advantage.	___, administration.
masilahi(N) (nafuu)	"	"	___,	see masilaha.	___
masjala(N)	tasji:l	تَسْجِيل	مَكْتَب تَسْجِيل تَسْجِيلٌ.	registration office, registry.	___, recording.
maskan(N)	maskan	مَسْكَن	___	home, dwelling place, residence.	___, house, abode habitation, domicile.
maskini(N) (fukara)	miski:n	مِسْكِين	___	poor, beggar, miserable, luckless.	___,
maslahi(N)	maslaḥa(t)	مَصْلَحَة	___	see masilaha.	___
masrufu(N) (also masarifu)	maṣru:f	مَصْرُوف	___	see masarifu.	___
matamanio(N)	tamaṉi(n)	تَمَنٍّ	___	desire, hope, longing, lust, wish.	___, aspiration, demand.
mathalani(conj.) (kwa mfano)	mathalan	مَثَلاً	___	for example, for instance.	___
mathubuti(N)	muthbit	مُثْبِت	___ ثَابِت	confirmation, support, proof.	___,established, positive, sure.
matini(N)(also kitini)	matn	مَتْن	___	context.	___
maulidi(N) Rel.)	mawlid	المَوْلِد النَّبَوِي	___	the prophet's birthday.	___
mauti(N) (kifo)	mawt	مَوْت	___	death, decease, die.	___
mawaidha(N) (mashauri)	mauiḍha (t)	مَوْعِظَة	___	teachings, good advice, preaching.	___

Swahili word	Transcription of Arabic word	Arabic word	Arabic word in Swahili sense	Swahili usage	Arabic usage.
mauidha(N)	mawi:dha(t)	مَوْعِظَة	——	see mawaidha.	——
mazali(N)	ma:za:l	مَا / زَالَ	——	see madhali.	——
mazidisho(N)	izdiya:d	إِزْدِيَاد	—— إِضَافَة	addition, supplement, augmentation.	——
mbadala(N) (meth.)	muba:dala (t)	مُبَادَلَة	—— البَدِيل	substitution.	exchange.
mbadhiri(adj.)	mubadhir	مُبَذِّر	——	spendthrift, wastrel.	——
mbadhirifu(N)	"	"	——	see mbadhiri.	——
mbamia(N) [Persian]*	ba:mia	بَامِيَة	نَبَات البَامِيَة	a plant of Okra.	——
mbangi(N)[Persian]* (afyuni) (majuni)	bangu	البَنْقُو	نَبَات البَنْقُو	see bangi.	——, (local arabic)
mbashiri(N)	mubashir	مُبَشِّر	——	a prophet, bringer of news.	——
mbayana(N)	bayyin	بَيِّن	مَشْهُور	a well known, notorious.	clear, obvious, evident.
mbazazi(N) (laghai) (mdanganyifu)	ibtiza:z	اِبْتِزَاز / بَزَّاز	خِدَاع	cheat, sharper, trader, shopkeeper.	emblessment, peculation.
mbuni(N)	bunn	البُنّ	—— (نَبَاتٌ)	a plant of the coffee beans.	—— (plant)
mchai(N)(mi-)[orig. Chinese]*	sha:i	الشَّاى	—— (نَبَات)	tea-plant(Theosinensis).	see chai.
mdadisi(N) (mpelelezi) (mtafiti)	dassa:s	دَسَّاس	—— بَاحِث	a curious, prying person, investigator.	intrigant, conspirator.
mdai(N) (wa-)	mudaii:	المدّعى	——	plantiff, prosecutor, creditor, pretender.	——
mdaiwa(N)	mudaaa:	المدعى عليه	——	defendant in a case, debtor.	——

Swahili word	Transcription of Arabic word	Arabic word	Arabic word in Swahili sense	Swahili usage	Arabic usage.
mdhabidhabina(N) (sing)	mudhabdhab	مُذَبْذَب	___	hesitant, vacillating, hypocrite.	___
mdhalimu(N) (wa-)	ḍha:lim	ظَالِم	___	see dhalimu.	___, unjust, sinner.
mdhamini(N) (wa-)	ḍami:n	ضَامِن / ضَمِين	___ كَفِيل	trustee, sponsor, gurantor, hostage.	___
mduara(N) (mi-)	da:ira(t)	دَائِرَة	___ دَائِرِيّ مُحِيطُ الدَّائِرَة	circle, circumference.	___
mdudu(N) (wa-)	du:d	دُودَة / دِيدَان	___, (مِيكْرُوب) حَشَرَة	insect, small creeping and flying creatures, parasite.	worm, maggot, larva. caterpillar.
(a)**methali**(N) (also mithali)	mithl	مِثْل	___	<u>proverb</u>,** emblem, likeness, resemblance, similitude, equivalent.	___
(b) **methali**(N)	mathal	/ مَثَل	___, أَمْثَال	proverb, (please notice the difference).	___, lesson, example.
mfadhili(N) (wa-) (mkarimu)	fa:ḍil	فَاضِل / مِفْضَال	___, مُحْسِن كَرِيم	favour, sponsor, kindness, benefit.	___, very generous, /liberal, remaining.
mfadhiliwa(N)	fuḍu:li	فُضُولِى / المَفْضُول	___ الَّذِى يُحْسَنُ إِلَيْهِ	meddlesome, officious.	___
mfarakano(N) (mi-)	tafarruq	تَفَرُّق / تَفْرِيق	___	separation, division, disunion.	___
mfariji(N)	mufarrij	مُفَرِّج / فَارِج	___ فَارِجُ الكَرْبِ	one who dispells the grief sorrow from another.	___
mfasiri(N)	mufassir	مُفَسِّر	___	commentator, translator, <u>interpretor</u>.**	___
mfawidhi(N)	mufawaḍ	مُفَوَّض	___	authorized agent, proxy, mandatory steward, in charge of.	___

Swahili word	Transcription of Arabic word	Arabic word	Arabic word in Swahili sense	Swahili usage	Arabic usage.
mfigili(N)	fujl	فُجْل	—— (نَبَات)	radish.	____
mfilisi(N) (mufilisi)	muflis	مُفْلِس	____	bankrupt, insolvent.	____
mhadhara(N)	muḥa:ḍara(t)	مُحَاضَرَة	____	lecture.	____, discourse.
mhadhiri(N)	muḥa:ḍir	مُحَاضِر	____	lecturer.	____
mhadimu(N)	kha:dim	خَادِم	____	servant, attendant.	____, domestic, servant, maid.
mhaini(N)	kha:i̲n	خَائِن	____	see haini.	____
mhakiki(N)	muḥaqqiq	مُحَقِّق	____	investigator, inquisitor.	____, examining, magistrate.
mhalifu(N)	mukha:lif	مُخَالِف	____	see halifu.	____
mhamiaji(N)	ḥa:i̲m	حَائِم	____ مُهَاجِر رَحَّالَة	see hama.	____
mhamishi(N)	"	"	____ الذِى يُهَجِّر	one who causes departure for others.	(see hama).
mharibifu(N) (fisadi) (mbadhirifu) (mharabu)	mukharrib	مُخَرِّب	____	see haribu	destroyer, saboteur.
mhariri(N) (edita)	muḥarrir	مُحَرِّر	____	editor.	____
mhashamu(N)	ḥishma(t) (root)	(مِنْ الحِشَمَة)	مُحْتَرَم / مُعَظَّم	honored, respected man.	____
mhasi(N)	mukhaṣṣa	مُخَصَّى	____	see maksai.	____
mhasibu(N)	muḥa:sib	مُحَاسِب	____	accountant, bookkeeper.	____, auditor, comptroller.
mheshimiwa(N)(mwadhamu) (mhashamu)	ḥishma(t) (root)	(مِنْ الحِشْمَة)	مُحْتَرَم مُعَظَّم	honourable, respected man.	____

Swahili word	Transcription of Arabic word	Arabic word	Arabic word in Swahili sense	Swahili usage	Arabic usage.
mhimili(N) (mi-) (grafu ya mihimili)	maḥmal. ḥammala(t)	مَحْمَل / حَمَّالة (الباب)	____	that which carries(supports a beam, prop, girder, pier).	____(loc. Ar.)
mhina(N)	ḥinna:ā	الحِنَّاء	____ (نبات)	henna(plant) [Ar.]*	____, lawsonia.
mhisani(N) (mtu mwema)	muḥsin	مُحْسِن	____, كَرِيم فَاضِل	beneficant, charitable.	____
mhitaji(N)	muḥta:j	مُحْتَاج	____	one who needs, applicant, candidate in want, poor.	___, destitute, indigent.
mhubiri(N)	mukhbir	مُخْبِر	____ وَاعِظ	preacher, reporter.	____, detective.
mhudumu(N) (tec.)	mukhaddim	مُخَدِّم	____	steward.	(see mhadimu)
mhuni(N) (mseja) (muhuni)	kha:i̱n	خَائِن	____, عَازِب سَيِّءُ الخُلُقِ	a bachelor, a bad person.	disloyal, false, faithless.
mia(N) (kumi mara kumi)	miā(t)	مِائة	____	a hundred, hundredth.	____
miadi(N) (ahadi)	mi:ạ:d	مِيعَاد	____ مَوْعِد عَهْد / وَعَد	a promise.	____
mihirabu(N)	miḥra:b	مِحْرَاب	____	the apse of a mosque.	____
mikasi(N) (sing mkasi, makasi).	miqaṣṣ	مِقَصّ	____	a scissor (see makasi).	____
mila(N)(desturi za jamii)	milla(t)	مِلَّة	عَادَات تَقَالِيد	custom, usage, propensity habit.	religion, creed, faith.
(a) **miliki**(V) (tamataki) **ia/ika/iwa/isha/iana**	malak(a)	مَلَكَ	____	to possess, to give possession of, rule,be owner, to reign, control, property, possession, wealth.	____, seize, to dominate, to acquire.
(b) **miliki**(N)	milk	مِلْكٌ	____	property, possession, wealth.	____, fortune.

Swahili word	Transcription of Arabic word	Arabic word	Arabic word in Swahili sense	Swahili usage	Arabic usage.
mimbari(N)	mimbar	مِـنْبَر	____	pulpit, tribune.	____
minajili(adv.) (kwa ajili ya)	min/ȧjli	مِنْ أَجْـلِ	____	because of, for the sake of.	____, on account of.
minalfaizina(N)	minalfa:i̱-zi:n(a)	مِـنْ الفَائِزِين	____	successful, victorious (for idd celebration).	____, victor, winner.
minghairi(adv.) (bila ya) (pasipo) (ghairi ya)	min/ghayr (i)	مِـنْ غَيْـرِ	____	without, except.	____
mintarafa(conj.)	min/ṭaraf	مِـنْ طَرَف		concerning, regarding, on behalf, about, anent.	a part of, some, a bit of.
miski(N)	misk	مِـسْك	____	musk [skt,]*	____
miteen(N) (also mi-teni)	miătain	مِـائـتَيْنِ	____	two hundred.	____
miteni(N)	"	"	____	see miteen.	____
mithali(N) also me-thali	mithl	مِثْـلُ / مِثَـال مَـثَل	____	see methali(a,b).	____
mithili(adv.) (kama) (rare)	mithl	مِـثْـلُ	____	similar, similarity, li-keness.	____, equivalent.
mizani(N)	mi:za:n	مِـيزَان	____	balance, scales, weight, measure.	____, poetic, measure, justice.
mizania(N)	mi:za:nia	مِـيزَانِيَة	____	budget.	____, equilibrium.
mjadala(N) (mi-)	mujadala (t)	مُـجَادَلَـة	____, نِقَـاشٌ جِدَال	argument, discussion.	____, dispute, quarrel.

Swahili word	Transcription of Arabic word	Arabic word	Arabic word in Swahili sense	Swahili usage	Arabic usage.
mjasiri(N)(wa-)	jasu:r	جَسُورٌ	جَرِيءٌ , ____	bold, brave, daring, forward, fearless, fool hardly, venturesome.	___, courageous, impudent, audacious.
mjeuri(N)	ja:i̲r	جَائِرٌ	____	unjust, oppressor, unfair.	____, despot, tyrant.
mjumuiko(N)	tajammuạ	تَجَمُّع	____	coming together, meeting, crowd gathering, agglomeration.	___, agglutination.
mkabala(N)	muqa:bala (t)	مُقَابَلَة	مُقَابِل ____	infront of, facing, opposite, future.	___, equivalent.
mkabidhi(N) (wa-)	muqbiḍ/ qa:biḍ	مُقْبِض قَابِض	حَافِظٌ , ___	one who keeps, holds things for others, trustee, also a miser.	_____, costive.
mkabili shamsi(N) (mgangani)	muqa:bil ashams	مُقَابِل الشَّمْسِ	عَبَّاد الشَّمْسِ دَوَّارُ الشَّمْسِ	facing the sun, sunflower	____,
mkadiriaji(N) estimator, assessor,	muqaddir	مُقَدِّر	____	estimator, see kadiria.	____, appraiser, taxer assessor.
mkahaba(N)	qaḥba(t)	قَحْبَة	مُومِسٌ , ____ عَاهِر/ عَاهِرَة دَاعِر/ فَاسِقٌ	a prostitute, whorish.	_____, whore, harlot.
(a)**mkahawa**(N) (mi-) (hoteli)	qahwa	قَهْوَة	مَقْهَى مطعم	coffee-house.	see kahawa.
mkahawa(N) (mi-) (mbuni)	"	(البُنّ) قَهْوَة	(نَبَاتُ) ____	coffee plant.	see kahawa.
mkaidi(N)(asiyemtiifu) (mbishi)	ka:i̲d	كَائِدٌ	عَنِيدٌ	obstinate, argumantative person.	one who deceive, dupe.

Swahili word	Transcription of Arabic word	Arabic word	Arabic word in Swahili sense	Swahili usage	Arabic usage.
mkalimani(N) (mtarjumani)	kilima:ny	كِلِمَانٌ	مُتَرْجِم	interpretor, translator.	eloquent.
mkarimu(N)	kari:m	كَرِيمٌ	——	generous, liberal, hospitable.	___, benefactor.
mkasa(N) (mi-)	qiṣṣ a(t)	قِصَّة	حَادِث	event, news, happening.	story, (see kisa)
mkasi(N) (mi-)	miqaṣṣ	مِقَصٌّ	——	see makasi.	____
mkataba(N) (mi-)	muka:taba (t)	مُكَاتَبَة	—— عَقْدٌ اتفاقية	engagement, contract, constitution.	____
mkutubi(N) (wa-)	âmi:n-al-maktaba (t)	أمين المكتبة	—— قيّم	librarian.	____
mlaanifu(N) (wa-)	malu:n	مَلْعُون / لَعِين	——	see laanifu.	____
mlaghai(N) (wa-)	laghw(un)	لَغْوٌ		see laghai.	nonsense, null.
mlozi(N) (mi-)	lawz	لَوْزٌ		see lozi-(an almond plant).	____
mnaana(N) (mi-)	naạnaạ	نَعْنَاع	—— (نبات)	a mint plant.	____
mnada(N) (mi-)	muna:da:(t)	مُنَادَاة	—— دِلاَلَة	auction, public sale.	____, announcement.
mnadi(N)	muna:di(n)	مُنَادٍ	____, دَلاَّل	auctioneer, announcer.	___, herald.
mnadi sala(N) (mwadhini) (Rel.) (rare)	muna:di(n)	مُنَادٍ للصَّلاَة	مُؤَذِّنٌ	Muezzin, announcer of the hour of Prayer.	____
mnafiki(N) (wa-) (**mzandiki**)	muna:fiq	مُنَافِقٌ	——	hypocrite, dissembler, liar, <u>pretender</u>.**	____, herald.
mnajimu(N) (wa-)	munajjim	مُنَجِّم	—— مُشَعْوِذ	astrologer.	____
mnajisi(N) (mi-) (mchafu)	najis/ munajjis	نَجِس مُنَجِّس	الذي يغتصب النساء	unclean, impure, <u>profane</u>,** dirty, <u>naping(of a woman)</u>.**	___, polluter, difiled

Swahili word	Transcription of Arabic word	Arabic word	Arabic word in Swahili sense	Swahili usage	Arabic usage.
mnanasi(N) (mi-) [Persian]**	ánana:s	أَنَنَاس	____ (نبات)	a pineapple plant.	____
mnara(N) (mi-)	mana:ra(t)	مَنَارَة / مَنَائِر (جمع)	____, بُرْج	tower, light-house, mina-ret[Ar.]* steeple.	____
mnasaba(N) (mi-) (uhusiano)	muna:saba (t)	مُنَاسَبَة	____	suitableness, correlation, kinship, relationship.	____, **opportunity**, analogy.
mnasara(N) (mkristo) (rare)	naṣara:ny	النَّصْرَانِيّ	____	a christian.	____
mnubi(N)	Nubyyi	النُّوبِيّ	____ السُّودَانِيّ	see Kinubi, Sudanese.	____
mnururisho(N)	Tanwi:r	تَنْوِير	____	illumination, lighting.	____, enlighten-ment.
mola(N) (Rel.)	mawla	المَوْلَى	____ الرَّبّ	Allah, Lord(God), God.	____
mraba(N) (mi-)	murabbaạ	مُرَبَّع	____	square.	____
mradi(N) (conj.) (mi-) (nia) (kusudi)	mura:d	المُرَاد	____	intention, purpose, desi-gn, wanted.	____, desired, intended.
mrasimu(N) (wa-)	rasmy	رَسْمِيّ	____	one who deals officially.	official, formal.
mratibu(N)	murattib	المرتّب	____ المُنَسِّق	co-ordinator.	____
mrehani(N) (mi-)	rayḥa:n	الرَّيْحَان (نبات)	____, الحبق	sweet basil (ocimum basi-licum).	____
mrihani(N) (mi-)	rayḥa:n	"	____, الحبق	see mrehani.	____
mrithi(N) (wa-)	wa:rith	الوَارِث	____, الوَرِيث	heir, inheritor.	____
mrithishi(N) (wa-)	muwarrith	المُوَرِّث	____, المُوصِي	legator, testator, execu-tor.	____
mroho(N)	Ru:ḥ(root)	(مِنْ الرُّوح)	شَرِه / نَهِم	glutton, greedy.	spirit, evil-spirit.

Swahili word	Transcription of Arabic word	Arabic word	Arabic word in Swahili sense	Swahili usage	Arabic usage.
mrua(N) (also murua)	muru:ā(t)	المُرُوءَة	____	politeness, good behavior, to be manly.	___, obligingness.
Mrumi(N)	rumyy	رُومِىّ	____	see Kirumi.	____
Mrusi(N)	rusyy	روسى	____	see Kirusi.	____
msaada(N)	musa:ạada (t)	مساعدة	____	help, assistance, aid, support.	____, encouragement.
msaala(N)	muṣalla(n)	مُصَلّى	سِجَّادٍ للصَّلَاة / حَصِير	a prayer mat.	place of Prayer, oratory.
msafara(N) (safari)	safar	(مِنْ السَّفَر)	قَافِلَة	caravan, expedition, crowd people, journey.	travel, trip, journey.
msafiri(N)	musa:fir	مُسَافِر	____	traveller.	____
msafirishaji(N)	tasfi:r	تَسْفِير	نَقْل / انْتِقَال	exporter, transportation.	____
msafishaji(N)	ṣa:fi(n)	صَافٍ (صَافِى)	عَامِلُ النَّظَافَةِ	cleaner, charwoman.	clean.
msafu(N) (mi-)	mus'ḥaf	مُصْحَف	____	see msahafu.	____
msahafu(N) (mi-) (Rel.)	mus'ḥaf	"	____	book(holy Koran), Bible** (rare).	____
msahala(N) (med.) (mi-)	mus hil	مُسْهِل	دَوَاءٌ مُسْهِلٌ للأَمْعَاءِ	laxative purgative salt.	____
msahaulifu(N) (wa-)	sahwa:n	سَهْوَان	____	absent-minded, inattentive, headless.	____, forgetful.
msahaulizi(N)	"	"	____	see msahaulifu.	____
msaidizi(N)	musa:ịd	مُسَاعِد	____	accomplice, assistant, helper, aide.	____, adjutant.
msajili(N) (tec.)	musajjil	مُسَجِّل	____	registrar, recorder.	____, tape recorder.
(a) **msala**(N) (mi-)	muṣalla(n)	مُصَلَّى	سِجَّادٌ للصَّلَاةِ	prayer mat.	a place of Prayer.

Swahili word	Transcription of Arabic word	Arabic word	Arabic word in Swahili sense	Swahili usage	Arabic usage.
(b) **msala**(N) (mi-)	muṣalla(n)	مُصَلًّى	مِرْحَاض	toilet(us. msalani), lavatory.	*
msalaba(N) (mi-) (Rel.)	ṣali:b	صَلِيب	———	cross.	———
msalata(N) (wa-) (also msaliti)	mutusalliṭ	مُتَسَلِّط	الخَائِن (وَطَنَهُ) طَاغِيَة مُسْتَبِدّ	slanderer, despot, traitor.	despot.
msalheri(N)	masa:ā -al khair.	مَسَاءُ الخَيْرِ	———	good evening(salutation).	———
msalihina(N)	ṣa:liḥi:n (a)	صَالِحِين (جمع)	صَالِح	devout, virtuous, honest, pious, Godly.	———, good, right,
msalimina(N) (wa-)	musa:limi:n(a)	مُسَالِمِين	مُسَالِم / صَالِح	see msalihina.	linient, peaceful, peaceable, gentle.
msaliti(N) (wa-) (haini) (mfitini)	mutusalliṭ	مُتَسَلِّط	———, خَائِنٌ وَطَنَهُ	see msalata.	———
msamaha(N) (mi-)	musa:maḥa (t)	مُسَامَحَة	———	Pardon, forgiveness, salvation, deliverance.	———
msamehe(N)	"	"	———	see msamaha.	———
msamiati(N) (mi-)	musammaya:t	المُسَمَّيَات (ج) (مُسَمًّى)	——— مُفْرَدَات	vocabulary.	sense, meaning of word.
msana(N) (wa-)	ṣa:niạ	صَانِعٌ	——— حَدَّاد	metal worker, smith.	———
msanaa(N)	"	"	———	see msani.	———
msani(N) (wa-)	ṣa:niạ	صَانِعٌ	مَاهِرٌ / المُتَخَصِّص الاختصاص	skillfull, craftsman, specialist.	———, artisan. expert.
msanifu (wa-)	muṣannif.	مُصَنِّف	——— كاتب	writer, author.	———
msanii (wa-)	ṣa:niạ	صَانِعٌ	———	see msani.	

Swahili word	Transcription of Arabic word	Arabic word	Arabic word in Swahili sense	Swahili usage	Arabic usage.
msarifu(N) (wa-)	ṣarra:f	صَرَّاف	___	cashier, money changer.	___
mshahara(N) (mi-)	musha:hara (t)	مشاهرة	راتب (شهرى)	salary, payment.	___, monthly, per month.
mshahara halisi(N) (tec.)	mush. kha: liṣa(t)	مشاهرة خالصة	___ الراتب الصافى	net salary.	___
mshahara wa jumla(N) (tec.)	mush. jum-la	المُشَاهَرَة بالجملة	الراتب الاجمالى	gross salary.	___
mshairi(N) (wa-)	sha:ir	شَاعِرٌ	___	poet.	___
mshari(N) (wa-)	shirri:r	شِرِّير	___ مُؤذٍ	strife, an evil person, mischief, jinx.	___
mshauri(N) (wa-) (mwongozi)	mustasha:r	مُسْتَشَار	___, نَاصِحٌ	advisor, counsellor, <u>friend</u>,** <u>presentative</u>,** <u>delegate</u>.**	___, consultant.
mshaushi(N) (wa-) (himizo)	mushawish	مُشَوِّش	___	temper, one who persuades.	___
mshikaki(N) (mi-) (also mshikiki)	mushaqqaq	مُشَقَّق	(لَحْمٌ مَشْوِىٌّ) مشقق	sprit, skewer, a bit of meat toasted on skewer.	splinter, piece.
mshiriki(N) (wa-)	musha:rik	مُشَارِك	___	participant, partner.	___
mshirikina(N) (wa-)	mushrik	مُشْرِك / مُشْرِكين	___ خُرَافِى	superstitious person.	godess, fidle.
mshitaki(N) (wa-)	mushtaki	مُشْتَكٍ	___ شَاكٍ المُدَّعِى	tale-bearer, plaintiff, complainant.	___
mshitakiwa(N)	mushku:w	مَشْكُوٌّ	___ مُتَّهَمٌ المَدَّعَى عَلَيْهِ	defendant, accused.	___
mshitiri(N) (wa-) (also mshtiri)	mushtary	مُشْتَرِى	___ الزَّبُون	buyer, purchaser, customer, <u>vendor</u>,** client.	___

Swahili word	Transcription of Arabic word	Arabic word	Arabic word in Swahili sense	Swahili usage	Arabic usage.
mshokishoki(N) (mi-)	shawk shawk	شَوْك شَوْك	فَاكِهَة ثِمَارُهَا ذَاتُ شَوْكٍ	a kind of tree which bears edible fruit (Nephelium lappaceum).	thorn, spine.
mshtaka(N) (mi-)	shakwa:	شَكْوَى	——	complaint, charge, accusation.	___, grievance.
mshtiri(N) (wa-) (mzabuni) (mnadi)	mushtari	مُشْتَرٍ (مُشْتَرِى)	——	see mshitiri.	
mshumaa(N) (mi-)	shamạ	شَمْع	——	wax, candle, candle stick.	___, spark plug.
mshurutisho(N) (mi-)	ishtira:ṭ	اشْتِرَاطٌ	—— قَسْرٌ/إِلْزَامٌ	compulsion, pressure, force.	___,condition.
msiba(N) (mi-)	muṣi:ba(t)	مُصِيبَة	——	misfortune, disaster, calamity, accident, sadness poverty, mourning.	___
msifu(N) (wa-)	waṣṣa:f	وَصَّاف	مُتَمَلِّق / مُدَاهِن مَادِح / مُتَزَلِّف	eulogist, toady, flatters.	describer, depicter.
msikiti(N) (wa-) (Rel.)	masjid	مَسْجِد	——	mosque [Ar.]*.	___
msimu(N) (mi-) (also musimu)	mawsim	مَوْسِم	—— فَصْلٌ أَوَان	season, period.	___
msiri(N) (wa-)	ka:tim sir	كَاتِمُ السِّرِّ	——	confident, accomplice.	___
mstaarabu(N) (wa-)	mustaạrib	مُسْتَعْرِب	مُتَحَضِّر	civilized person, intelligentsia.	Arabist.
mstahiki(N)(mheshimiwa)	mustaḥiqq	مُسْتَحِقّ	... فَخَامَة مُحْتَرَم	His Excellency,honourable,respected man.	entitled, claiming,beneficiary, deserving.
mstarehe(N)	mustari:ḥ	مُسْتَرِيح	——	rest, quiet, recreation, relaxation.	resting, relaxing, calm.
mstari(N) (mfuo) (foleni)	saṭr	سَطْرٌ	مِسْطَرَة خَطّ	line, row, ruler.	line.
mstatili(N)	mustaṭi:l	مُسْتَطِيلٌ	——	rectangle, oblong.	___

Swahili word	Transcription of Arabic word	Arabic word	Arabic word in Swahili sense	Swahili usage	Arabic usage.
msuaki(N) (mi-) (also mswaki)	miswa:k	مِسْوَاك	———	toothbrush, a stick or twig for cleaning the teeth.	———
msufi(N) (mi-)	ṣu:f	صُوف	القَبَك	kapok tree (Bombax, rhodognaphlon).	wool.
msuluhishi(N) (wa-)	muṣliḥ	مُصْلِح	———	see suluhishaji.	———
msuluhisho(N)	ṣulḥ	صُلْحٌ	———	peace make, mediator, conciliator.	———
msuluhishaji(N) (wa-) (mpatanishi)	muṣlih	مُصْلِحٌ	———	a peace-maker, reconciler.	———
msuluhivu(N) (wa-)	muṣlih		———	see msuluhishi	———
msumari(N) (mi-)	misma:r	مِسْمَارٌ	———	nail, sting, pin, spur, screw.	———, tack, rivet, peg.
msunobari(N) (mi-)	ṣanawbar	صَنَوْبَر	———	pine, pinetree.	———
mswahili(N) (wa-) (mjanja)	sawahili:	سَوَاحِلِيّ	———	(1) a person whose mother tongue is Swahili language. (2) a person who dwells on the East African coast. (3) a sly, a mart, deceitful, a cunning person. (4) a muslim (us. heard).	from sahil means coast.
mswaki(N) (mi-) (also muswaki)	miswa:k	مِسْوَاك	———	see mswaki.	———
mtaala(N) (mi-)	muṭa:la ạa (t)	مُطَالَعَة	———	study, reading, practice, curriculum development.	reading, study.
mtaalamu(N) (wa-)	mutaạllim	مُتَعَلِّم	———	educated person, scholar.	———
mtabiri(N) (wa-)	muạabbir	مُعَبِّر	———	soothsayer, commentator, forecaster, meteorologist.	one who announces or foretells events.

Swahili word	Transcription of Arabic word	Arabic word	Arabic word in Swahili sense	Swahili usage	Arabic usage.
mtahini(N) (wa-)	mumtaḥin	مُمْتَحِن	___	examiner, tester.	___
mtahiniwa(N) (wa-)	mumtaḥan	مُمْتَحَن	___	examinee, candidate, examined, tested.	___
mtalaka (N)	muṭallaqa (t)	مُطَلَّقَة	___	divorcee, divorced woman.	___
mtalii(N) (wa-)	muṭṭalii̦	مُطَّلِع	___	tourist.	viewer, observer.
mtanabahisho(N) (mi-) (mzinduo)	Tambi:h	تَنْبِيه	——— اِنْتِبَاه اِسْتِيقَاظ	a wakening, rousing.	___, alerting.
mtanashati(N) (wa-) (nadhifu) (bashashi)	nashi:ṭ	نَشِيط	___	clean.	active, anergetic.
mtawafu(N) (wa-) (Rel.)	muṭawwif	مُطَوِّف	___	one who guides the pilgrims during the pilgrimage.	___
mtawala(N) (wa-)	wa:li(n)	وَالٍ	___ حَاكِم	ruler, governor.	___
mtawalia (N) (wa-) (also mtawalio)	mutawa:lia (t)	مُتَوَالِيَة	___	continuously, sequence, sequency, one by one.	___
mtihani(N) (mi-)	imtiḥa:n	اِمْتِحَان	___	examination, experiment.	___
mtii(N) (wa-)	muṭi:ạ	مُطِيع	___	see mtiifu.	___
mtiifu(N) (wa-)	muṭi:ạ	"	___	obedient, submissive, docile.	___
mtini(N) (mi-)	ti:n	تِين	نَبَات التِّين	figtree (firus carica).	___
mtofaa(N) (mi-) (also mtofaha, mtufaha)	tuffa:ḥ	تُفَّاح	←——— (نَبَات)	the rose-apple tree.	an apple.
muadhini(N) (wa-)	muādhin	مُؤَذِّن	___	see adhini(V).	___

Swahili word	Transcription of Arabic word	Arabic word	Arabic word in Swahili sense	Swahili usage	Arabic usage.
muainisho(N)(mi-) (Ling)	taayi:n	تَعْيِين	تَصْنِيف	classfication.	specification, nomination, itemization.
muda(N) (kipindi maalum) (nafasi)	mudda(t)	مُدَّة	___	period, space of time, chance.	___
mudiri(N)	mudi:r	مُدِير	___	head, (department),a chief.	___, director, administrator, manager.
muflisi(N)	muflis	مُفْلِس	___	see mfilisi.	___
mufti(N) (ma-) (sheikh mkuu) (profesa)	mufti:	مُفْتِى ، بروفيسور علّامة	___	(1) deliverer of formal legal opinions, official expounder of Islamic law, mufti, (2) a Proffesor**	___
muhafidhina(N)	muha:fidhi:n	مُحَافِظِين (ج)	مُحَافِظ	conservative, gardian, caretaker.	___, custodian.
muhali(N) (mi-)	muha:l	مُحَال	___	impossible, anything difficult.	___, unreasonable
muhashamu(N)	muhtasham	مُحْتَشَم	مُحْتَم	see mheshimiwa.	
muhimu(adj.)	muhimm	مُهِمّ	___	important, urgent, serious, significant.	___, momentous.
muhtasari(N)	mukhtasar	مُخْتَصَر	___	summary, abridgement, brief, abstract, outline.	___, concise, short.
muhula(N) (mi-)	muhla(t)	مُهْلَة	مُدَّة (سمستر)	term, interval.	___, respite, a delay, time to think.
muhuni(N) (wa-)	kha:in	خَائِن	___	see haini.	___
muhuri(N) (mi-) (also mhuri)	muhr	مُهْر	___	seal signet.	___
mujibu (adv.)	mu:jib	مُوجِب	___	according to, on account of.	

Swahili word	Transcription of Arabic word	Arabic word	Arabic word in Swahili sense	Swahili usage	Arabic usage.
muktadha (N) (mada)	muqtaḍa:	مُقتضى	____	according to, in conformity with.	____
mumini (N) (wa-)	mũ:min	مُؤمِن	____ تَابِع	a true Muslim, <u>a true believer</u>,** a very faithfulman.	____
muminina (N) (wa-)	mũmini:n (a)	مُؤمِنِين (ج)	مُؤمِن	see mumini.	____
munkani (N)	munkar	مُنْكَر	____	abomination, forbidden.	____ denied.
muradi (N) (conj.)	mura:d	المُرَاد	____	see mradi.	____
murua (N) (tabia mjema) (heshima)	muru:ā(t)	مُرُوءَة	____	see mrua.	____
mushawara (N) (Ref. Mfanyakazi.TZ.)	musha:wara (t)	مُشَاوَرَة	____	consultation, deliberation, conference.	____
mushkil (N) (mi-) (wasiwasi) (kasoro)	mushkila (t)	مُشْكِلَة/ مُشْكِل	____	problem, difficulty, doubt, disquiet.	____, issue.
mushkili (N) (mi-) (also mushikil)	"	"	____	see mushkil.	____
musimu (N)	mawsim	مَوْسِم	____	see msimu.	____
mustakbadhi (N)	istiqba:ḍ	اسْتِقْبَاض	____	receipt, voucher.	receiving, grasping.
mustakbal (N)	mustaqbal	مُسْتَقْبَل	____	future.	____
mustarehe (N)	mustari:ḥ	مُسْتَرِيح	____	see mstarehe.	____
mutasari (N) (mi-)	mukhtaṣar	مُخْتَصَر	____	see muhtasari.	____
muswada (N) (mi-)	musaw̲ada (t)	مُسَوَّدَة	____	draft, roughcopy, proof sheet.	____, rough sketch.

Swahili word	Transcription of Arabic word	Arabic word	Arabic word in Swahili sense	Swahili usage	Arabic usage.
muujiza(N) (ml-) (shani) (ajabu)	muạjiza(t)	مُعْجِزَة	—— كَرَامَة أعْجُوبَة	miracle, honour, marval.	____, respect.
muumini(N) (wa-)	mū:min	مُؤْمِن	——	see mumini.	____
muadhamu(N) (mheshimiwa)	muạd̲h̲am	مُعَظَّم	—— مُحْتَرَم	glorified, sublime, august.	____
mwadhamu(N) (muhtaramu) (mheshimiwa)	"	"	—— مُحْتَرَم	see muadhamu.	____
mwadhini(N) (Rel.)	muād̲h̲in	مُؤَذِّن	——	see adhini.	____
mwafaka(N)	muwa:faqa (t)	مُوَافَقَة	——	see afikiano.	____
mwajiri(N) (wa-)	muājjir	مُؤَجِّر	——	landlord, lessor.	____
mwajiriwa(N) (wa-)	muājjar	مُؤَجَّر	——، المُسْتَأْجِر	lessee, lease holder, employer,	____, tenant.
(mwana)damu(N) (wa-)	(ibn)Adam	(اِبْنُ) آدَم	—— الأنْسَان	see binadamu.	____
(mwana) halali(N) (wa-)	(ibn) ḥala:l	(اِبْنُ) حَلَال	——، اِبْنٌ شَرْعِيّ	see halali.	____
(mwana)haramu(wa-)	(ibn) ḥara:m	(اِبْنُ) حَرَام	—— اِبْنٌ غَيْرُ شَرْعِيّ	see haramu.	____
(mwana)hewa(N) (wa-) (rubani)	(____)hawa: ā	(مِنْ الهَوَاء)	—— طَيَّان	pilot.	____
mwalimu(N) (wa-)	muạllim	مُعَلِّم	—— لَقَب احْتِرَام	teacher, master.	____
mwarabu(N) (wa-)	Ạrabiyy (un)	عَرَبِيّ	——	Arabian.	____, Arabic.
mwasharati(N) (wa-)	muạ:shir	مُعَاشِر	زَانٍ	see asherati.	companion, fellow, friend, associate, comrade.

Swahili word	Transcription of Arabic word	Arabic word	Arabic word in Swahili sense	Swahili usage	Arabic usage.
mwasherati(N) (wa-)	muạ:shir	مُعَاشِر	—— زَانٍ	see asherati	——
mwasi(N) (wa-) (mkaidi)	ạ:ṣi(n)	عَاصٍ	—— مُتَمَرِّد	disobedient, rebel, sinful.	——
mwasisi(N) (wa-)	muāssis	مُؤَسِّس	——	founder, originator.	——
Mwislamu(N) (wa-)	muslim	مُسْلِم	——	a muslim(moslem).	——
Myahudi(N) (wa-)	Yuhu:dy	يَهُودِيّ	——	Jew, Hebrew.	——
mzabibu(N) (mi-)	zabi:b	زَبِيب	(نَبَات) عِنَب	grape vine.	grape.
mzabuni(N) (wa-) (mnada) (mshitiri)	zabu:n	زَبُون	——، المُزَايِد	a bidder at a sale.	customer.
mzaha(N) (mi-)	miza:ḥ	مِزَاح	——	joke, fun, joking, jest.	——
mzaituni(N) (mi-)	zaitu:n	زَيْتُون	——، (نَبَات)	olive-tree.	olive.
mzandiki(N) (wa-)	zindi:q	زِنْدِيق	——، مُنَافِق	see mnafiki.	——
mzeituni(N) (mi-)	zaitu:n	زَيْتُون	——، (نَبَات)	see mzaituni.	——
mzinifu(N) (wa-)	zani(n)	زَانٍ	——، زَانِيَة عَاهِرَة	adulterer, adulteress, prostitute.	——
		N			
naam(inter.) (ndiyo) (vema)	naạm	نَعَمْ	——	yes, certainly, surely, it is so.	——
nabii(N) (ma-)	nabiyy(un)	نَبِيّ	—— رَسُولٌ	a prophet.	——
nadharia(N) (mawazo) (maelezo)	nadḥaria	نَظَرِيَّة	——	theory, look, attention, consideration.	——
nadhifu(N) (safi)	nadḥi:f	نَظِيفٌ	—— أَنِيق	clean, well kept, tidy, neat.	——, well tended.

Swahili word	Transcription of Arabic word	Arabic word	Arabic word in Swahili sense	Swahili usage	Arabic usage.
nadra(N) (haba) (chache) (kidogo)	na:dir	نَادِر	____ نُدْرَة	rare, uncommon, seldom, rarely.	____, odd, unusual.
nafaka(N)	nafaqa(t)	نَفَقَة	حُبُوب	grain, corn, seeds, berries.	sustenance, expence.
nafasi(N) (muda)	nafas	نَفَس	____	opportunity, breathing time, relief, interval, space, time.	____
nafsi(N) (roho) (mwenyewe) (kiini au dhati ya kitu)	nafs.	نَفْس	____	mind, spirit, soul, person, breath self.	____, essence
nafuu(N) (wepesi) (urahisi) (ahueni) (hujambo)	nafa̤	نَفْعٌ	____ فَائدَة	use, usefulness, benefit, profit, avail, advantage, gain,	____,
nahau(N) (sarufi)	naḥau	النَّحْو	____	(1) idiom (2) grammar.	grammar, syntax, way, method.
nai(N) [Persian]*	nai	نَاى	____	reed, flute.	____
naibu(N) (ma-)	na:i̱b	نَائِب	____	deputy, agent, on behalf of.	___, vice ___, representative.
najisi(N) (sio tohara)	najs	نَجْسٌ	____	unclean, impure, dirty, defile, profane.	___, stained, polluted.
najisi(V) **ia/ika/isha/iwa/iana.**	najjas(a)	نَجَّس	____, اغْتَصَبَ	defile, pollute, contaminate, profane, <u>violate</u>.**	____,
nakala(N)	naql	نَقْل	____, نُسْخَة	a copy, a single book.	coping, transfer, removal, conveyance.
nakili(N)	naqal(a)	نَقَلَ	____, نَسَخَ	to copy, transcribe.	____, to remove, to communicate, to transport.
nakshi(N) (chora) (pamba)	naqsh	نَقْش	____, تَزْيِين حفر	engraving, carving.	____,painting.

Swahili word	Transcription of Arabic word	Arabic word	Arabic word in Swahili sense	Swahili usage	Arabic usage.
nanaa(N)	naạna:ạ	نَعْنَاع	____	mint	____
nanasi(N) (ma-) [Persian]*	ànana:s	أَنَنَاس	____	pine-apple	
nasaba(N)	nasab	نَسَبٌ	____	lineage, pedigree, descent, kinship, relationship genealogy.	____, ancestral line.
naṣaha(N)	naṣa:ḥa(t)	نَصَاحَة	____	advice, counsel, guidance.	____
nasara(N) (ma-) (mkristo)	naṣa:ra(t)	نَصَارَى (ج)	نَصْرَانِيّ ,	a christian.	christians.
nasibisha(V) (husisha na) **ia/ika/iwa/ana**	nasab(a)	نَسَبَ / نَاسَبَ	____	relate, correlate, reffer pertain.	____, to trace back the ancestry.
nasibu(N) (bahati)	naṣi:b	نَصِيب	____	fortune, lot.	____
nasihi(V) **ia/ika/isha/iwa/iana**	naṣaḥ(a)	نَصَحَ / نَاصَحَ	____	to advise, to give good advice, consult.	___, to give sincerely.
nauli(N)	naul/ nawa:l	نَوْل / نَوَال	أُجْرَة النَّقْلِ	fare, passage, money, charge for freight.	giving, granting.
natija(N) (matokeo mazuri) (tija)	nati:ja(t)	نَتِيجَة	____	a good result.	a result.
(a) **nawiri**(V) (nenepa)	naw̱ar(a)	نَوَّرَ	____, أَصْبَحَ نَيِّرًا	shine(only for a person's countenance).	to be luminous, shining.
(b) **nawiri**(V) **ia/ika /isha.**	naw̱ar	نَوَّر	أَنَارَ	to shine, give light, to be clean, be illuminated, be enlightened.	____, to flower, blossom, to shed light.
neema(N) (baraka) (ustawi) (riziki)	niạma(t)	نِعْمَة	____	blessing, boom, rich, favour, grace, ease, comfort	___, benefit, benefaction, kindness.

Swahili word	Transcription of Arabic word	Arabic word	Arabic word in Swahili sense	Swahili usage	Arabic usage.
neemeka(V) esha	tanaạm(a)	تنَعَّمَ	___	to be delighted, to live in comfort, to lead a life of ease and luxury.	___
neemefu(adj.)	mutunaịim	مُتَنَعِّم	___	abundant, plentiful, one whose life is easy and comfortable.	___
neemevu(adj.)	"	"	___	see neemefu.	___
nia(N) (kusudio)	nia/niyya (t)	نِيَة / نِيَّة	___	intention, purpose, will, heart, mind, thought, idea, disposition.	___, tendency, plan, determination, volition.
niaba(N)	niaba	نِيَابَة	___	on behalf of, in place of, in stead of, acting, deputy, by proxy.	___
nidhamu(N) (adabu) (utaratibu mzuri)	niḍha:m	نظَام	___	proper arrangement, order system, regularity, discipline.	___, organization, rule.
nifasi(N) (Rel.)	nifa:s	نِفَاس	___	childbed, parturition, delivery, accouchment.	___, confinement, childbirth.
nikahi(N) (ndoa) (akidi) (Rel.)	nika:ḥ	نِكَاح	___	marriage, wedding, matrimony.	___, wedlock.
nishani(N) (local Arabic) [Persian]*	ni:sha:n	نِيشَان	___	medal, mark, sign, decoration, badge.	___, target, goal, aim
nishati(N)	nasha:ṭ	نَشَاط	طَاقَة	energy, strength, power, activeness, exertion.	___, activity, briskness, animation, liveliness.
nufaika(V) (faidika) /**esha.**	intafaạ(a)	انْتَفَعَ	___	to get profit, prosper, gain.	___,

Swahili word	Transcription of Arabic word	Arabic word	Arabic word in Swahili sense	Swahili usage	Arabic usage.
nuia(V) (waza) (tabana) (azimu) **lia/lika/za/wa.**	nawa:	نَوَى	___	to intend, purpose, have in mind, consider, resolve.	___, determine.
nuhusi(N) (balaa) (kisirani) (mkosi)	naḥs	نَحْس	___	misfortune, badluck, disaster, failure.	___
nuksani(N) (rare) (also nuksi)	nuqṣa:n	نُقْصَان	مِحْنَة/نحس بَلِيّة/ سُوءُ الحَظّ	misfortune, disaster, badluck, calamity, failure, disappointment.	shortage, damage, loss, decrease, diminution, gap.
nuksi(N) (also nuksani, nuhusi)	naqṣ	نَقْص	نَحْس	see nukdani.	___
nukta(N) (sekunde)	nuqṭa(t)	نُقْطَة	___ عَلامة ثانِيَة (زمن)	dot, mark, spot, point, punctuation.	___, period, full stop, affair matter, place, branch, item.
nukulu(N) (rare)	naqal(a)	نَقَلَ (ف)	___	see nakili.	___
nukuu(N) (also nakili) **lia/lika/lisha/liana.**	"	"	___	see nakili.	___
nurisha (V)	ána:r(a)	أَنَارَ (ف)	___	illuminate, brighten, to light, reflect.	___, to shed light, clarify.
nuru(N)	nu:r	نُور	___	light, brightness, illumination.	___, light beam, gleam.
nusra(N) (tahafifu) (also nusura)	nuṣra(t)	نُصْرَة	___, انْقَاذ	help, aid, backing, assistance, support, protection, defence.	___, save.
nusu(N) (local Arabic)	niṣf/nuṣf	نِصْفٌ	___	half, portion, bit, part.	half, middle, semi, mid.

Swahili word	Transcription of Arabic word	Arabic word	Arabic word in Swahili sense	Swahili usage	Arabic usage.
nusuru(V)(salimisha) (okoa) (ponyesha) (auni) (saidia) **ia/ ika/isha/iwa.**	naṣar(a)	نَصَر	___ , أنقذ	to help, aid, assist, protect, support, defend, <u>save</u>,** seek to support.	___, keep, totriumph, to guard.
nuwia(V) (dhamiria) (kusudia)	nawa:	نَوى	___ أضْمَرَ	see nuia.	____
nyadhifa(N) (pl. of wadhifa)	waḍhi:fa (t)	وَظِيفَة	وَظَائِف	see wadhifa.	____
nyakati(N) (pl. of wakati)	waqt	وَقْتٌ	أوْقَات	see wakati.	____
nyaraka(N) (pl. of waraka)	waraqa(t)	وَرَقَة	(الأرْشيف) سِجِلّات	archives, (also see waraka)	see waraka.
nyiradi(N) (pl. of uradi)	ʾawra:d	أوْرَاد	___ ذِكْرٌ	see uradi.	____
okota(N)	laqaṭ(a)	لَقَطَ (ف)	___	pick up, find, gather, obtain something without effort, come upon by chance, not expected.	___, collect, glean bargain.
ole(conj.) (N) (adj)	wail/(a)	وَيْل / وَيْلَة	___	owe! grief, fat, lot, detiny.	___, distress, disaster, affliction, misfortune, adversity, calamity.
orodha(N)	ạrḍ istịara:ḍ	عَرْض اسْتِعْرَاضٌ	قَائِمَة	list, invoice, time-table, catalogue, inventory.	(1) parade, review, (2) presention, submission, (3) display, exhibition, (4) width, breadth.

Swahili word	Transcription of Arabic word	Arabic word	Arabic word in Swahili sense	Swahili usage	Arabic usage.
orodhohali(N) (loc. Ar.)	ardha:l	عَرْضُحَال (عَرْض حَالٍ)	___ , طَلب	application.	___, petition.
orofa(N) (also ghorofa, gorofa)	ghurfa)t)	غُرْفَة	طَابق / دَوْر عِمَارة	(upper) floor or room, story of a house.	room, chamber, upper chamber, cabinet.
		P			
pahala(N) (mahali)	maḥall	مَحَلّ	___	place, situation, position, country, room, space interval.	___
pahali(N) (also pahala)	"	"	___	see pahala.	___
		R			
Rabi(N) (Mola) (Mungu)	Rabb	رَبّ	___ اله (اللهُ تعَالى)	Lord, Master (refferring to God)	___, boss.
radhi(N)	riḍ a(n)	رِضَا / رِضً	___	pardon, apology, contentedness, contentment, agreement, blessing.	___, assent, sanction, satisfaction, acceptance.
radi(N)	raạd	رَعْدٌ	___	thunder, clap of thunder	___
rafiki(N) (ma-) (sahibu) (mwandani)	rafi:q	رَفِيقٌ	___	companion, comrade, friend, partner.	___, attendant, associate, gentle, mild.

Swahili word	Transcription of Arabic word	Arabic word	Arabic word in Swahili sense	Swahili usage	Arabic usage.
rafu(N) (shubaka)	raff	رَفٌّ	___	shelf, wall at the back of a reccess**.	___
raghibu(V) **ia/ika/isha/iwa/iana.**	raghib(a)	رَغِبَ	___	to wish, desire.	___
raha(N)	ra:ḥa(t)	رَاحَةٌ	___	comfort, rest, peace, bliss.	___
rahani(N) (also rihani)	rahn	رَهْنٌ	___ الأرْتِهَان	pawn, deposite as security, pledge, mortage.	___, hostage, hypothec.
rahisi(adj.)	rakhi:ṣ	رَخِيص	___ سَهْل	easy,** cheap, low-priced, in expensive.	___, low, soft, supple, base, tender.
rahisi(V)**ia/ika/isha/iwa**	rakhuṣ(a)	رَخُصَ	___ سَهَّلَ قَلَّلَ البَيْع	to become cheap, be little, make cheap, reduce the price.	___, to be supple.
rai(N) (fikira) (siha) (nguvu)	raay	رَأْيٌ	___	idea, opinion, view, advice, suggestion.	___, notion, conception, proposal.
raia(N)	raịya(t)	رَعِيَة	___ مُوَاطِن	fold, citizen, subject.	___, herd.
rais(N) (ma-) (kiongozi wa nchi, shirika, kampuni, au chama)	rai:s	رَئِيس	___	president, chairman.	___, leader, incharge of, head, boss, chairman.
raka(N) (ma-) (also kiraka)	ruqạa(t)	رُقْعَة	___	a patch.	___
rakaa(N) (Rel.)	rakạa(t)	رَكْعَة	___	act of bowing with the hands on the knees doing by a Muslim during the Prayers.	___

Swahili word	Transcription of Arabic word	Arabic word	Arabic word in Swahili sense	Swahili usage	Arabic usage.
rakaateni(N) (rakaa mbili)	rakạatain	رَكْعَتَيْنِ	___	two(rakaa) which see.	___
rakibu(V) (also re-kebisha)	rakkab(a)	رَكَّبَ (ف)	___, جَمَعَ	assemble, put together, construct.	___, compose, to set, fix.
Ramadhani(N) (Rel.)	Ramḍa:n	رَمَضَان	___	a month of fasting (for Muslims).	___
ramli(N)	raml	رَمْل	الشَعْوَذَة	soothsaying from figures in sand/divine.	sand.
rasharasha(N) (mvua nyepesi)	rasha(t)	رَشّة (المَطَرِ)	___	shower of rain.	___
(a) **rasi**(N)	raàs	رَأْس	___ (الكاب) ارض داخلة في البحرِ	cape, promontory, head-land.	___
(b) **ras** (N) (poet.) (kichwa)	raàs	"	___	head.	___, mind, intellect.
rasilimali(N)	ras-ma:l	رَأْسُ مَالٍ	___ (رَأْسمال)	capital, fund, assets, property.	___
rasisi(V) **ia/ika/isha**	raṣṣaṣ(a)	رَصَّصَ	___, طَلَى بالرَّصَاصِ	to cover, lay, with lead, plate with tin.	___
rasmi(adv.)	rasmiy	رَسْمِيٌ	___	official, formal.	___, regular.
ratiba(N)	rati:b	رَتِيب	على نسق واحِدٍ / بَرْنَامِج	arrangement, method, system, order, neatness.	routine, monotonous, regular course.
ratibu(V) **ia/ika/isha/iwa/iana.**	rattab(a)	رَتَّبَ	___	set in proper order, arrange, adjust.	___, prepare.
rehani(N)	rahn	رَهْنٌ	___	see rahani.	___

Swahili word	Transcription of Arabic word	Arabic word	Arabic word in Swahili sense	Swahili usage	Arabic usage.
rehema(N)	raḥma(t)	رَحْمَة	——	mercy, pity, clemency, compassion.	——
rehemu(V) **ea/eka/ esha/ewa.**	raḥim(a)	رَحِمَ	——	compassionate, pity, to have mercy	——
rejareja(V)	rajaạ/ rajaạ	رَجَعَ / رَجَعَ	قَطّاعي	returnable(of selling re- tial).	go and return.
rejea(V) (rudi) **lea/ leka/sha/za/wa/ana.**	rajaạ(a)	رَجَعَ	—— عَادَة	to return, go, come back, refer, to revoke, relate to, relate to, begin aga- in.	——
rekebisha(V)	rakkab(a)	رَكّب	——	see rakibu	——
rekebisho(N) (ma-)	tarki:b	تَرْكِيبٌ	——	assembling, making, pre- paration, construction, setting.	___, installation, composition, build.
riadha(N)	ria:ḍ a(t)	رِيَاضَة	——	athletics, sport.	____, gymnastics, practice.
riahi(N) (rare)	riaḥ	رِيَاح	——	gas in the stomach, wind.	___, flatulence.
riba(N)	riba:	الرِّبَا	——	interest, usury.	——
ridhaa(N)	riḍa:	رِضا / رِضَى	——	acceptance, consent, as- sent.	_____, satisfacti- on, pleasure.
ridhi (V) **ia/ika/ isha/iwa/iana.**	raḍiya	رَضِيَ	——	please, content, accept, satisfy, approve.	___, agree, wish, desive.
ridhiko(V) (ma-) (ridhaa)	riḍa:ā	رِضَاء	——	contentedness, agreement, consent,assent, accepta- nce.	___, conciliation, saction, approval.
riha(N) (rihi) (ha- rufu)	raịḥa(t) ri:ḥa(t)	رَائِحَة رِيحَة	——	odor, odour, smell.	——

Swahili word	Transcription of Arabic word	Arabic word	Arabic word in Swahili sense	Swahili usage	Arabic usage.
risala(N)	risa:la(t)	رِسَالَة	_____	message, epistle, consignment, letter.	_____, radio message, vocation.
risasi(N)	raṣa:s	رَصَاص	____	lead, bullet, solder, tin**	_____
ritadi(V) (Rel.)	irtadda	اِرْتَدَّ	_____ عَنْ الاسْلَام	retire, fall back, retreat, withdraw, (from Islamic religion).	_____
rithi(V) **ia/ika/isha /iwa/iana.**	warith(a)	وَرِثَ	____	to inherit, to bring on (by inheritance).	_____, to be heir.
riwaya(N)	riwa:ya(t)	رِوَايَة	____	story, narrative, tale, novel, play, drama.	_____, report, account.
riziki(N)	rizq	رِزْق	____	means of living, livelihood, food, maintenance, subsistance.	_____, blessing(of God) fortune, wealth.
robota(N)(ma-)	rabṭa(t)	رَبْطَة	____ رِزْمَة / حِزْمَة / طَرْد	parcel,packet, bundle, bale.	____, package.
roho(N)	ru:ḥ	رُوح	____	spirit, soul, breath of life, Ghost, throat, character, greediness,	___, vital force.
roshani(N)[Persian]* (ghorofa)	roshan (rushan)	رَوْشَن	____	storey(in a building).	window.(loc. Ar.).
rotoba(N) (bunda) (tunda)	ruṭu:ba(t)	رُطُوبَة	____	dampness, moisture.	_____, humidity, wetness.
rubani(N) (ma-)	rubba:n	رُبَّان	____	pilot, captain of ship, helmsman, a guide.	_____
rudi(N) (rejea) (onya), **ia/ika/isha ishiana**	radda	رَدَّ	_____	turn, give, send(back), correct, reverse, contradict, reprove, shrink.	____, throw, drive(back).
rudufu(N) (ma-)	mardu:f	مَرْدُوف/مُرَادِف	_____	double, two fold.	____, synonym.

Swahili word	Transcription of Arabic word	Arabic word	Arabic word in Swahili sense	Swahili usage	Arabic usage.
rudufu(V) **ia/ika/ isha/iwa.**	radaf(a)	رَدَف	___	to double.	___, to come next, follow, ride behind.
rufaa(N) (rufani)	mura:faạa (t)	مُرَافَعَة	___, اسْتِئْناف	appeal.	___, speech for the defence.
rufani(N)	"	"	___	see rufaa.	___
ruhan(N) (ma-)	ru:ḥa:ni	رُوحَانِي	___	a kind of djjin.	spiritual, immaterial, divine, holy sacred, elergyman.
ruhusa(N)(idhini) (kibali)	rukhṣa(t)	رُخْصَة	___	permission, leave, authorization, liberty, holiday.	___, admission.
ruhusu(V)(kibali)	rak͟has(a)	رخّص	___	to authorise, to permit, to license.	___
ruiya(also ruya) (rare)	ruũya:	رُؤْيَا	___	dream, vision.	___
ruksa(N)(also ruhusa)	rukhṣa(t)	رُخْصَة	___	see ruhusa.	___
rukuu(V)(Rel.)	rakaạ(a)	رَكَع	___	to kneel down, to bend the body, see rakaa.	___
rushwa(N)	rushwa(t)	رُشْوَة	___	bribe, corruption, bribery.	___
rutba(N)(also rutuba)	ruṭu:ba(t)	رُطُوبَة	___	see rutuba.	___
rutuba(N)	ruṭu:ba(t)	"	___	moisture, humidity, dampness.	___, wetness.

Swahili word	Transcription of Arabic word	Arabic word	Arabic word in Swahili sense	Swahili usage	Arabic usage.
rutubika(V) **isha/ ishia/ishwa**	raṭṭab(a)	رَطَّبَ	____	to moisten, make damp or wet, to be cooled, refreshed, relieved.	____
ruya(N)(ndoto) (ujozi)	ruūya:	رُؤْيَا	____	see ruiya.	____
ruzuku(V)(Rel.)	razaq(a)	رَزَقَ	____	maintain, support, to provide with means of live, to bless with.	____, endow.
		S			
saa(N)	sa:ạa(t)	سَاعَة	____	an hour,time, watch, clock, timepiece.	___at once, instantly.
saba(N) (also sabaa)	sabạ a(t)	سَبْعَة	____	سَبْع	seven, seventh, sometimes for (juma) means <u>week,**</u> <u>honey month.**</u>	____
sababisna(V) **ia/ika/ iwa**	sabbab(a)	سَبَّبَ	____	to cause, to bring on.	____
sababu(N), (conj.) (ajili) (maana) (kisa).	sabab	سَبَب	____	reason, motive, cause, means, medium.	____, origin.
sabaini(N) (also sabini)	sabị:n	سَبْعِين	____, سَبْعُونَ	seventy,(70), seventieth.	____
sabalkheri(inter) (also subalkheri)	ṣaba:ḥ-a.-khair	صَبَاحُ الخَيْرِ	____	good morning.	____
sabihi(V) (Rel.) **ia/ika/iwa**	sabbaḥ(a)	سَبَّحَ	____	to praise, glorify(for God only).	____
Sabiini(N) (makumi saba)	sabi:n	سَبْعِين	____ سَبْعُون	see sabaini.	

Swahili word	Transcription of Arabic word	Arabic word	Arabic word in Swahili sense	Swahili usage	Arabic usage.
sabiki(V) (rare) (tangulia) (takadamu) **ia/ika/isha/iwa**	sabaq(a)	سَبَقَ	____ سَبَقَ	to precede, go before, to leave behind.	____, to beat.
sabini(N)	sabi:n	سَبْعِينَ	____ سَبْعُون	see sabaini.	____
sabuni(N) [Persian]*	ṣa:bu:n	صَابُون	____ ، الغَاسُول	soap.	____
sadaka(N) (kafara) (dhabihu) (tambiko)	ṣadaq a(t)	صَدَقَة	____ ، إِحْسَان	charity, alms, sacrifice, a religious offering.	____
sadfa(N) (rare)	ṣudfa(t)	صُدْفَة	____	chance, accident, by-chance, accidentally, co-incidence.	____
sadifu(V)	ṣa:da(a)	صَادَفَ	____	to happen by chance, to chance, to meet unexpectedly.	____
sadiki(V) (Rel.) (amini) **ia/ika/isha.**	ṣaddaq(a)	صَدَّقَ	____	to believe, say or tell the truth, to fulfil, give credence.	____, be sincere, to fit exactly.
sadikifu(adj.)	ṣadiq	صَادِق	____ أَمِين مُخْلِص	truthful, true, faithful, sincere.	____, veracious, candid.
(a) **safari**(N)	safar	سَفَر	____	journey, travel, voyage, departure, expedition.	____
(b) **safari**(N)(mara)	safar	سَفَر	مَرَّة / وَقْت	time, onetime, once, on one occasion only.	*
safi(adj.) (hakika) (-kweli)	ṣa:fi	صَافٍ	____	clean, clear, pure, net, straight, honest, sincere friend, limpid, undisturbed, in order, correct bright, lucid.	____, unmixed, sheer, untroubled. candid, open hearted, cloudless.
safi(V) **ia/ika/isha/iwa.**	ṣaffa:	صَفَّى	____	become clear, to clarify, to net, make clear, correct, set to right.	____, rectify, purify, to select.
safina(N) (Rel.)	safi:na(t)	سَفِينَة	سَفِينَةُ نُوحٍ عَلَيْهِ السَّلَام	the ship of Prophet Noah.	a ship, boat.

Swahili word	Transcription of Arabic word	Arabic word	Arabic word in Swahili sense	Swahili usage	Arabic usage.
safiri(V) **ia/ika/isha/iwa/iana.**	sa:far(a)	سَافَرَ	____ سَفَّرَ	travel, to send on a journey.	____, send away, dispatch.
safisha(V)	ṣaffa:	صَفَّى	____	see safi(V).	____
safu(N) (mstari) (tabaka)	ṣaff	صَفّ	____ خَطّ	line, row, range, rank, series.	____, class, division.
saga(V) **ia/ika/isha/iwa/iana.**	saḥaq(a)	سَحَق	____ طَحَنَ	to crush to bits, <u>grind</u>,** pulverize, triturate, oppress.	___, destroy, bruise, to pound.
sagaji(N) (tec.) (msagaji)	musaḥiqa (t)	مُسَاحِقَة	____	lesbian.	____
sahaba(N) (ma-)	ṣaḥa:ba(t)	صَحَابة (ج)	صَحَابِيّ	the companion of the Prophet Muhammad. (sing).	the companion of the Prophet Muhammad. (Pl.)
sahali(adj.) (wepesi) (urahisi) (rahisi) (siyo gumu)	sahl	سَهْل	____	easy, simple, facile, light, not heavy.	___, smooth, level plain, fluent, convenient.
sahani(N)	saḥ n	صَحْنٌ	____	dish, plate, bowl.	____, disk, plane surface, meal, yard, courtyard.
sahau(V) (ghafilika) **lia/lika/lisha/liwa.**	saha: yas'hu	سَهَا / يَسْهُو	نَسِىَ	absent-minded, to be inattentive, forget.	___, neglect, omit, overlook.
sahau(N) (tabia ya (kughafirika)	sahw(un)	سَهْوٌ	النّسْيَان	absent-mindedness, alapse of memory, forgetfulness, inattention, distractedness.	___, negligence, neglectfullness.
sahaulifu(adj.)	sahwa:n	سَهْوَان	الّذي يَنْسَى كثيرا	forgetful, inattentive, absent-minded.	___, heedless.
sahibu(N) (ma-) (rafiki) (mwenzi)	ṣa:ḥib	صَاحِب	الرّفِيق ____ الزَّمِيل	companion, comrade, follower, friend.	___, associate, master, lord, owner.

Swahili word	Transcription of Arabic word	Arabic word	Arabic word in Swahili sense	Swahili usage	Arabic usage.
sahifa(N) (ukurasa) (also sahifu)	ṣaḥi:fa(t)	صَحِيفَة	___	page, leaf of a book.	____, paper, newspaper, journal, daily.
(a) **sahihi**(V) **ia/ika /isha/iwa.**	ṣaḥḥaḥ(a)	صَحَّحَ /	___ صَحَّ	correct, to be true, put right.	____, to recover.
(b) **sahihi**(adj.) (sawa sawa)	ṣaḥi:ḥ	صَحِيح	___	correct, valid, right, true, genuine.	___proper, legal.
(c) **sahihi**(N)(saini)	"	"	التَوْقِيع / الإِمْضَاء	signature, attestation, guarantee.	*
sahihisha(V)	ṣaḥḥaḥ	صَحَّحَ	___	see sahihi(a).	____, rectfy, confirm.
sahihisho(N) (ma-) (rekebisho)	Taṣḥ:h	تَصْحِيح	___	correctness, rightness, truth, verity.	___, faultlessness.
sahili(adj.)	sahl	سَهْل	___	see sahali.	____
sahili(V) (rahisisha) **ia/ika/isha/iwa**	sahul(a)	سَهُلَ / سَهَّل	___	to be smooth, level, make easy, ease, facilitate, make light.	___, relieve, mild.
saidia(V) (auni) **ka/ sha/ana**	sa:ạd(a)	سَاعَدَ	___	help, assist, aid, support, contribute,	___, back, favor.
saili(V) (uliza swahili) (hoji)	saal(a)	سَأَلَ	___	ask, examine, request, question.	____, demand, claim.
sajili(V) (rajisi) **ia/ika/isha/iwa.**	sajjal(a)	سَجَّلَ	___	register, make an entry, to note down.	___, record.
sakafu(N)	saqf	سَقْف	الأَرْضِيَة	floor, roof of a flat-roofed, stone building.	roof, ceiling.
sakafu(V) (pigilia) **ia/ika/isha/iwa**	saqqaf(a)	سَقَّفَ	___	make a roof, floor, or pavement of concrete.	provide with a roofing or ceiling.

Swahili word	Transcription of Arabic word	Arabic word	Arabic word in Swahili sense	Swahili usage	Arabic usage.
sakarati(N)	sakara:t	سَكَرَات	___ (المَوْت)	agony of death.	___
sakifu(V) (also sa-kafu(V)	saqqaf(a)	سَقَّفَ	___	see sakafu(v).	___
sala(N) (dua) (maombi)	ṣala:(t)	صَلَاة	___ دُعَاء	salat, the official Islamic Prayer/ritual invocation, imploration.	___, supplication.
salaam(U) (N)	salaam	سَلَام	___	greeting, salutation, compliments.	___,safety, peacefulness, soundness
salala(conj.)	salla:ạlai hi	صَلَّى اللّٰهُ عَلَيْهِ وَسَلَّم	___	in exclamation, God forbid(concern Prophet Muhammad(S.A.W)	___, God bless him.
salama(N) (adv.)	sala:ma(t)	سَلَامَة	___	security, safety, sound health, peace.	___, well-being.
salamu(N)	sala:m (yu/salli)	سَلَام	___	see salaam(N).	___
sali(V) (Rel.) ia/ika/isha/iwa	ṣalla:	صَلَّى	___	pray, worship, bless, to implore.	___
salimina(adv.)	sa:limin (a)	سَالِمِين	___, سَالِمُونَ	in safety,safely.	___, (Pl. in Arabic).
salimu(V) **ia/ika/iwa /iana** (silimu) (toa) (amkia) (kabidhi) (kubali kushindwa)	sallam(a)	سَلَّمَ	___	greet, salute, to submit, deliver, consign, resign, surrender, yield, save, cause to be save, hand-over.	___, get, obtain takeover, take possession.
(a) **saliti**(V) (fitini) (danganya) (ghushi) **ia/ika/isha/iwa /iana.**	tasallaṭ (a)	تَسَلَّطَ	اضطهد / طعن	be domineering, sarcastic, betray, <u>adultrate</u>,** cause trouble, hold sway.	__, establish as ruler, impose, reign.
(b) **saliti**(V) (changanya pamoja) **ia/ika isha/iwa.**	sallaṭ	سَلَّطَ	خَلَط	mix, adultrate.	*

Swahili word	Transcription of Arabic word	Arabic word	Arabic word in Swahili sense	Swahili usage	Arabic usage.
samadi(N) (mbolea) (mavi ya wanyama)	sama:d	سَمَاد	——	dung, fertilizer, manure.	——
samahani(interj.)	sama:ḥ	سَمَاح	عَفْوًا / أُعْفُ عَنِّ / سَامِحْنِي	forgive me, pardon me, excuse me.	pardon, forgiveness.
samahani(N) (msamaha)	musa:maḥa (t)	مُسَامَحَة	——	pardon, forgiveness, tolerance.	for bearance.
samaki(N)	samak	سَمَك	——	fish.	——
samawati(N) (aina ya rangi)	sama:wa:t	سَمَوَات	سَمَاوِى (لَوْن)	sky-colour, blue, azure.	——, sky(pl. in Ar.)
samehe(V) **ea/eka/esha/ewa/ana.**	samaḥ(a)	سَمَحَ	——	forgive, pardon, remit, apologize.	——, to allow, permit.
samli(N)	samn	سَمْن	——	ghee, cooking butter.	——
sana(N) (mno)(zaidi)	sana:â	سَنَاه	جِدًّا / كَثِيرًا	very much, just so, certainly.	high, sublime, exalted, excellence.
sana(V) (rare) (fua)	ṣanaạ(a)	صنعة / صناعة صَنَع	——	hammer, strike, beat(metal)	to make, fabricate.
sanaa(N)	ṣanaạ(t)	صَنْعَة / صَنَاعَة	——	art, workmanship, craft, artistic, skill, proffession.	——, work, business vccation, manufacture.
sanamu(N)[Persian]*	ṣanam	صَنَم	—— تِمْثَال	statue, image, likeness, idol.	idol, image.
sanda(N) (bafta ya kuzikia maiti) (mazishi) (satini) (ubani)	1. sanad 2. misnad/ masnad.	سَنَد مِسْنَد مَسْنَد	كَفَن	shroud, winding, sheet burial cloth.	support, prop, stay, back, rest, (2) pillow, cushion.
sandali(N)	ṣandal	صَنْدَل	——	sandal-wood. sandals.	——

Swahili word	Transcription of Arabic word	Arabic word	Arabic word in Swahili sense	Swahili usage	Arabic usage.
sanduku(N) (ma-) (kasha)	ṣandu:q	صَنْدُوق	____ صَنْدُوق البَرِيد	box, chest, trunk, crate, case, S.L.P = (P.O.Box).	____, suitcase, cabinet, till.
sanifu(V) **ia/ika/ isha/iwa/**	ṣannaf(a)	صَنَّفَ	____	classify, to compile, compose, invent, do work with skill.	____, categorize, assort, write a book.
sanifu(adj.)	muṣanaf	مُصَنَّف	مِقْيَاس / مِعْيَار	standard.	literary work.
sanii(V)	sanaạ(a)	صَنَعَ	____	to produce, to design.	____., build, arrange.
sarafu(N) (rare)	ṣarf	صَرْف	____ عُمْلَة	coin, exchange, a small mental or ornament worn on the neck.	changing of money, spending.
sarifu(V) (panga) **ia/ika/isha/iwa/iana**	ṣarraf(a)	صَرَّفَ	(تَصْرِيف الأفعَال)	to arrange, set in order (esp. of language.)	to inflect or decline, a word, to conjugate.
(a) **saruji**(N) [Persian]*	ṣa:ru:j	صَارُوج	____ الأَسْمَنْت	cement, concrete.	____
(b) **saruji**(N) (matandiko ya farasi) (rare)	sarj	سَرْج	____	saddle(for a horse).	____
saujika(V) (also sawijika)	saw̱a:	سَوَّى	____	see sawijika.	____
(a) **saumu**(N) (Rel.) (mfunguo) (fungo)	ṣawm	الصَّوْم	____	fasting, fast.	____
(b) **saumu**(N) (thomo) (thumu) (somu)	thu:m	ثُوم	____	garlic.	____
sauti(N)	ṣawt.	صَوْت	____	sound, voice, noise.	____

Swahili word	Transcription of Arabic word	Arabic word	Arabic word in Swahili sense	Swahili usage	Arabic usage.
sawa(adj.) (n)	sawi:y	سَوِى	———	like, egual, same, fair, right, level. smooth, straight, likeness, flatness.	___,correct, proper, regular, even, together.
sawajika(V) (also sawjika) (rare)	iswadd(a)	اِسْوَدَّ	يَنْحَل / يهزل يضعف	disfigured, emaciated from illness.	become black, blacken.
sawasawa(adj.)	sawa:a bi-sawa:a	سَوَاء بِسَوَاء	———	equally, evenly, all the same.	___, without distinction.
sawazisha(V) (weka sawa) (rekebisha)	sa:wa:	سَاوَى	———	cause to be equal, like, compare.	_____, equalize.
sawia(adv.) (wakati ule ule)	sawiyya(n)	سَوِيًّا	آنَذَاك	then, at that time, on the spot.	together, in common, jointly.
sawidi(V)	sawad(a)	سوّد	———	to make draft, rough copy.	———
sawijika(V) (sawajika) isha	iswadd(a)	اسْوَدّ	نَحَلَ / ضَعُفَ هَزَلَ	see sawajika.	———
sawiri(V) **ia/ika/ isha/iwa.** (rare)	ṣawar(a)	صَوَّر	———	make a picture, fashion, form.	___, to imagine.
sayidi(N) (bwana) (rare)	sayyid	سَيِّد	———	lord, master.	———
sefu(N) (poet.)(ma-) (upanga) (rare)	saif	سَيْف	———	sword.	———
sefule(N) (rare)	asfal	أسْفَل	———	low fellow, lower person.	lower, bottom, below, underneath.
sehemu(N) (baadhi) (upande wa mahali)	sah m suhaim (dimin)	سَهْمٌ سُهَيْمٌ	جُزْء / حِصَّة	part, portion, share, piece, lot.	____, arrow, dart.
selaha(N) (silaha)	sila:ḥ	سِلَاح	———	arms, weapon,(see silaha).	———

Swahili word	Transcription of Arabic word	Arabic word	Arabic word in Swahili sense	Swahili usage	Arabic usage.
(a) **sera**(N)	si:ra(t)	سِيرَة	____	way of life, behavior, biography.	____
(b) **sera**(N) (ngome) (gereza) (boma) (buruji) (rare)	su:r	سُور	حِصْنٌ / قَلْعَة	fortness, castle, strong hold.	wall, fence.
(c) **sera**(N) (rare)	*		*	bee wax, wax.	*
setiri(V)	satar(a)	سَتَر	____	see sitiri.	____
shaba(N)	shabb(at)	شَبّ / شَبَّة	____	alum.	____, (local Ar.).
shabu(N) (shaba)	"	"	____	alum.	____(local Arabic).
(a) **shabaha**(N) (lengo) (makusudi)	shabaḥ	شَبَحٌ	هَدَفٌ / قَصْدٌ	target, aim.	object of vision.
(b) **shabaha**(N) (adj)	tasha:buh	شِبْه / تَشَابُه	____ تَمَاثُل	similarity, likeness, same as, like.	____, resemblance.
shabihi(V) ia/ika/isha/iwa/iana	shabbah(a)	شَبَّه	____	be like, to liken, to resemble, look like.	____, imitate, to similar.
shabiki(N)(mshabiki)	shabiq.	شَبِق	ولع بـ/ مُحِبٌّ لـ	one who likes something very much.	lustful, lecherous, libidinous.
shada(N) (ling.)	shadda(t)	شَدَّة	____, نَبِرَة	accent, stress, emphasis	doubled letter.
(a) **shahada**(N) (digrii)(stashahada)	shaha:da (t)	شَهَادَة	____ (دِبْلُوم)	certificate, testimonial, diploma.	____, evidence.
(b) **shahada**(N)(Rel.)	shaha:da (t)	شَهَادَة	____ (مِنْ أَرْكَانِ الإسْلَام)	the first step to be comverted to Islam.	____
(c) **shahada**(N) (kidole cha shahada)	shahada(t)	شَهَادَة	السَّبَابَة	the forefinger.	*
shahamu(N) (mafuta ya mnyama)	shaḥ m	شَحْم	____	fat, greese, lard.	____, lubricant, suit.

Swahili word	Transcription of Arabic word	Arabic word	Arabic word in Swahili sense	Swahili usage	Arabic usage.
shahawa(N) (manii)	shahwa(t)	شَهْوَة	مَنِيّ	semen.	lust, greed, desire, eagerness, appetit.
(a) **shahidi**(N) (ma-)	sha:hid	شَاهِد	____	witness, martyr,** an authority, one who gives evidence or proof, who attests or guarantees.	____
(b) **shahidi**(N) (ma-)	shahi:d	شَهِيد	____	martyr.	____
shairi(N) (ma-) (utenzi) (beti)	shiạr	شِعْر	____	poetry, verse, a song, a poem.	____, versification.
shaitani(N) (ma-)	shaiṭa:n	شَيْطَان	____	satan, devil, an evil, spirit, demon.	____
shajiisha(V)	shajjaạ(a)	شَجَّع	____	encourage, hearten, embolden.	____, pluckup courage.
shaka(N) (wasiwasi) (tuhuma)	shakk	شَكّ	____, وَسْوَاس	doubt, uncertainly, suspicion, scruple.	____
(a) **shamiri**(V)(enea) (zagaa) (tapakaa) **ia/ika/isha/iwa.**	shammar(a)	شَمَّر	____	togather up, put together spread.	___, to tuck, to buckle.
(b) **shamiri**(V) (tia risasi au shindilia baruti) **ia/ika/isha/iwa.**	shammar(a)	شَمَّرَ	صَوَّبَ للضَّرْبِ	loud, a gun, to prepare gun ready for shooting.	to bare the upper arm,make ready for to recede, to retract.
shamirisho(N) (kielezi)(ling.)	shammar(a)	(مِنْ شَمَّرَ)	حَالٌ / ظَرْفٌ	adverb.	*
shani(N) (ajabu) (kioja) (mwujiza)	shaạn	شَأْن	____	accident, wonder, novelty curiosity.	matter, importance, affair, concern, case.
sharabati(N)	sharba:t	مُشْرُوبَات (شربات)	____	sherbet. [Ar.]*.	____

Swahili word	Transcription of Arabic word	Arabic word	Arabic word in Swahili sense	Swahili usage	Arabic usage.
shari(N) (ugomvi)	sharr	شَرٌّ	____	evil, mischief, harm, malice, ill luck, calamity, disaster, injustice.	____, sin, wickedness, damage, injury, vice.
(a) **Sharia**(N) (sheria) (Rel.)	shari:ạ a(t)	شَرِيعَة	الشَّرِيعَة الاسْلامِيَة	sharia, law of Islam	____
(b) **sharia** (N) (usu. sheria)	shari:ạ a(t)	"	قَانُون	see sheria	____
(a) **sharifu**(N) (ma-)	shari:f	شَرِيف	____	esteamed person	____
(b) **sharifu**(N) (ma-) (Rel.)	"	"	مِنْ آلِ البَيْتِ	sherif, a title of the descendants of the Prophet Muhammad (S.A.W.)	____
sharabu(V) (tec.) **ika/isha/iwa/iana.**	sharib(a)	شَرِبَ/ تَشَرَّبَ	أمْتَصَّ / تَشَرَّبَ	absorb, soak up, imbibe	____, to drink, to sip, toast.
sharti(N) (ma-) (lazima) (kanuni)	sharṭ	شَرْط	____	incision, condition, an obligation, stipulation, necessity, by-law, wager.	___, provision, clause.
sharubati(N) (sharabati)	sharba:t	شربات/ مشروبات	____	see sharabati.	____
sharubu (N) (ma-)	sha:rib	شَارِب	____	mustache.	____
sharuti(N) (azima)	sharṭ	شَرْط	____	see sharti.	____
sharutisha(V) (shurutisha) **ia/ika/iwa/iana.**	sharaṭ(a)	شَرَط	____, أَلْزَمَ اشْتَرَطَ	press with arguement, force, compel, wager, stipulate.	____
shashi(N)	sha:sh	شَاش	____	muslin, white cloth, <u>tissue paper</u>**	____
shaufu(adv.) (-enye majisifu)	shaufa(t)	شَوْفَة	المُعْجب بنفسهِ	a shameless person, one without manners, one disposed to show off.	sight, view, spectacle.

Swahili word	Transcription of Arabic word	Arabic word	Arabic word in Swahili sense	Swahili usage	Arabic usage.
shauri(V) **ia/ika/ isha/iwa/iana**	istasha:r (a)	اسْتَشَار	___	advise, to consult, suggest, cause to get advice. consult together.	___
shauri(N) (ma-) (maoni) (rai) (nasaha) (jambo)	istisha:ra (t)	اسْتِشَارة	تَشَاوُر , ___	consultation, guidance, advice, discussion, intention, design, plan.	___, counsel, deliberation.
shawishi(V) **ia/ika/ iwa/iana**	shaw̱ash(a)	شَوَّش	___	confuse, disturb, muddle, persuade, entice, temp.	___, confound, complicate, jumble.
shayiri(N) (bot.)	shaị:r	شَعِير	___	barley.	___
shebaha(N) (shabaha)	tasha:buh	تَشَابُه	___	see shabaha (a) and (b).	___
sheha(N) (ma-)	shaikh	شَيْخ	شَيْخُ القَبِيلَة	a chief of a (village or tribe).	___
shehe(N) (ma-) (mkubwa) (mzee) (mwalimu) (mfalme) (sheikh)	shaikh	شَيْخ	___ مُسِنّ	old man, elder, sheik, chief, title of respect, reverence, councillor, teacher, an important person.	___, ruler.
shehena(N)	shaḥn	شَحْن	___	freight, cargo, charge, load.	___
sheheni(V) **ia/ika/ iwa.**	shaḥan(a)	شَحَنَ	___	to load, fill up with cargo.	
sheikh(N) (shehe)	shaikh	شَيْخ	___	see shehe.	___
sheitani(N)(shetani)	shaiṭa:n	شَيْطَان	___	see shaitani.	___
(a) **sherehe**(N) (tamasha)	inshira:ḥ	انْشِرَاح	___	demonstration, triumph, cheer, rejoicing, pomp, gait.	relaxation, joy, glee, delight, gaiety.
(b)sherehe(N)(ufafanuzi wa kitabu)	sharḥ	شَرْح	___	explanation, expounding, elucidation, commentation.	___ exposition.

Swahili word	Transcription of Arabic word	Arabic word	Arabic word in Swahili sense	Swahili usage	Arabic usage.
(c) **sherehe**(N) (faharasạ) (ufafanuzi)	sharḥ	شَرْحٌ	____, فِهْرِس	index, a list of words which is explained in the last of a book, appendix.	see **sherehe**(b).
sherehi(V) (fafanua) ia/ika/iwa.	sharaḥ(a)	شَرَحَ	____	to explain, expand, comment, interprete.	____, inquire, explicate.
sheria(N)	shari:ạ(a)	شَرِيعَة	قانُون / دُسْتُور	law, a written or statute law, basic rule, constitution, canon[Gr.], *legal.	Islamic law, law, statute, lawful.
sherifu(N) (sharifu)	shari:f	شَرِيف	____	see sharifu(a)(b).	____
shetani(N) (ibilisi) (habithi)	shaiṭa:n	شَيْطَان	____	see shaitani.	____
shiba(V) **ia/ika/isha /wa/ana**	shabiạ(a)	شَبِعَ (ف)	____	satisfy, feed, eat ones, fill, to be full,	____, to be loaded or charged.
shibe(N)	shabạ	شَبَعٌ	____	fullness, satisfaction, satiety, completion, repletion.	____
shibiri(N) (rare)	shibr	شِبْرٌ	____	span.	____
(a) **shida**(N) (taabu) (msiba) (dhiki) (matata)	shidda(t)	شِدَّة	____ بَلِيَّة ضِيق	difficulty, problem, distress, hardship, calamity, adversity.	____, violence, force, power, hardness.
(b) **shida**(N) (haba) (chache) (adimu)	"	"	قِلَّة	hardly to get, rareness, seldom, scarceness, want.	scarceness, rareness.
shibli(N) (poet.)	shibl	شِبْل	____	lion cub, proper name.	____
(a) **shifaa**(N) (shufaa)	shifa:ā (t)	شِفَاء	____	cure, healing, gratification, recovery, restoration.	____, satisfaction.
(b) **shifaa**(N) (shufaa)	shafa:ạ a (t)	شَفَاعَة	____	mediation, intercession.	____, advocacy.

Swahili word	Transcription of Arabic word	Arabic word	Arabic word in Swahili sense	Swahili usage	Arabic usage.
shirika(N) (ma-)	sharika(t)	شَرِكَة	___, مُؤَسَّسَة	partnership, company, communion, corporation.	___, companionship
(a) **shiriki**(V) **ia/ika/isha/iwa/iana**	sha:rak(a)	شَارَكَ	___, اشْتَرَكَ	to be a partner to, associate with, share, act together, participate.	___, sympathize, to cooperate.
(b) **shiriki**(V)(Rel.) **isha.**	àshrak(a)	أَشْرَكَ (بِاللّٰهِ)	___	to be a polytheist, an idolator, to set up or attribute associates to God.	___
shirikisho(N)	ishtira:k	اشْتِرَاك	مُشَارَكَة ___ اِتِّحَاد / تَعَاوُنٌ	copartnership, participation, jointness, co-operation.	___, collaboration.
shitadi(V) (zidi)	ishtadd(a)	اشْتَدَّ	___	to become strong, vigorous, increase.	___
shitaka(N) (ma-) (shtaka)	shakwa:	شَكْوَى	___	accusation, complaint, grievance.	___, suffering.
shitaki(V) (shtaki) **ia/ika/isha/iwa/iana**	ishtaka:	اشْتَكَى	___	to complain, accuse, prosecute,charge.	___
(a) **shoga**(N) (dada) (somo)	shawq	شَوْقٌ	مُحْبُوبَة	a term of endearment or familiarity between women	longing, wish, desire, craving, yearning.
(b)**shoga**(N) (hanithi) (msenge) (rambuza)	shawq	"	المَأْبُون / غُلَام شَاذٌّ جِنْسِيًّا	catamite.	see shoga(a).
shokishoki(N) (ma-)	shawk shawk	شَوْكٌ شَوْكٌ	نَوْعٌ مِنْ الفَوَاكِه	the fruit of Rambutan-tree.	thorn, spine, spike, sting, prickle.
shokshok(N) (ma-)	"	"	"	see shokishoki.	___
shtaka(N) (ma-)	shakwa:	شَكْوَى	___	see shitaka.	___

Swahili word	Transcription of Arabic word	Arabic word	Arabic word in Swahili sense	Swahili usage	Arabic usage.
shtaki(V) **ia/ika/ iwa/iana**	ishtaka:	اشتكى	____	see shitaki.	____
shubaka(N) (ma-) (daka) (dirisha) (mwangaza)	shubba:k	شُبَّاك	____, نافذة صغيرة	a small window, a blind window, light-hole, port-hole, embrasure, loop-hole.	window, wicket.
(a) **shubiri**(N) (shi-biri)	shibr	شِبْر	____	see shibr.	____
(b) **shubiri**(N) (su-bili)	ṣabir(ṣa-bar)	صَبِرٌ/ الصَبِر	____	a biter, medicine used for stomack.	____, aloes.
shudu(N) (ma-)	shadd	شَدٌّ	الكَسْب: الثُفْل بَعْدَ عَصْرِ الزَيْتِ	oil-cake.	to compress.
shufa(N)	shafạ	شَفْعٌ	____, عَدَدٌ زوجِى	even number, double, ali-quot.	____
shufaa(N) (nafuu) (ahueni) (hujambo)	shifa:ā(t)	شِفَاء	____	see shifaa.	____
shufaka(N) (poet.) (huruma)	shafaqa(t)	شَفَقَة	____, رَحْمَة	pity, tenderness, compa-ssion,kindness.	____, affectiona-teness.
shufu(V) (poet.) (tazama) (angalia)	sha:f(a)	شَاف	____ رَأَى	look at, see, lookforward perceive.	____
shufwa(N)	shafạ	شَفْع	____, عَدَدٌ زَوْجِى	see shufa.	____
shughuli(N) (kazi)	shughl	شُغْل	____	occupation, activity, bu-siness, engagement, anx-iety, concern, worry, trouble.	____, detention, prevention, work, job.
shughulika(V) **isha**.	ishtaghal (a)	اشْتَغَلَ	____	busy, give trouble, enga-ge, occupy, disturb, to be worried.	____, take up, fill, distract.
shuhuda(N) (ma-) (shahidi)	shuhu:d	شُهُود	شَاهِدٌ	see shahidi.	____

Swahili word	Transcription of Arabic word	Arabic word	Arabic word in Swahili sense	Swahili usage	Arabic usage.
shuhudia(V) (kuwa shahidi) lia/lika/lisha/wa/ana.	shahid(a)	شَهِد	____	give evidence, confirm, allest, proof, be witness to swear by God.	____
shujaa(N) (ma-)	shuja:ạ	شُجَاع	____	brave, hero, courageous, bold.	____, audacious.
shukran(N)(shukrani)	shukran	شُكْراً / شُكْرَان	____ شَكْرَان	thanks, gratitude.	____
shukrani(N)	"	"	____	see shukran.	____
shuku(V) (kuwa na wasiwasi) (dhani) (tuhumu) ia/ika/isha/iwa.	shakk(a)	شَكَّ	____	suspect, be doubtful.	____
shukurani(N)	shukran	شُكْرَان / شُكْرًا	____	see shukran.	____
shukuru(V) (toa shukurani) ia/ika/isha/iwa/iana	shakar(a)	شَكَرَ	____	to thank, be grateful, thankful, become contented.	____, to praise, laud.
shumari(N)	shama:r	شَمَار	____	fennel(bot.).	____
shuruti(adv.) (sharti) (lazima)	shart̤ shuru:t̤ (Pl.)	شَرْط شُرُوط (جَمْع)	____	see sharti.	____
shurutisha(V) (lazimisha) ia/ika/iwa/iana.	ishtarat̤ (a)	اشْتَرَط	____, أَلْزَمَ	compel, stipulate, make, conditional, oblige.	____, scarify.
shutumu(V) (laumu) ia/ika/isha/iwa/iana	shatam(a)	شَتَمَ	____	to abuse, curse, vilify, reproach, revile, upbraid, blame, scold.	____, heap.
shutumu(N) (ma-) (lawama) (singizio)	shatm	شَتْم	____	abuse, insult, railing, vilification.	____, vituperation.

Swahili word	Transcription of Arabic word	Arabic word	Arabic word in Swahili sense	Swahili usage	Arabic usage.
siaha(N)	ṣi aḥ	صِيَاح	___	a loud cry, crying with much noise.	___
siahi(N) (ukelele mkali) (yowe)	ṣi aḥ	"	___	see siaha.	___
siasa(N) (taratibu) (polepole)	siasa(t)	سِيَاسَة	___	politics, carefulness, orderliness, policy, diplomacy, gentleness.	___, administration, management.
sibabi(V) (tukana) **ia/ika/isha/iwa.**	sabb(a)	سَبَّ	___	slander, revile, calumniate, defame, insult, abuse, curse.	___, rail.
(a) **sibu**(V) (sibabi)	"	"	___	see sibabi(V).	___
(b) **sibu**(V)	àṣa:b(a)	أَصَاب	تَكَهَّنَ / تَنَبَّأَ	foretell event(bad or good).	to score, make goals.
(c) **sibu**(V)	āṣa:b(a)	"	___	afflict, happen, to be hardhit.	___, to suffer a loss.
sidiria(N) (kanchiri) (rare)	ṣudra(t)	صُدْرَة / صُدَيْرِيَة	___	a cloth worn by some women just below the breast to support them.	waist coat, vest.
sifa(N)	ṣifa(t)	صِفَة	___	characteristic, fame,** reputation,** praise, applause,** flattery,** an adjective(gram).	___, property, attribute, description.
sifu(V) **ia/ika/isha/iwa**	waṣaf(a)	وَصَفَ	___	praise, flatter,**commend, recommend, to praise.	___, to describe, credit, characterize.
(ji) sifu(V)	waṣaf(a)	وَصَفَ (نَفْسَه)	___, تَفَاخَر مَدَحَ نَفْسَه	to brag, to praise, boast (oneself).	*
(a)**sifuri**(N)	ṣifr	صِفْر	___,	zero, [Ar.]* cipher, nought	___, empty, void.
(b)**sifuri**(N)	ṣufr	صُفْر	___ نُحَاس أَصْفَر	brass.	___, bronze.

Swahili word	Transcription of Arabic word	Arabic word	Arabic word in Swahili sense	Swahili usage	Arabic usage.
sigha(N) (ZNZ)	ṣiġha(t)	صِيغَة	___	word form(wording).	___, shape, form.
siha(N) (nguvu) (afya/uzima)	ṣiḥḥa(t)	صِحَّة	___	health, strength.	___, rightness, verity, correctness, soundness.
sihi(V) **ia/ika/isha/wa/iana**	ṣaḥḥ(a)	صَحّ	___ جَازَ	be acceptable, be suitable, correct, to be true.	___, to be sound, to health, rectify.
sihiri(N) (uchawi)	siḥr	سِحْر	___	witch craft, magic.	___
sihiri(V) (roga) (fanya uchawi) **ia/ika/isha/iwa/iana**	saḥar(a)	سَحَر (ف)	___	be witch, fascinate.	___
sijida(N)	sajda(t)	سَجْدَة	___	prostration in [Islamic prayer].	___
silaha(N)	sila:ḥ	سِلَاح	___	arms, weapon, armor.	___
silika(N) (tabia) (sifa) (mwenda)	sulu:k	سُلُوك	___	instinct, character, mien disposition, manners, behaviour.	___, attitude, conduct.
silimisha(V) (Rel.)	ȧslam(a)	أَسْلَم	___	see silimu.	___
silimu(V) (Rel.) (kuwa Mwislamu) **ia/ika/iwa/isha**.	ȧslam(a)	أَسْلَم	___	be converted to Islam.	___, to yield, submit, surrender.
silisili(N) (mnyororo) (pingu) (rare)	silsila(t)	سِلْسِلَة	___	iron chain, bonds.	___, backbone, line of ancestor.
simadi(N) (samadi)	sama:d	سَمَاد	___	see samadi.	___
simsim(N) (ufuta) (rare)(Ref.Radio/Tz)	simsim	سِمْسِم	___, جُلْجُلَان	sesame.[Ar.]*(usu. heard ufuta).	___

Swahili word	Transcription of Arabic word	Arabic word	Arabic word in Swahili sense	Swahili usage	Arabic usage.
simulia(V) (hubiri) (hubiri) (hadithi) (ambia habari) **ka/sha/za/wa/ana.**	samur(a)	سَمُرَ (ف)	___	tell a story, narrate, relate, give an account, report.	___, chart, talk, converse.
sinia(N) (sahani) (chano)	ṣi:ni:ya (t)	صِينِيَة	___	tray, salver[Sp.]*	___
siraji(N) (poet.) (taa)	sira:j	سِرَاج	___	lamp, torch, night light.	___
sirati(N) (Rel.)	ṣira:ṭ	صِرَاط	___	the way to heaven or hell, a way, road.	___, path.
siri(N) (faragha) (ficha)	sirr	سِرٌّ	___	a secret, secrecy, mystery, privacy, puzzle, confidential.	___
sirika(N) (silika)	sulu:k	سُلُوك	___	see silika.	___
sita(N) (tandatu).	sitta(t)	سِتَّة	___ سِتٌّ	six, sixth(6).	___
(a) **sitaha**(N) (also staha)	saṭḥ	سَطْح	ظَهْرُ المُرْكَبِ	deck.	roof, platform.
(b) **sitaha** (N) (also staha)	istiḥya:ā	اسْتِحْيَاء	___	see staha(b).	___
sitahi(V) (stahi) **ia/ika/isha/iwa/iana**	istaḥa:	اسْتَحَى	___	see stahi.	___
sitara(N) (kificho) (stara)	istiạ:ra (t)	اسْتِعَارَة	___	see stara.	___
sitashara(N) (PMB)	sitta-t-ạshra(t)	سِتَّةَ عَشْرَ	___ سِتَّ عَشْرَة	sixteen, sixteenth.	___
sitawi(V) (stawi) **ia/ika/isha/**	istawa:	اسْتَوَى	___	see stawa.	___

Swahili word	Transcription of Arabic word	Arabic word	Arabic word in Swahili sense	Swahili usage	Arabic usage.
siti(N) (mwana) (bibi) [Persian]*	sitt	السِّتّ	___	lady, madam.	___
sitiari(N)(also sitiara)	istiạ:ra (t)	اسْتِعَارَة	___	metaphor.	___
sitini(N)	sitti:n	سِتِّين	___ سِتُّون	sixty, sixties.	___
sitiri(V) (ficha aibu) **ia/ika/isha/iwa/iana.** (also stiri)	satar(a)	سَتَرَ	___, أَخْفَى	hide, conceal, cover up, disguise, a tone for.	___, protect, veil, shield, shelter.
sogea(V) **lea/leka**	sa:g(a)	سَاقَ	يَقْتَرِب / يَدْنُو يَدْفَع إِلَى الأَمَام	move nearer, draw near.	to draw out, to be driven, drive, urge on, to harmonize, to drift.
soko(N) (ma-) (chete)	su:q	سُوق	___	market, mart, market-place, emporium.	___
(a) **somo**(N) (ma-) (rafiki)	sami:y	سَمِيّ	___	namesake, <u>friend.</u>**	___
(b) **somo**(N) (ma-)	*	*	*	subject(e.g. mathematic, geography, history, etc.).	*
somu(N) (saumu)	ṣawm	صَوْم	___, صِيَام	see saumu.	___
staafu(V) **ia/ika/isha/iwa.**	istuạfia	اسْتَعْفَى	___, تَقَاعَدَ	to retire.	to resign.
staajabu(V) (ona ajabu((shangaa) **ia/ika/isha/iwa.**	istaạjab (a)	اسْتَعْجَبَ	___	suprise, astonished, marvel, be amezed.	___
staarabika(V)	staạrab(a)	اسْتَعْرَبَ	تَحَضَّرَ	be civilized, be wise, get understanding.	to adopt the custom of the Arabs.

Swahili word	Transcription of Arabic word	Arabic word	Arabic word in Swahili sense	Swahili usage	Arabic usage.
staarabisha(V)	"	اسْتَعْرَبَ	___	see staarabu.	___
staftahi(V) **ia/ika/ isha/iwa** (rare)	istaftaḥ (a)	اسْتَفْتَحَ	تَنَاوَلَ طَعَامَ الأفْطار	eat the breakfast.	start, begin, incept, commence.
(a) **staha**(N)	saṭḥ	سَطْح	ظَهْرُ المَرْكَبِ	deck.	roof, platform.
(b) **staha**(N)	istiḥya:a	اسْتِحْيَاء	___	shame, bashfulness, respect, shyness, honour, reverence.	___, diffidence, timidity.
stahamala(N) (ustahamilivu)	[taḥammul/ istiḥma:l]	تَحَمُّل احتمال/اسْتِحْمَال	___	bearing, endurance, sufferance, durability, strength, patience.	___, solidity, sturdiness.
stahamali(V) (vumilia) (stahimili)	istaḥma:l (a)/taḥammal(a)	اسْتَحْمَل تَحَمَّل	___	endure, support, tolerate, put up with, suffer, be patient, persevere.	___, sustain, resist.
stahimilivu(adj.) (stahimilivu)	mustaḥmil.	مُسْتَحْمِل	حَمُول	long-suffering, persevering, patient.	___, gentle.
stahi(V) (heshimu) **ia/ika/isha/iwa**	istaḥa: istaḥya:	اسْتَحَى	___ خَجِلَ	to blush, be ashamed, bashful, shy, give honour to, to respect.	___, diffident.
stahifu(adj.) (-a heshima)(-a adabu)	mustaḥi(n)	مُسْتَحِي مستحيٍ مُسْتَحٍ	جَدِيرٌ بالاحْتِرَامِ والإجْلَالِ.	estimable, honourable, deserving, of respect.	___,
stahiki(V) **ia/ika/ isha/iwa.**	istaḥaqqh (a)	اسْتَحَقَّ	___	be (worthy, fitting, proper, suitable deserving, a duty.).	___, to demand, to right.
stahili(V)	istaḥall (a)	اسْتَحَلَّ	___	to deem lawful, be due, merit, declare, deserving, make worthy, be qualified for.	___

Swahili word	Transcription of Arabic word	Arabic word	Arabic word in Swahili sense	Swahili usage	Arabic usage.
stahimili(V) (stahamili) ia/ika/isha/iwa.	istaḥmal (a)	اسْتَحْمَل	____	see stahamili(V).	____
stahimilivu(adj.) (stahamilivu)	mustaḥmil	مُسْتَحْمِل / مُتَحَمِّل	حَمُول , ____	see stahamilivu.	____
stakabadhi(N) (risiti)	istiqba:ḍ	اسْتِقْبَاض	إِيصَال	receipt, acknowledgement, quittance, pledge, earnest, money.	receiving, receipt cashing.
stakabadhi(V) (kabidhi) ia/ika/isha/iwa	istaqbaḍ (a)	اسْتَقْبَضَ	____	to receive, to cash, (see kabidhi)	____
stanji(V) (Rel.)	istanja:	اسْتَنْجَى	____	to cleanse oneself after defecation.	____
starehe(V) (kuwa na raha) ea/eka/esha/ewa.	istara:ḥ (a)	اسْتَرَاحَ	____	to rest, relax, live in peace, to find rest, refresh, be saved, relieve, be confortable.	___, to be calm, be pleased.
starehe(N)	raḥa(t)	رَاحَة اسْتِرَاحة	____	rest, repose, comfort, recreation, peace, bliss.	____, vacation, leisure.
stashahada(N) (shahada)	shahada(t)	شَهَادَة	____	see shahada.	____
stawi(V) ia/ika/isha	istawa: sawa:	اسْتَوَى سَوَّى	____	to equalize, make good, arrange, to regulate, put in order, to be equivalent.	____, become ripe, dispute settle.
stiara(N) (also stiari)	istiạ:ra (t)	اسْتِعَارَة	____	metaphor.	____, borrowing.
stiari(N) (also sitiari)	"	"	____	see sitiari.	____

Swahili word	Transcription of Arabic word	Arabic word	Arabic word in Swahili sense	Swahili usage	Arabic usage.
stihizai(V) (kejeli) (hizaya) (fanyia mzaha wa dharau) **ia/ika/isha/iwa.** (rare)	istahzaȧ (a)	اسْتَهْزَأْ	____	disgrace, dishonour, put to shame, insult, ridicule, mock, deride.	____, make fun, jeer, sneer, scoff.
stihizai(N) (kejeli) (rare)	istihza:ā	اسْتِهْزَاء	____	derision, contempt, mockey, scorn, ridicule.	____, disdain.
stiri(V) (sitiri) **ia/ika/isha/iwa.**	satar(a)	سَتَرَ	____	see sitiri(V).	____
suali(N) (swala)	suā:l	سُؤَال	____	question, inquiry, request, <u>problem</u>.**	____, claim, demand.
subalkheri(conj.) (also sabalkheri)	ṣaba:ḥ-al-khair.	صَبَاحُ الخَيْرِ	____	see saballkheri.	____
subili(N) (shubiri)	ṣabir	الصَّبِر/ الألوة	____ دَوَاءٌ مُرّ	(see shubiri(b).	____
subira(N)	ṣabr	صَبْرٌ	____	patience, forbearance, firmness.	___, equanimity, composure.
subiri(V) (stahamili) **ia/ika/isha/iwa**	ṣabar(a)	صَبَرَ	____	be patient, persevere, confort, wait patiently. <u>wait</u>.**	_____, fetter.
(a) **subu**(V) (tukana) **ia/ika/isha/iwa.** (rare)	sabb(a)	سَبَّ	_____	see sibu(V).	____
(b) **subu**(V) **ia/ika/ iwa.** (rare)	ṣabb(a)	صَبَّ	____	cast, to found (mental).	____,
subutu(V) (thubutu) **isha**	thabat(a)	ثَبَتَ	___, تجرأ	have courage to, dare, venture.	to stand firm, to prove, to be brave.
subutu(conj.) (thubutu)	thaba:t	ثَبَات	____	courage, daring.	firmness, stability.

Swahili word	Transcription of Arabic word	Arabic word	Arabic word in Swahili sense	Swahili usage	Arabic usage.
sudusi(N) ($^1/_6$)	sudus (or) suds	سُدُس سُدْس	___, كَسْر/ جُزْء	one-sixth, a sixth part, the fraction.	___
(a) **sufi**(N)	ṣu:f	صُوف	كتلة ألياف حريرية تكتنف بزور شجرة السيبة تستعمل لملء الحشايا	the fine soft silky cotton from the pods of Kapok tree(msufi).	wool.
(b) **sufi**(N) (also sufu)	ṣu:f	صُوف	___	wool.	___
sufii(N) (mtawa) (walii) (mcha Mungu)	ṣu:fiy	صُوفِيّ	___ مُتَصَوِّف	sufi, Islamic mystic, hermit, holy person, dervish [Persian]*.	___
sufu(N) (usufu) (rare)	ṣu:f	صُوف	___	see sufi.	___
sufufu(adj.) (-ingi) (rare)	ṣufu:f	صُفُوف	كثيرًا	many, much, plenty.	aligning, or arranging in a line or row, lines, rows.
sufuri(N) (sifuri)	ṣifr	صِفْر	___	see sifuri (a) (b).	___
sufuria(N) (ma-)	ṣufr	صُفْر	قِدْرِ الطَّبْخ (حَلَّة)	metal cooking-pot.(usu. large).	copper, brass.
sujudu(V) (Rel.) **ia/ika/isha/iwa.**	sajad(a)	سَجَدَ	___	to bow in worship, prostrate, to worship. (God)	___, adore.
sukari(N)[orig.Skr]* [Persian]*	sukkar	سُكَّر	___	sugar.	___
Sultani(N) (ma-) (rare)	sulṭa:n	سُلْطَان	___	Sultan[Ar.]*, king,ruler, chief.	___
sulubu(V) **ia/ika/ isha/iwa.**	ṣalab(a)	صلب	___	to crucify, hang on a cross.	___

Swahili word	Transcription of Arabic word	Arabic word	Arabic word in Swahili sense	Swahili usage	Arabic usage.
sulubu(N) (usulubu) (rare) (nguvu) (bi-dii) (ushupavu)	ṣala:ba(t)	صَلَابَة	___	firmness, vigour, strength, hard, hardness.	___
suluhia(V) **ika/isha/iwa/iana**	àṣlaḥ(a)	أَصْلَح	___	cause to agree, to foster peace, to mend, reconcile, make peace (between), conciliate.	___, compromise, to make amends, compensate.
suluhisha(V) (patanisha)	"	"	___	see suluhia(V).	___
(a) **suluhisho**(N) (ma-)	isla:h	إِصْلَاح	___	restoration, mending, repair, overhauling.	___, correction, reconditioning.
(b) **suluhisho**(N) (ma-)	muṣa:laḥ a (t)	مُصَالَحَة	___	peace, compromise, consiliation, settlement.	___, composition.
suluhu(V)	ṣaluḥ(a)	صَلُحَ	___	to put in order, righteous, improve, to be useful usable, reconcile.	___, settle, restore, restitute, rebuild.
sumu(N)	summ/simm samm/	سُمّ / سِمّ سَمّ	___	poison.	___, toxin, venom
sumu(V) (lisha sumu) (tilia sumu) (rare)	sammam(a)	سَمَّمَ	___	to put poison, to poison.	___
sumulia(V) (simulia)	samur	سَمَرَ	___	see simulia.	___
sunna(Rel.) (kitendo cha hiari cha thawabu)	sunna(t)	سُنَّة	___	sunna of the Prophet Muhammad. eg.(his saying and doings).	___
sunobari(N)	ṣanwbar	صَنَوْبَر	___	deal, pine-wood.	___
sundusi(N) (rare)	sundus	سُنْدُس	___ حَرِير رَقِيق	sarcenet.	___

Swahili word	Transcription of Arabic word	Arabic word	Arabic word in Swahili sense	Swahili usage	Arabic usage.
sunni(N) (Rel.)	sunny	السُّنِّي	أَهْلُ السُّنَّة واحد من أهل السنة	sunnites, orthodox Muslims.	____
sunu(V) (rel.) **ia/isha/iwa.**	sunn(a)	سَنَّ	____	to prescribe a rule (see sunna).	____
(a) **sura**(N) (umbile) (uso) (jinsi) (mandhari) (tabia) (mfano)	ṣu:ra(t)	صُورَة	شَكْلٌ / مَظْهَرٌ	form, face, appearance, likeness, <u>expression</u>,** shape, look, prospect.	___, picture, image.
(b) **sura**(N) (mlango) (faslu)	ṣu:ra(t)	صُورَة	فَصْل	chapter of a book.	*
(c) **sura**(N) (sura ya Koran)	su:ra(t)	سُورَة	____	sura, chapter of Holy Koran.	____
suruale(N) (also suruali)	(surwa:l) sara:wi:l	(سُرْوَال) سَرَاوِيل (مُفْرَد)	سَرَاوِيل (مُفْرَد) أو بَنْطَلون)	see suruali.	____
suruali(N)[Persian]*	"	"	____	trousers.	____, pants, drawers, panties.
sus(N) (rare)	su:s	سُوس	____	liquarice, licorice.	____, woodworm, moth.
susa(N)	tasaw̱us	تَسَوُّس	____	tartar(of teeth) decay, worn-hole.	____,
(a) **swala**(N) (ma-) (suali) (uliza)	suā:l	سُؤَال	____	see suali.	____
(b) **swala**(N) (sala) (Rel.)	ṣala:(t)	صَلَاة	____	see sala.	____
(c) **swala** (N)	*	*	*	gazelle[Ar.]*.	*
swali(V) (sali) (Rel.) **ia/ika/isha/iwa**	ṣala;	صَلَّى	____	see sali(V).	____

Swahili word	Transcription of Arabic word	Arabic word	Arabic word in Swahili sense	Swahili usage	Arabic usage.
taabani(adv.) (hoi)	taạba:n	تعبان	متعب مرهق	tired, fatiqued (because of illness).	____
taabika(V) (sumbuka) (hangaika) (dhikika) isha.	taạib(a)	تعب	____ سئم	be fatiqued, become tired, tire, labour, toil, to give trouble, anxious.	___, weary, to work hard.
taabini(N)	taȧbi:n	تأبين	____	eulogy(of a dead person).	____
taabu(N)	taạb	تعب	____	trouble, inconvenience, difficulty, fatique, distress, toil, tiredness.	____, nuisance, burden, drudgery.
taadabu(V) (shika adabu)	taȧddab(a)	تأدب	____	be polite, civil, be with good manners.	____
taadhima(N) (heshima) (utukufu) (unyenyekevu)	taạḍhi:m	تعظيم	____ احترام	honour, glorification, exaltation, respect, aggrandizement.	___, military salute.
taadhimu(V) (tukuza) **ia/ika/isha/iwa**	adham(a)	عظم	____	glorify, exalt, revere.	____
taahari(V) (kawia) **isha**	taȧkhar (a)	تأخر	____	see ahiri.	____
taahiri(N) (ukawiaji) (ulimatiaji)	taȧkhi:r	تأخير	____	postponement, delay.	____, retardation.
taajabu(V) (staajabu) **ia/ika/isha/iwa.**	taạjjab(a)	تعجب	____	see staajabu.	____
taala(adj.) (Rel.)	taạ:la:	تعالى	____ الله تعالى	God is exalted, is most-high.	____
taalim(N) (taalimu)	taạli:m	تعليم	____	see elimu.	____
taalimu(N) (elimu)	"	"	____	see elimu.	____

Swahili word	Transcription of Arabic word	Arabic word	Arabic word in Swahili sense	Swahili usage	Arabic usage.
taaluma(N)	taạli:m	تَعْلِيم (عَالٍ)	أكادِيمِي	academic studies, teaching, education, schooling, training, higher education.	____, information announcement.
taamali(V) (fikiri)	taȧmmal(a)	تَأَمَّل	تَفَكَّر	to look attentively, contemplate, meditate, consider, think over.	____, to hope, expect, regard, ponder, reflect.
taamuli(N)(fikiri)	taȧmmul	تَأَمُّل	تَفَكُّر	consideration, meditation thought, contemplation, thoughtfulness.	____
taarabu(N) (also tarabu)	ṭarab	طَرَب	____	entertainment with music, joy, music, amusement.	____, pleasure, delight, rapture.
taaradhi(V) (dadisi) (uliza uliza hodari) **ia/ika/isha/iwa/iana**	taạraḍ(a)	تَعَرَّض	____	meddle, interfere in a person's affairs, cross-question.	resist, work against, oppose, contradict, protest.
taaradhia(V) (rare)	"	"	____	see taaradhia(V).	____
taarifa(V) (habari)	taạri:fa (t)	تَعْرِيفَة	____	information, a report.	information, notification, tarriff [Ar.],*(Price list).
taarifu(V) (arifu)	taạrraf(a)	تَعَرَّف	____	see arifu.	explorate, realize.
taashira(N) (also ishara)	taȧshi:ra(t)	تَأْشِيرَة	أشَارَة	see ishara.	visa, transit visa.
taasisi(N)	taȧsis	تَأْسِيس	مَعْهَد	institute.	institution, establishment, foundation.
taathira(N) (kasoro) (dosari) **(doa)**	taȧthi:r	تَأْثِير	____	influence, effect, impression(see athari).	____
taazia(N) (also tazia) **(tanzia)**	taạzia(t)	تَعْزِيَة	____	consolation, condolence, death-notice.	____, solace, comfort.

Swahili word	Transcription of Arabic word	Arabic word	Arabic word in Swahili sense	Swahili usage	Arabic usage.
tabaka(N) (tabaki)	ṭabaqa(t)	طَبَقَة	———	anything laid on another, stage, layer, stratum, class, category.	____, floor, story of building.
tabaruku(V) (also tabaruki) **ia/ika/ isha/iwa.**	tabarrak (a)	تَبَرَّك	———,	<u>join together in prayer or meeting for conversation</u>,** to obtain or seek the blessing of.	———
tabasamu(V) **ia/ika/ isha/iwa/iana**	tabassam (a)	تَبَسَّمَ	———, ابتَسَمَ	to smile.	———
tabasamu(N)	tabassum	تَبَسُّم	——, ابْتِسام	smile, smiling.	———
tabasuri(V) (kuwa na busara) (rare)	tabaṣṣar (a)	تَبَصَّرَ (ف)	تبصر	consider, contemplate.	———
tabawali(V) (kojoa) **ia/ika/isha/iwa**	tabaw̱al(a)	تَبَوَّلَ	———	urinate.	———
tabia(N) (sifa) (madhehebu) (hali) (desturi) (sura) (moyo) (umbo)	ṭabi:ạa(t)	طَبِيعَة	———	(1) nature, disposition, constitution, (2) habits, attainment, humour, character, (3) physical feature, weather, climate.	_____, regular, normal manner, individuality, peculiarity.
tabibu(N) (mganga) (daktari) (rare)	ṭabi:b	طَبِيب	———	doctor, physician, medical man.	———
tabiri(V)	ạbbar(a)	عَبَّرَ	——— تَنَبَّأَ	to interpret(a dream), explain, expound of a fortune-teller, foretell, predict.	____, to state clearly, express, declare, to acknowledge a quality.
tabu(N) (usumbufu) (shida) (dhiki) (mashaka)	taạb	تَعْب	———	see taabu.	———

Swahili word	Transcription of Arabic word	Arabic word	Arabic word in Swahili sense	Swahili usage	Arabic usage.
tadaraki(V) (also tadaruki) ia/ika/ isha/iwa/iana.	ădrak(a)	أَدْرَكَ	لَحِقَ ، ———	be in time, be able, reach, <u>succeed</u>,**guarantee,** undertake, <u>venture</u>,** <u>manage</u>,** attain, <u>arrange</u>.**	———, to pursue, to ripen, mature, know, realize, to perceive, obtain, to come to age, to catch up, arrive.
(a) **tafadhali**(adv.)	tafaḍḍal	تَفَضَّل	مِنْ فَضْلِكَ	please, if you please.	see tafadhali(V).
(b) **tafadhali**(V) (fanya hisani) /isha	tafaḍḍal	تَفَضَّل	———	please, be good to, do a kindness to.	———, to favour, oblige.
tafakari(V) (zingatia) (waza) ia/ika/ isha/iwa.	tafakkar (a)	تَفَكَّرَ	———	think, consider, meditate contemplate, ponder, reflect, cogitate.	———, speculate, muse, to remind, recall, think over.
tafakuri(N) (taamuli) (mazingatio)	tafakkur	تَفَكُّر	تَفْكِير ، ———	thinking, contemplation, reflection, consideration cogitation,	———, thought, speculation, meditation.
tafakuri(V) (tafakari) ia/ika/isha/iwa	tafakkar (a)	تَفَكَّر	———	see tafakari(a)(b).	———
tafaraji(V) (also tafaruji) (tafuta faraja)	tafarraj (a)	تَفَرَّج	———	to comfort, to be dispelled, <u>go to an entertainment</u>,** look at a pleasant sight, become gay.	———, observe, view, regard, relieve, relax, to open, part, separate.
tafauti(N) (also tofauti) (rare)	tafaut	تَفَاوُت	———	see tofauti.	———
taflisi(N) (adv.)	tafli:s	تَفْلِيس	إِفْلَاس ، ———	bankruptcy, insolvency.	----, failure.
tafrija(N) (sherehe)	tafarruj	تَفَرُّج	فَرَح	relaxation, enjoyment, amusement, rest, comfort, pleasant, entertainment.	relief, happy ending, relaxation.

Swahili word	Transcription of Arabic word	Arabic word	Arabic word in Swahili sense	Swahili usage	Arabic usage.
tafsiri(V) (fasiri) **ia/ika/isha/iwa/iana**	fassar(a)	فَسَّرَ	____	see fasiri(V).	____
tafsiri(N)	tafsi:r̜	تَفْسِير	____	explanation, translation.	___, interpretation, commentary, explication, exposition.
taghafali(V) (ghafilika) **ika/isha/iwa**	taghaffal (a)	تَغَفَّلَ	____ غَفُلَ	see ghafilika(V).	____
tahadhari(V) **ia/ika/isha/iwa.**	taḥadhar (a)	تَحَذَّرَ	____	be cautious, avoid, put on guard.	____, be careful.
tahadhari(N) (hadhari)	taḥdhi:r	تَحْذِير	____	warning, coutioning, prudence.	____, care.
tahafifu(N) (adj.0	takhfi:f	تَخْفِيف	____, خفيف	insignificant, trifling, valueless.	___, lightening, reduction, slight.
tahajia(N)	taḥjia	التَهْجِيَة	____ تَهَجٍّ حُرُوف الهِجَاء	alphabet, spelling, othography.	_____
tahakiki(N)	taḥqi:q	تَحْقِيق	____	realization, investigation, inquiry.	____, implementation, identification.
tahalili(N) (Rel.) (halili)	tahli:l	تَهْلِيل	____	praising God, funeral song, coranach, dirge, (usu. saying of La,ila:ha illa Allah) it means "there is no god but God"	____,
taharak(V) (babaika) (ingiwa na wasiwasi) **ia/ika/isha/iwa.**	taḥarrak (a)	تَحَرَّكَ	____, أَثَارَ	be in a hurry, be excited, be bustled.	set in motion, agitate, stimulate excite, stir.

Swahili word	Transcription of Arabic word	Arabic word	Arabic word in Swahili sense	Swahili usage	Arabic usage.
taharaki(V)(taharak) (taharuki) (stahara-ki) ia/ika/isha/iwa.	taḥarrak (a)	تَحَرَّكَ	———	see taharak(V).	———
taharuki(N) (wasi wasi) (mababaiko)	taḥarruk	تَحَرُّك	———, إِثَارَة	excitement, bustle, haste hurry.	start, motion, movement, departure.
taharuki(V) ia/ika/isha/iwa	taḥarrak (a)	تَحَرَّكَ (ف)	———	see taharak(V).	———
tahayari(V) ia/ika/isha/iwa.	taḥayyar (a)	تَحَيَّرَ	خَجِلَ	be(shy, ashamed, abashed, humilitated), ashame, abash, become embarrassed.	to become confused, be at a loss, hesitate, confuse.
tahayuri(N)(fedheha) (soni)	taḥayyur	تَحَيُّر	خَجَل	shame, confusion, disgrace, shyness.	confusion, embarrassment, dismay.
tahini(V) ia/ika/isha/iwa.	imtaḥan(a)	اِمْتَحَنَ	———	to examine, test, put to the test.	———
tahiri(V) (tia tohara) (kata kinembe) ia/ika/isha/iwa.	ṭahhar(a)	طَهَّرَ	خَتَنَ	to circumcise** (local Arabic), cleanse.	———, to clean, purify, sterilize, circumcise (loc. Ar.).
Tahiyatu(N) (Rel.)	taḥiyya:t	تَحِيَّات	———	to say special "requests" to God. It means "tahiyatu"	———, regards, compliments.
tahlili(N) (Rel.)	tahli:l	تَهْلِيل	———	see halili	———
taifa(N) (ma-)	ṭa:i̱fa (root)	طَائِفَة	———, أُمَّة / شَعْب / قَوْم	nation, race, tribe.	people, sect, party, denomination, confession.
taifisha(V) ia/ika/iwa	ta:i̱fa(t)	(مِنْ طَائِفَة)	أَمَّمَ (يُؤَمِّم)	nationalize, convert into national property.	*
tajamala(i)(N)(rare)	tajammul	تَجَمُّل	مَعْرُوف / مِنَّة فَضْل	a favour, kindness, agreement.	embelishment, decoration.

Swahili word	Transcription of Arabic word	Arabic word	Arabic word in Swahili sense	Swahili usage	Arabic usage.
tajamali(V) (rare)	tajammal	تَجَمَّل	يَمُنُّ على / يدعم	do a favour, help, show favour, assist.	to embelish.
taji(N)	ta:j	تَاج	____	crown, coronet, diadem.	____
tajiri(N) (mwenye mali nyingi) (mfanya biashara) (mtu anayeajiri mtu mwingine.) (kwasi)	ta:jir	تَاجِر	____ غَنِيّ	merchant, business man, trader, capitalist, man of wealth, <u>lessor</u>,**<u>landlord</u>.*	____
tajirika(V) (kuwa tajiri) **isha**.	ta:jar(a)	أتَّجَرَ/ تَاجَرَ	____, أَثْرَى	to become wealthy, be rich, enrich.	____
tajiwidi(N) (also tajuwidi)	tajwi:d	التَّجْوِيد	____	art of reciting the Koran reading, intonation.	____
tajuwidi(N)	"	"	____	see tajiwidi.	____
taka(V) (tamani) (penda) (hitaji) (elekea) **ia/ika/isha wa/ana**.	taq(a)	تَاقَ	____ يَشْتَهِي يُرِيدُ / يَرْغَبُ	want, desire, wish, need, require, ask, request, seem to want.	to long, wish, yearn, desire, crave, hanken.
taka(N)	*	*	*	dirt, rubbish, filth, sweepings.	*
takabadhi(V) (kabidhi) **iwa**	qabaḍ(a)	قَبَض	____	see kabidhi(V).	____
takabali(V) (Rel.) **ia/ika/iwa**.	taqabbal (a)	تَقَبَّل	____	to grant or hear(a prayer).	____
takabari(V) (jiona) **ia/ika/isha**.	takabbar (a)	تَكَبَّر	____	to be proud or haughty, display arrogance.	____
takadamu(V) (tangulia) (anza)	taqaddam (a)	تَقَدَّم	____	go before, go forward, lead the way, precede, to advance, proceed.	____, progress, improve, surpass.
takalifu(V) (kalifu)	takallaf (a)	تَكَلَّف	____	take pains over work.	____

Swahili word	Transcription of Arabic word	Arabic word	Arabic word in Swahili sense	Swahili usage	Arabic usage.
takalifu(N)	takli:f	تَكْلِيف	———	trouble, discomfort, annoyance, worry.	———, inconvenience, farmality, ceremony.
takarima(N) (karama) (takrima) (takirima)	takri:m	تَكْرِيمٌ / تكرمة	——— مَأْدُبَة / إِكْرَامُ الوِفَادَةِ	feast, a festive entertainment, banquet.	honouring, tribute.
takarimu(V) (karimu)	takarrm(a)	تَكَرَّم	———	see karimu(V).	———
takbira(N) (Rel.)	takbi:ra (t)	تَكْبِيرَة	———	"to say Allahu Akbar", it means God is Greater.	———
takdiri(N) (kadari) (majaaliwa)	taqdi:r	تَقْدِير	——— قَدَرٌ	fate, destiny, predestination.	———
takilifu(N)	takli:f	تَكْلِيف	———	see takalifu(N).	———
takirima(N)	takri:ma (t)	تَكْرِمَة	——— تَكْرِيم إِكْرَامُ الوِفَادَةِ	see takarima(N).	———
takriban(adv.)	taqri:ban	تَقْرِيباً	———	nearly, almost, approximately.	———, roughly, about.
takwa(N) (Rel.)	taqwa:	التَّقْوَى	———	godiness, piety, devoutness.	———
takwimu(N)	taqwi:m	تَقْوِيم	——— إِحْصَاء	<u>statistics</u>,** calendar.	reformation, valuation, estimation, gazetteer
talaka(N) (kuachana)	ṭala:q	طَلَاق	———	divorce, talak, definite divorce.	———
talakimu(N) (uradi)	talqi:n	تَلْقِين	———	the Islamic burial prayers.	———.
talasimu(N) (hirizi) (dawa) (kago)	ṭalasim	طَلَاسِم	——— طِلَّسْم	talisman [Ar.],* magical combination of words, cryptic characters, charm.	———, a seal.

Swahili word	Transcription of Arabic word	Arabic word	Arabic word in Swahili sense	Swahili usage	Arabic usage.
taliki(V) (acha) (toa talaka)	ṭallaq(a)	طَلَّقَ	____	divorce, repudiate.	____
talkini(N) (Rel.)	talqi:n	تلقِين	____	see talakimu(N).	____
tama(V)	tamm(a)	تَمَّ	____	be finished, complete, come to an end.	___, done, execute.
tama(adj.) (kweli)	ta:mm	تامّ	____	final, decisive, complete, perfect, matter, finishing, really.**	___, entire, sterling, consummate, genuine.
tama(N) (tamati)	ta:mm	تامّ	تمام	see tamati, also end, final stage, conclusion.	see tamati.
tamaa(N) (shauku) (roho) (rare)	ṭamaạ	طَمَعٌ	____	greed, avidity, greediness, ambition, lust, desire, cupidity, avarice.	___, covetousness, object of desire.
tamaduni(V) (staarabu) (rare)	tamaddan (a)	تَمَدَّنَ	____	become civilized.	____
tamani(V) (kuwa na tamaa) **ia/ika/isha/iwa/iana.**	tamanna:	تَمَنَّى	____	desire, long for, like, covet, lust after, want.	___, be able/capable.
tamani(N)	tamanni(n)	تَمَنٍّ	____, أُمْنِيَة	desire, longing, lust, trust, hope.	____, demand, claim aspiration.
tamanio(N) (ma-)	ŭmniya(t)	أُمْنِيَة	____, أَمَان	desire, wish, object of desire.	____
tamati(N) (mwisho wa jambo)	tamma t	تَمَّتْ	____	end,finish (of poem or story).	____
tamthilia(N) (tec.)	tamthilia	تَمْثِيلِيَة	____	play.	____
tamu(adj.) (-enye kufurahisha)	taạm	طَعْمٌ	حُلْوَ	sweet, nice, pleasant, agreeable, dilightful, tasty, mild, gentle.	tast, flavour.

Swahili word	Transcription of Arabic word	Arabic word	Arabic word in Swahili sense	Swahili usage	Arabic usage.
tanabahi(V) (kumbuka) (fahamu) (tafakari) **ia/ika/isha.**	tanabbah (a)	تَنَبَّهَ	———	notice, pay attention, remember, perceive, cause to remember, be awake to, alert, understand.	___, awake, to warn against danger, or offence.
tanashati(adj.)	nashi:ṭ	نَشِيطٌ	نَظِيفٌ	clean, well dressed, neat pretty, fresh.	active, energetic.
tania(V) (dhihaki) (fyua) **lia/lika/wa/ana**	waṭan (root)	(مِنْ الوَطَنِ)	مزح	make fun, jest, to joke.	see utani.
tanzia(N) (taazia)	taʿzia(t)	تَعْزِيَة	———	see taazia.	———
tarabu(N) (taarabu)	ṭarab	طَرَب	———	see taarabu(N).	———
taradhia(V) **lia/lika /wa/ana.**	taʿraḍ(a)	تعرض	تَعَرَّض	(1) warn, give advice, reproach, admonish, (2) see radhi.	see taaradhia(V).
tarafa(N) (tarafu)	ṭaraf	طَرَف	مَنْطِقَة / مُقَاطَعَة	district, share, part, duty, business, parish, task, work.	part, edge, end, border, region, area section.
tarakimu(N) (rare)	tarqi:m	تَرْقِيم	———	figure, written numeral digit.	pointing, numeration, numbering.
taratibu(N) (pole pole)	tarti:b	تَرْتِيب	———	order, system, organization, sturucture , procedure, method.	___, arrangement, provision, sequence.
tarawehe(N) (Rel.)	tara:wi:ḥ	تَرَاوِيح	———	prayer pronounced after prayer of "isha:a" during Ramadan.	———
tarawehi(N)(tarawehe)	tara:wi:ḥ		———	see tarawehe.	———
tarazaki(V) **ia/ika.**	tarazzaq (a)	تَرَزَّقَ	———	see ruzuku.	———

Swahili word	Transcription of Arabic word	Arabic word	Arabic word in Swahili sense	Swahili usage	Arabic usage.
tarehe(N)	ta:ri:kh	تاريخ	____	date, chronology, annals.	___, history, cronicle.
tarekhe(N)	ta:ri:kh		____	see tarehe.	____
tarjumi(V) (tafsiri) (rare)	tarjam(a)	ترجم	____	see tafsiri(V).	translate, interpret, render, explain.
tarjumi(N) (tafsiri)	tarjama(t)	ترجمة	____	see tafsiri(N).	translation, interpretation, biography.
tartibu(N)	tarti:b	ترتيب	____	see taratibu.	____
tasa(N) (bakuli)	ṭa:sa(t)	طاسة	____	tasa, a small metal vessel.	____
tasawari(V) (aminika) (elekea) (ingia akilini) **ia/ika/isha**	taṣawar	تصوّر	____	be fully able,** competent, be capable.	to imagine fancy, conceive, appear, seem, think.
tasawari(N)	taṣawur	تصوُّر	____	practicability, competence, feasibility.	imagination, fancy conception, idea.
tasbihi(N) (Rel.) (himidi) (sifu)	tasbi:ḥ	تسبيح	____	ascription of praise to God, rosary, Praise, glorification of God.	____, exclaiming.
tashwishi(N)(wasiwasi)(mashaka)	tashwi:sh	تشويش	____	doubt, confusion, uncertaity.	____, confounding, disturbance, ailment.
tasihili(adv.) (upesi) (rare)	tas'hi:l	تسهيل	____	quickly, with, speed.	facilitation.
tasjila(N)	tasji:l	تسجيل	____	see masjala.	____

Swahili word	Transcription of Arabic word	Arabic word	Arabic word in Swahili sense	Swahili usage	Arabic usage.
taslimu(adj.) (kamili)	taslim	تَسْلِيم	—— نَقْدًا	in cash, direct delivery.	delivery, salutation, submission, recognition.
tasliti(V)	tasallaṭ (a)	تَسَلَّطَ	——	cause trouble, betray, deceive, annoy, incite.	hold stay, rule, reign, control, command.
taswira(N) (maono) (picha) (mchoro) (sanamu)	taṣwi:ra (t)	تَصْوِيرَة	——	picture, portrait, likeness, drawing, surface of the earth.	image, picture, pictorial/representation, illustration.
tathmini(V)(thamini)	thamman(a)	ثَمَّنَ	——	to appraise, estimate, estimation, appraisal, valuation.	___, to price.
tathmini(N)	tathmi:n	تَثْمِين	—— تَقْدِير	estimation, appraisal, valuation.	___, rating.
taurati(N) (torati) (Rel.)	tawra:t	التَوْرَاة	——	Pentateuch, the law of Moses.	___
tausi(N) (kibibi)	ta:ū:s	طَاوُوس	——	peacock.	___
(a) **tawadha**(V)(Rel.)	tawaḍḍaȧ	تَوَضَّأَ	——	ceremonial washing, ablution.	___
(b) **tawadha**(V) (safisha kwa maji)	waḍuȧ	وَضُأَ	——, نَظُفَ	clean, to be clean, pure.	___
tawafu(N)(Rel.)	ṭawa:f	الطَّوَاف	——	curcumambulation of the Kaaba.	___, round, circuit.
tawakali(V) (rare)	tawakkal (a)	تَوَكَّلَ	——	trust, rely on (God) have confidence, take courage, hope.	___
tawala(V)	tawalla:	تَوَلَّى	——	rule, govern, cause to rule, come to power, inaugurate.	___, undertake.

Swahili word	Transcription of Arabic word	Arabic word	Arabic word in Swahili sense	Swahili usage	Arabic usage.
tawili(adj.) (-refu) (ZNZ)	ṭawi:l	طويل	____	long, tall.	____
tawilisha(V) (refusha) isha.	aṭa:L(a)	أطال	____, مدّ	lengthen, prolong, grow long.	
tena(adv.)	tha:ni	ثانٍ / ثانية	____	then, next, again, further.	next, second.
thabiti(adj.)(-enye nguvu) (imara) (-a kweli)	tha:bit	ثابت	____ راسخ	firm, brave, strong, constant secure, resolute, proved, reliable, true, genuine, character.	____, verification, permanent, fearless, confirmed.
thakili(N) (adj.) (mashaka) (dhiki) (zito) (ZNZ)	thaqi:l	ثقيل	____	one who casts a gloom upon others.	____
thalathini(N) (also thelathini)	thala:thi:n	ثلاثين	____ ثلاثون	thirty.(30).	____
thamani(N)	thaman	ثمن	____	price, value, estimation.	____, cost
thamanini(N)	thama:ni:n	ثمانين	____ ثمانون	eighty,	____, fourscore.
(a) **thamini**(V) (tathmini)	thamman(a)	ثمّن	____	appraise, value, evaluate estimate, assess.	____, to price.
(b) **thamini**(V) (heshimu) **ia/ika/isha/iwa/iana.**	thamman(a)	ثمّن	____ قدّر	respect, characterize, appreciate.	____, fruit, effect result, gain, profit.
thamra(N) (mkarafu)	thamra(t)	ثمرة	—	cloves in the first stage of growth.	fruit, result, affection, yield, benefit, product.
thania(N) (tec.)	thuna:i̱	ثنائي	____	bilingual.	double, dual, binary, two fold, biradical.

Swahili word	Transcription of Arabic word	Arabic word	Arabic word in Swahili sense	Swahili usage	Arabic usage.
thawabu(N) (jaza)	thawa:b	ثَـوَاب	جَـزَاء	reward, recompense, gift (from God).	___, requital, merit.
thelatha(N) (rare)	thala:tha (t)	ثلاثة	___	three, third.	___
thelathini(N)	thala:thi:n	ثلاثين	ثلاثون	thirty, (30).	___
theluji(N)	thalj	ثلج	جَليد	snow.	___, ice, snow-flake.
theluthi(N) (thulu-thi)	thuluth	ثُـلُـث	___	a third, ($^1/_3$).	___
themanini(N)	thama:ni:n	ثَمَانين	ثَمَانُونَ	eighty.	fourscore.
themuni(N)	thumn	ثُـمْـنٌ	___	an eighth, ($^1/_8$).	___
thenashara(N) (rare)	ithna a̱-shar	إِثْنَى عَشَر (اِثْنَا عَشَر)	___	twelve.	___
theneen(N) (-wili)	ithnain	إِثْنَين	إِثْنَانِ	two.	___
theneni(N) (-wili)	"	"	___	see theneen.	___
thibiti(V) ika/isha.	thabat(a)	ثَـبَـتَ	أَثْبَتَ	be fixed, to stand firm, stable, strong, streng-then, to prove guilty, convict, stead fast, establish.	___, defy, resist, to remain, stay, to maintain, con-firm, consolidate, assert, determine, identify.
thibitisho(N) (haki-kisho)	ithba:t	إِثْبَات	___	confirmation, establish-ment, assertion, proof, demonstration.	___, evidence, verification, recording.
thinashara(N) kumi na mbili) (rare)	ithna a̱-shar	إِثْنَا عَشَر إِثْنَى عَشَر	___	twelve, twelveth.	___

Swahili word	Transcription of Arabic word	Arabic word	Arabic word in Swahili sense	Swahili usage	Arabic usage.
thomo(N) (saumu)	thu:m	ثُومٌ	____	garlic.	____
thubutu(V) (subutu) **ika/isha.**	thabat(a)	ثَبَتَ	____ يَجْرُؤُ يَجْسُر	dare, have courage to, venture.	___, to be brave.
thulathiya(N) (tec.)	thula:thi:	ثُلاثِيّ	____	trilingual.	tripartite, tri-
thumu(N) (thomo) (tumu)	thu:m	ثُوم	____	garlic.	____
thumuni(N) (thumni)	thumn	ثُمْن	____	an eighth.	____
thurea(N) (kilimia)	thurayya:	الثُّرَيَّا	____	chandelier, pleiades.	____
tiba(N)	ṭibb	طِبٌّ	____	medicine, medical treatment.	____,
tibu(V) (ganga) **ia/ ika/iwa/iana**	ṭabbab(a)	طَبَّبَ	____ عَالَج	to treat medically, consult a doctor.	____, seek.
tii(V) (fuata amri) **ia/ika/isha/iwa/iana**	aṭa:a̦(a)	أَطَاعَ	____	to obey, render, submit to, be obedient.	____, yield, accede.
tija(N) (natija)	nati:ja(t)	نَتِيجَة	____	see natija.	____
tilifika(V) (tilifu)	atlaf(a)	أَتْلَفَ	____	see tilifu(V).	____
tilifu(V) **ika/isha.**	talif(a)	تَلِفَ	____	waste, destroy, become damaged, spoil, injure, decrease, be lost, ruin.	____, break, get broken.
timamu(adj.)(kamili)	itma:m	اِتْمَام	____ اِنْجَاز	completion, completed state, conclusion.	____
timilifu(adj.)	ta:mm	تَامٌّ	____ كَامِل	complete, perfect, consummate.	___, full, genuine.
timu(V) **ia/iza/iwa**	tamma	تَمَّ	____	be complete, finish, conclude, to come to an end, fulfill, perfect, done.	____, execute, achieve, terminate, wind up.

Swahili word	Transcription of Arabic word	Arabic word	Arabic word in Swahili sense	Swahili usage	Arabic usage.
timu(N)	*	*	*	team.	*
tini(N)	ti:n	تِين	___	a fig.	___
tisa(N) (kenda)	tisa̤a(t)	تِسْعَة	___ تِسْع التَّاسِع	nine, nineth,(9).	___
tisini(N)	tisi̤:n	تِسْعِين	___ تِسْعُون	ninety, ninetieth.	___
toba(N)	tawba(t)	تَوْبَة	___	penitence, repentance, contrition, regret, remorse.	___, penance.
tofaa(N) (tufaha)	tuffa:ḥ	تُفَّاح	___	the rose-apple.	an apple.
tofali(N) (ma-) (tufali)	ṭufa:l	الطُّفَال	___	brick, tile.	argil, potter's clay, loam, clay.
tofauti(N) (tafauti. R.)	tafa:ut	تَفَاوُت	مُتَفَاوِت	difference, distinction, interval, discrepancy, dispute, excess,** want** quarrel,* blame,* fault.**	___, differ.
tohara(N)	ṭaha:ra(t)	طَهَارَة	___ خِتَان خِفَاض	ritual purity, circumcision.**	___,
toharika(V) **isha**	ṭahur(a) ṭahhar(a)	طَهُرَ طَهَّرَ	___	to be circumcised, circumcise.	___ (loc.Ar.).
torati(N) (Rel.)	tawra:t	التَّوْرَاة	___	see taurati.	
toroka(V) **sha**	tarak(a)	تَرَكَ	هَرَبَ / هَرَبَ	run away, scape, desert, play truant.	to leave, give up to abandon, let, to allow, to let alone.
tubia(V) (Rel.)	ta:b(a)	تَابَ	___ أَنَابَ إِلَى	repent of a fault, repent before God.	___

Swahili word	Transcription of Arabic word	Arabic word	Arabic word in Swahili sense	Swahili usage	Arabic usage.
tubu(V) (juta) (sikitika) **ia/isha**	ta:b(a)	تَـابَ	____	repent, feel remorse, regret, be penitent, correct, chastise.	____
tufaha(N) (tofaa)	tuffa:ḥa (t)	تُفَّـاحَة	____	see tofaa.	
tufali(N) (ma-) (tofali)	ṭufa:l	الطُّـفَال	____	see tofali.	
tufani(N) (dhoruba) (kimbunga)	ṭu:fa:n	طُـوفَـان		storm, tempest, gale, hurricane.	flood, deluge, inundition.
tufe(N) (___, ma-)	ṭauf	طَـوْف	كُرَة / جِسْمٌ كُرَوِي	a ball, a game of ball, sphere.	circuit, round, beat.
tufu(V) (Rel.)	ṭa:f(a)	طَـافَ	___	to perform the circumambulation of the Kaaba, encircle.	______
tuhma(N) (also tuhuma)	tuhma(t)	تُهْمَـة	____	accusation, suspicion.	___, charge, insinuation.
tuhuma(N) (shaka)	"			see tuhma.	___
tuhumu(V) **ia/ika/isha/iwa/iana.**	ittaham(a)	اتَّهَمَ	____	suspect, accuse, reproach, charge with something.	___,to frame a person, doubt.
tumai(V) (tumaini) **ia/ika/isha/iwa/iana**	tamanna:	تَمَـنَّى	____	see tumaini.	
tumaini(N) (ma-)	tamanni(n)	تَمَـنٍّ	____	أَمَـلٌ	desire, belief, confidence, trust.	____,hope, faith, expectation.
tumaini(V) (kuwa na tamaa) **ia/ika/isha/iwa/iana.**	tamanna:	تَمَـنَّى	____	desire, long for, hope for, yearn for, expect, trust, rely on, be confident.	_____

Swahili word	Transcription of Arabic word	Arabic word	Arabic word in Swahili sense	Swahili usage	Arabic usage.
tumainifu(adj.)	mutmai̱nn	مُطْمِئِنّ	ثِقَة ___	confident, hopeful, reliable, trust-worthy.	___, peacefulness, secure, tranguil, calm.
tumbako(N) [Hindostani]*(also tumbaku)	tumba:k	تُمْبَاك	تَبْغ ___	toba co, snuff.	___
tumu(N) (thumu)	thu:m	ثُوم (U)	___	garlic.	___
uadhimishaji(N)	ṭaạḍhi:m	تَعْظِيم	مَهْرَجَان / مَرَاسِم تَشْرِيفَات اِبْتِهَاج.	festival, ceremony.	glorification, exaltation, aggrandizament, military salute.
uadilifu(N)	ạda:la(t)	عَدَالَة	___	justice, integrity, fairness, honesty.	___, probity, decency, equitableness.
uadui(N) (ugomvi) (uhasama)	ada:wa:	عَدَاوَة عَدَاء	خُصُومَة ___	enmity, ill-will, hostility.	___, animosity, antagonism.
uahirisho(N)	taạkhi:r	تَأْخِير	تَأْجِيل تَأَخُّر ___	delay, postponement.	___, deferment, obstruction.
uajemi(N)	ạjam	عَجَم / (عُجْمَة)	إِيرَان بِلَادُ الفُرْسِ ___	Persia, Persians, Iran.	___, non-Arabs.
uajiri(N)	ụjra(t)	أُجْرَة	___	see ujira.	___
uajuza(N) (uzee wa kike)	ụju:z	العَجُوز	___	old age(for women only).	old age (for men, and women)
ualimu(N)	taạli:m	تَعْلِيم	تَدْرِيس ___	teaching, teaching profession, instruction, education.	___
uamini(N)	áma:na(t)	أَمَانَة	___	see uaminifu.	___
uaminifu(N)	áma:na(t)	"	___	confidence, trust, faithfulness, trustworthiness, honesty, accuracy.	___, trusteeship, straightforwardness.

Swahili word	Transcription of Arabic word	Arabic word	Arabic word in Swahili sense	Swahili usage	Arabic usage.
uamiri(N) (ukuu wa cheo)	ima:ra(t)	إِمَارَة	____,	position of, rank of, general.	power, authority, emirate.
uanadamu(N) (ubina-damu)	ãdamiya(t)	الآدَمِيّة	الإنْسَانِيّة	humanity, human nature.	____, humanness, humanism.
(uana) **halali**(N)	bunu:wa-al-ḥill	بُنُوّة الحِلّ	بُنُوّة شَرْعِيّة	sonship of lawful, filiation.	____
(uana) **haramu**(N)	bunu:wa-al-ḥurma(t)	بُنُوّة الحُرْمة	بُنُوّة غَيْر شَرْعِيّة	illegal sonship, without filiation.	____
(uana) **hewa**(N)	(from) hawa:ā	(مِن الهَواء)	البِلاَحَة الجَوّيّة (الطّيرَان)	aviation.	*
(uana) **jeshi**(N)	(from) ja-ish	(و مِن الجَيْش)	الشُّؤُون العَسْكَريّة	military affairs.	*
(uana) **sheria** (N)	(from) shari:aa (t)	(مِن الشَّريعَة)	الأُمُور الشَّرْعِيّة	legal matter, practice of law.	*
uarabu(N)	uru:ba(t)	العُرُوبة	____	the Arab idea, Arabism, Arabdom.	____, the Arab character.
uarabuni(N) (nchi za Waarabu)	albila:d al-Arabia (t)	البِلاَد العَربِيّة	____	the Arab countries.	____
uasherati(N)	mua:shara (t)	المُعَاشَرة	الفُسُوق ، علاقة جِنْسِيّة غَيْر شَرْعِيّة	immorality, debauchery, profligacy, adultery.	____, intimacy.
uasi(N)	isya:n	عِصْيَان	____	mutiny, insurrection, rebellion, disobedience.	____, revolt, sedition.
uaskari(N)	askariya (t)	عَسْكَريّة	____	military service, military profession, soldiership.	____, militarism, soldiery, soldierliness.
uaskofu(N)	usqufiya	الأُسْقُفيّة	____	bishopric, episcopate.	____

Swahili word	Transcription of Arabic word	Arabic word	Arabic word in Swahili sense	Swahili usage	Arabic usage.
ubadhiri(N)	tabdhi:r	تَبْذِير	إِسْرَاف ,———	see ubadhirifu.	———
ubadhirifu(N) (upotevu)	tabdhi:r	تَبْذِير	إسْرَاف ,———	waste, prodigality, extravagance, immoderation, lack of restraint.	———, dissipation, squandering.
ubadili(N)	ibda:l	إِبْدَال	———	see ubadilifu.	———
ubadilifu(N)	ibda:l	"	تَبَادُل ———	change, changeableness, exchange, interchange.	———, substitution
ubadiliko(N) (ma-)	tabaddul	تَبَدُّل	مُبَادَلَة ———	change of circumstances, conditions.	———
ubadilishaji(N)	istibda:l	اسْتِبْدَال تَبَادُل	تَعْدِيل تَقَلُّب ———	changeableness, revisionism, fickleness.	———, replacement.
ubahaimu(N)	bahi:mi:ya (t)	بَهِيمِيَّة	الحَيْوَانِيَّة	brutishness, bestiality.	———,brutality.
ubaharia(N)	ibḥa:r	ابْحَار"	المِلَاحَة ———	navigation, shipping.	———
ubahili(N)	bukhl	بُخْل"	———	miserliness, avarice.	———, greed, cupidity.
ubainifu(N) (ubaini) (ujuaji)	bayyina(t)	بَيِّنَة	———	proof, certainly, evidence.	———,
ubalehe(N)	bulu:gh	بُلُوغ	سِنُّ الرُّشْدِ ———	puberty, maturity, marriageble age.	———, reaching, arrival, legal majority.
ubalighishaji(N) (ufikishaji)	Ibla:gh	إِبْلَاغ	تَبْلِيغ ———	conveyance, notification, transmission.	———, information, announcement.
ubani(N)	luba:n	لُبَان	———	frankincense.	———
ubaridi(N)	buru:da(t)	بُرُودَة	———	coldness, coolness, indifference reserve, kindness, gentleness.	———, frigidity, emotional.

Swahili word	Transcription of Arabic word	Arabic word	Arabic word in Swahili sense	Swahili usage	Arabic usage.
ubashasha(N)	basha:sha (t)	بَشَاشَة	____	smile, happy mien.	____
ubashashi(N)	"	"	____	see ubashasha.	____
ubashiri(N)	tabshi:r	تَبْشِير	____, نُبُوَّة، تَنَبُّؤ	prophecy, <u>prediction</u>,** proclamation, announcement.	____, evangelization, missionary activity.
ubatili(N)	butla:n	بُطْلَان	____	worthlessness, uselessness, emptiness, futility, falsity.	____, untruth, nullity, invalidity.
ubatilifu(N)	butla:n	"	____	see ubatilifu.	____
ubayana(N) (ubainifu)	bayyina(t)	البَيِّنَة	____	see ubainifu.	____
ubedui(N)	bada:wa(t)	البَدَاوَة	____	bedouin[Ar.]* life, momadism.	____, desert life, bedouinism.
ubeti(N)	bait(poem)	بَيْت (الشِعْر)	____,	verse, section, <u>paragraph</u>,** strophe.	___, house, building family.
ubikira(N)	baka:ra(t)	البَكَارَة	____, غشاءُ البَكَارة	virginity, celibacy, hymen	____
ubilisi(N)	ibli:si:y	إبْلِيسِي	____, إغْرَاء	temptation, satanic.	_____, devilish.
ubinadamu(N)	ā:damiya (t)	الآدَمِيَّة	____ الإنسانِيَّة	see uanadamu.	____
ubinafsi(N)	(from) nafs	(مِنْ النَّفْسِ)	الشَخْصِيَّة / الذَاتِيَّة المُمَيَّزَة	personaly, selfishness.	person, soul, humanbeing, individual.
(a) **ubini**(N)	banawiy	بَنَوِي	تَزْوِيرٌ / تَزْيِيفٌ	forgery, counterfeiting, act of forging.	filial.
(b) **ubini**(N)	bunu:wa(t)	بُنُوَّة	لقَب/ كُنْيَة	family name, surname.	sonship, filiation.

Swahili word	Transcription of Arabic word	Arabic word	Arabic word in Swahili sense	Swahili usage	Arabic usage.
uburudisho(N)	buru:d	البُرُود	اِنْتِعَاش اِسْتِجْمَام	coolness, refreshment, recreation, rest, relief.	coolness, coldness frigidity, emotional coldness.
udadisi(N) (upelelezi)	dasi:sa(t)	دَسِيسَة دَسّ	بَحْثٌ / تَحْقِيقٌ حُبُّ الِاسْتِطْلَاعِ	inquisitiveness, curiosity, indiscretion.	intrique, machination, plot.
udalali(N)	dila:la(t)	دِلَالَة	——— سَمْسَرَة عُمُولَة	auctioneering, commission.	____, brokerage.
udhahiri(N)	iḍhha:r	اظْهَار	———	manifestation, demonstration, testimony, evidence, obviousness, plainness, clarity.	____, declaration, display, announcement, disclosure.
udhalilifu(N)	iḍh ha:r	اِظْهَار	———	see udhahiri.	____
udhaifu(N)	ḍuaf	ضُعْفٌ	———, خِسَّة حَقَارَة	weakness, infirmity, meanness, baseness, paltriness, insignificance.	____, feebleness, debiltation, fraility.
udhalifu(N) (udhilifu)	idhla:l	اِذْلَال	——— ذِلَّة حَقَارَة	abasement, humiliation, submissiveness.	____, degradation.
udhalimu(N)	ḍhulm.	ظُلْمٌ	———	injustice, wrong, oppression, aggression, tyranny, unfairness.	____, iniquity, suppression.
udhamini(N)	ḍama:n	ضَمَان	——— كَفَالَة مِنْحَة / رَهْن	pledge, sponsorship,** guarantee, surety, trusteeship.	___, liability.
udhani(N)	ḍhann	ظَنٌّ	———, المَظِنَّة	suspicion, assumption, guess, view.	____, opinion, idea.
udhanifu(N) (udhani)	ḍhann		———	see udhani.	____
udhi(N)	ȧdhia(t)	أذِيَّة	———	annoy, hurt, disturb, worry, bore, tire.	____

Swahili word	Transcription of Arabic word	Arabic word	Arabic word in Swahili sense	Swahili usage	Arabic usage.
udhia(N)	ȧdha:	أذى	____	trouble, anoyance, harm, difficulty, confussion, disorder.	___,damage, offense, insult.
udhibiti(N)	ḍabt	ضَبْطٌ	____	control.	____,restraint.
udhihirifu(N)	idhha:r	إظْهَار	____	see udhahirifu.	____
udhiki(N)	ḍi:q	ضِيقٌ	____	narrowness, lack of space, distress.	___,trouble.
udhiko(N)	ȧdha:	أذَى	____	see udhia.	____
udhilifu(N) (udhalilifu)	idhla:l	إذْلال	____	see udhalilifu(N).	____
udhoofu	duạf	ضُعْفٌ	—	see udhaifu.	____
udhu(N)(Rel.)	wuḍū	وُضُوء	____	ritual ablution, purity, cleanness.	____
udhuru(N) (hoja) (sababu) (dharura)	ụdhr	عُذْر	____	excuse, pretext, reason.**	____
udil(N)	ụ:d	عُود	____ خَشَبٌ عِطْرٌ	aloe-wood.	____, stick, lute.
udibaji(N)[Persian]*	tadbi:j	تَدْبِيج	____ تَزْيِينٌ تهذيب	ornamentation, decoration, refinement.	____, embellishment, adornment.
uduni(N)	du:nia(t)	دُونِيَة	____	low, inadequate, inferior, bad.	____, lowly, poor, meager.
ufadhili(N)	faḍl	فَضْل	____, احْسَان	kindness, favor, goodwill, affection, obligation, privilege.	____, merit, desert, advantage, honour.
ufahamifu(N)	fahm	فَهْمٌ	____ ذَكَاءٌ	intelligence, understanding, penetration, memory, quick-wittedness.	____, sagacity, comprehension.
ufahamivu(N)	fahm	"	____	see ufahamifu.	____

Swahili word	Transcription of Arabic word	Arabic word	Arabic word in Swahili sense	Swahili usage	Arabic usage.
ufahamu(N)	fahm	فَهْم	—	see ufahamifu.	—
ufahari(N)	fakhr	فَخْرٌ	—	glory, vanity, honour.	—
ufarisi(N) (rare)	fira:sa(t)	فِرَاسَةٌ	مَقْدِرَة عَقْلِيَة خِبْرَة	capability, experience, competence, expertness.	perspicacity, observation, acumen.
ufasaha(N) (ufasihi)	faṣa:ḥa(t)	فَصَاحَةٌ	—	eloquence, lucidity, clarity, elegance, goodteste.	—
ufasihi(N)	faṣa:ḥa(t)	فَصَاحَةٌ	—	see ufasaha.	—
ufasiki(N)	fusu:q fisq	فُسُوقٌ فِسْقٌ	—,	immorality, debauchery, vice, adultery, fornication.	—, sin, dissoluteness, libertanism.
ufaulu(N)	tafa:ūl	تَفَاؤُل	نَجَاح	success.	optimism.
ufedhuli(N)	fuḍu:l	فُضُول	مَجْرُفَة / تَكَبُّر وَقَاحَة	arrogance, impudence, insolence, outrage, temper, wanton, insults.	inquisitiveness, curiosity, meddling.
ufidhuli(N) (kiburi)	"	"	—	see ufedhuli.	—
ufilisi(N)	ifla:s	افْلَاس	—	bankruptcy, insolvency.	—, failure.
ufisadi(N) (maovu) (uharibifu)	fasa:d	فَسَاد	—	corruption, vice, viciousness.	—
ufitina(N)	fitna(t)	فِتْنَة	خِلَاف/ نِزَاع شِقَاق	dissension, discord, rebellion, agitation, intrique, revolt.	—, see fitina.
ufukara(N)	faqr	فَقْر	—	poverty, misery, begging, distress.	—, need, lack, want.

Swahili word	Transcription of Arabic word	Arabic word	Arabic word in Swahili sense	Swahili usage	Arabic usage.
ufununu(N) (tetesi) (dokezo)	funu:n	فُنُون	إِشَاعَة	rumour, gossip some knowledge.	kind, field of work, specialty art, scientific discipline.
ufurahi(N)	farah	فَرَح	___	delight, pleasure, joy.	___, glee, gaoetu, mirth, exhilaration.
ughaibu(N)	ghaib	غَيْب	___	absent, a distant place, condition of being unobtainable.	___
ughali(N)	ghala:ā	غَلَاء	___	high cost, high level of price, high price.	___
ughuna(N) (tec.)	ghunna(t)	غُنَّة	صَوْتٌ جَهُورٌ	voiced.	see ghuna.
ughushi(N)	ghish	غِشّ	___	adulteration, mixing, corruption.	____, fraud, deceit.
uhaba(N) (chache) (kidogo) (kitambo)	habba(t)	حَبَّة	قِلَّة/ نُدْرَة	fewness, rarity, scantiness, being too few.	grain, seed. see haba.
uhadimu(N)	khidma(t)	خِدْمَة	___	service, attendance.	____, job, operation.
uhafifu(N) (uduni) (unyonge) (dhaifu)	khiffa(t)	خِفَّة	___	lightness, slightness, insignificance, commonness, poor quality, worthlessness.	____, sprightliness, agility, buoyancy, nimbleness, fickleness.
uhai(N)	haya:(t)	حياة	___	life, lifeliness, animation.	____, life blood.
uhaini(N) (uasi) (usaliti)	khiya:na (t)	خِيَانَة	___	treachery, faithlessness, perfidy, betrayal.	___, treason, falseness, disloyalty,

Swahili word	Transcription of Arabic word	Arabic word	Arabic word in Swahili sense	Swahili usage	Arabic usage.
uhaji(N) (Rel.) (silimu) (enda jando) (linatumika katika msemo)	ḥajj (root)	(مِنْ الحَجّ)	أسْلَمَ اخْتَتَنَ	(1) convert to Islam, (2) to be circumcised.	*
uhakiki(N)(tahakiki)	taḥqi:q	تَحْقِيقٌ	____	see tahakiki.	____
uhakimu(N)	ḥukm	(مِنْ الحُكْمِ)	القَضَاء	judgement, authority, jurisdiction, sentence, trial, decision, jurisprudence, judgeship, power.	____, dominion caidemnation, judiciousness.
uhalifu(N)	khila:f	خِلَاف	____، عِصْيَان تمرد	rebellion, disobedience, transgression, naughtiness.	disagreement, difference, divergence, diviation.
uhamiaji(N)	ḥawm/ ḥawama:n	حَوْم / حَوَمَان	نُزُوحٌ / هِجْرَة ارْتِحَالَ	migration, immigration.	hovering.
uhamisho(N)	"		____	moval, resettlement, eviction, ejection.	see hama(V).
uhanithi(N) (ushoga)	takhannuth	تَخَنُّثٌ	لِوَاطٌ	sodomy, pederasty, sexual perversion.	effeminacy, effeminateness.
uharamia(N)	ḥara:m (root)	(مِنْ الحَرَام)	لُصُوصِيَّة / قَطْعُ طُرُقٍ	outlawry, brigandage, piracy.	see haramu.
uharamu(N)	ḥurma(t)	الحُرْمَة	____	unlawfulness, illegality.	____
uharara(N)	ḥarara(t)	الحَرَارَة	____	warmth, heat, impetuosity, fervour.	____
uharibifu(N) (uharibivu)	takhri:b	تَخْرِيب/ خَرَاب	____	spoiling, destruction, waste, corruption, mortality.	devastation, wrecking, sabotage, demolition, destruction.
uhariri(N) (kazi ya uhariri)	taḥri:r	تَحْرِير	____	editing, editorship, writing.	____, liberation, release.
uhasama(N) (uadui) (uhasimu)	khiṣa:m	خِصَامٌ	____ خُصُومَة نِزَاعٌ	enmity, sulkiness, violence, dispute.	____, quarrel, contention, litigation.

Swahili word	Transcription of Arabic word	Arabic word	Arabic word in Swahili sense	Swahili usage	Arabic usage.
uhasibu(N)	ḥisa:ba:t	الحِسَابَات	المُحَاسَبَة , ____	accounting.	____
uhasiḍi(N)	ḥasad	الحَسَد	____	envy, malignity, spite.	____, grudge, covetousness.
uhasimu(N) (uhasama)	khiṣa:m	خِصَام	____	see uhasama.	____
uhawara(N)	ḥawra:ā	حَوْرَاء	____	see hawara.	____
uhayawani(N) (unyama)	ḥaywa:niya (t)	الحَيْوَانِيَّة	____	animality, animal nature, bestiality.	____
uhiana(N)	khiana(t)	الخِيَانَة	____	see uhaini.	____
uhifadhi(N)	ḥifa:ḍh	حِفَاظ	حِمَايَة ____	guarding, careful watching, defence, protection.	____, preservation, maintenance.
uhitaji(V)(hitaji, ma-)	ihtiya:j.	اِحْتِيَاج	____	need, desire, want, indigence.	____, necessity, requirement.
uhodari(N)	ḥuḍu:r al badi:ha	حُضُورُ البَدِيهَة	ثَبَات/ شَجَاعَة	courage, stability.	presence of mind.
uhuni(N)	khiana(t)	خِيَانَة	مُخَالَفَةُ القَانُونِ التَّشَرُّد	lawlessness, vogabondage.	unfaithfulness, dishonesty, treason, perfidy.
uhuru(N)	ḥurriya(t)	الحُرِّيَّة	____	freedom, emancipation, liberty, independence.	____
uhusiano(N)	ikhtiṣa:sy	اِخْتِصَاص خَاصّ بِ	وَثَاقَة الصِّلَة , ____	relevancy, relative, pertinent, concerning.	____, designated, earmarked.
uimamu(N)	ima:ma(t)	اِمَامَة	____	leadership, chiefdom.	____
uimara(N) (uthabiti)	ima:ra(t)	العِمَارَة أو الإِمَارَة	القُوَّة المَتَانَة	firmness, stability, hardness, strength.	structure, real estate, tract lot, building, edifice.

Swahili word	Transcription of Arabic word	Arabic word	Arabic word in Swahili sense	Swahili usage	Arabic usage.
uimarisho(N)	taạmi:r Ima:ra(t)	التعمير العِمَارة	———	strengthening, establishment, installation, resolution, determination, securing.	———
Uislamu(N)	Isla:m	الإسلام	———	Islam.	———
ujabari(N)(poet.)	jabaru:t	الجَبَرُوت	———	omnipotence.	might, potency, power.
ujahili(N) (ujinga) (ukatili)	jaha:la(t)	الجَهَالَة	——— جَهْلٌ قساوة	cruelty, mercilessness, ignorance, foolishness.	———, folly, stupidity.
ujamaa(N) (udugu)	jama:ạ(t)	جَمَاعة	الِاشْتِرَاكِيَّة	brotherhood, relationship, kin, socialism.	company, party, community, set.
ujasiri(N) (ushujaa) (uhodari)	jasa:ra(t)	جَسَارَة	جرأة/ وَقَاحة جَسَارة/شَجَاعة	bravery, foolhardiness, venturesomeness, audacity.	———, boldness, nerve, courage.
ujasusi(N)	tajassus	تَجَسُّس	——— جَاسُوسِيَّة	betrayal, prying, inquisitiveness.	———, espionage.
ujeuri(N) (ufidhuli) (ustadi)	jaur	الجَوْر	——— اسْتِبْدَاد طُغْيَان	tyranny, violence, outrage, injustice, oppression, brutality.	———
ujihamu(N)	hima:ya(t)	الحِمَايَة (الذَّاتِيَّة)	———	self-defence.	*
ujini(N)	junu:n	الجُنُون	———	wickedness, guile, cunning, magic, sorcery, diabolical art.	madness, obsession, foolishness, folly, mania.
ujio(N)(kuja)	maji:	المَجِيء	———	arriving, comming.	———, see ja(V)).
ujira(N) (mshahara) (kodi)	ujra.	الأُجْرَة	——— الِإيجَار	wages, hire, pay, salary, fee.	———, lease, rent.

Swahili word	Transcription of Arabic word	Arabic word	Arabic word in Swahili sense	Swahili usage	Arabic usage.
ujirani(N)	ji:ra(t) jiwa:r	الجِيرَة الجِوَار	___	neighborliness, vicinity, neighborhood, environs.	___
ujitahidi(N)	ijtiha:d	الاِجْتِهَاد	___	see jitahidi.	___
ujitawala(N) (rare)	wila:ya(t)	وِلاَية	الحُكْمُ الذَّاتِي	self government, autonomy	sovereign power, rule, government.
ujuba(N)	ụjb	العُجْب	___ طُغْيَان وَقَاحَة / جَرَاءَة / اِسْتِبْدَاد / ظُلْمٌ	fearlessness,boldness, courage, turanny, oppression.	pride, vanity, conceit.
ujumla(N)	jumla(t)	جُمْلَة	وُحْدَة كَامِلَة كِمِّيَة كَبِيرَة	totality, great number, large quantity.	___, whole, sentence, clause.
ukabaila(N)	gabali	قَبَلِي	شُهْرَة قَبَلِيَّة أهَمِّيَة شَان طَبَقَة اِجْتِمَاعِيَّة	high social standing, importance, prominence, high position.	tribal.
ukabidhi(N) (u werevu)	qiba :ḍa (t)	قِبَاضَة	الاِقْتِصَاد	thriftiness, economy, hoarding.	collecting, levying, (of funds, of taxes).
ukabila(N)	qabi:la	قَبِيلَة	القَبَلِيّة العَصَبِيّة	nationality, tribalism, racism, citizenship.	tribe.
ukadhi(N)	qaḍa:ā	القَضَاء	___	judgement, jurisdiction, justice.	___, decision execution, law.
ukadiri(N) (also ukadirifu)	taqdi:r	التَقْدِير	___	estimation, appraisal, evaluation, computation, calculation, settlement, judgement, moderation.	___, appreciation, assessment, taxation.
ukafiri(N)	kufr	الكُفْر	___ كُفْرَان	blasphemy, sacrilege, apostasy, unbelief, infidelity.	___, profanity, godlessness, ingratitude.
ukahaba(N)	qaḥba(t)	القَحْبَة	بَغَاء	prostitution.	whore, prostitute.

Swahili word	Transcription of Arabic word	Arabic word	Arabic word in Swahili sense	Swahili usage	Arabic usage.
ukaidi(N) (ujeuri) . (ushupavu)	kaid	كَيْد	عِنَاد / مُعَانَدَة عِصْيَان / تَمَرُّد	disobedience, obstinacy, insubordination, stubborness, recalcitrance.	cunning, deceit, trick, dodge, ruse, slyness.
ukaimu(N) (usultani)	qiya:m	قِيَام (بالمَسْئُولِيَّة)	—— نِيَابَة	vice-regent, vice-royalty, deputy, agent, representative, position of substitute.	execution, discharge, performance, carrying out, working, functioning.
ukalifu(N) (usumbufu) (utaabishaji)	takli:f	تَكْلِيف	—— جَهْد شِدَّة	intensity, tension.	troubling, discomfort.
ukalimani(N)	kalma:ni	كَلْمَانى	التَرْجَمَة / التَفْسِير	interpreting, translating.	eleguent, fluent speaker.
ukamili(N)	kama:l	كَمَال	—— اكْمَال	completeness, perfection, unity, consummation, fulfilment.	___, completion, conclusion, wind-up, termination.
ukamilifu(N) (utimilifu)	kama:l	كَمَال	—— ، إِكْمَال	see ukamili.	______
ukamilisho(N)	takmi:l	تَكْمِيل	—— ،	completion, perfection.	____, execution, conclusion.
ukarimu(N)	karam	كَرَم	——	hospitality, charity, liberality, generosity, beneficence.	______
ukashifu(N)	kashf	كَشْف	طَعْنٌ / . قَذْفٌ	libel, slander, defamation.	disclosure, uncovering, unveiling.
ukasisi(N)	qusu:sa(t)	قُسُوسَة	——	priest hood, presbyterate.	____, ministry.
ukati(N) (wakati)	auqa:t	أَوْقَات (جَمْعٌ)	وَقْت	see wakati.	_____
ukatibu(N) (kazi ya katibu)	ka:tib (root)	كَاتِب	أَمَانَة السِّرّ (السَكرتيرية)	secretariat, position of clerk.	secretary, clerk, typist, registrar, writer, author.
ukatili(N) (ujahili) (uonevu) (udhalimu)	qita:l	قِتَال	قَتْلٌ وَحْشِيّ مَذْبَحَة سَفْكُ الدِّمَاء	bloodthirstiness, massacre, cruelty, atrocity.	fight, strugle, contention, strife, combat.

Swahili word	Transcription of Arabic word	Arabic word	Arabic word in Swahili sense	Swahili usage	Arabic usage.
ukinifu(N)	iqtina:ạ	اقتناع	____, اقناع	satisfaction, contentment, conceit, independence, self-satisfaction.	____,
ukiri(N)	iqra:r	إقرار	____ اعتراف، قبول	recognition, acknowledgement, acceptance, approval, assent, confession, admission.	____
ukubalifu(N) (kibali)	qabu:l	قبول	____	agreement, approval, assent, concord, harmony.	____, admittance, concent.
ukufuru(N) (also ukafiri)	kufr(root)	كفر	____ كفران	see ukafiri.	____
ukurasa(N) (kurasa)	kurra:sa (t)	كراسة	صفحة/ ورقة	page, sheet, leaf of a book, leaflet.	booklet, notebook, quire, brochure.
ukutubi(N)	ama:na(t) al maktaba (t)	أمانة المكتبة	____	librarianship.	____
ulaanifu(N)	laạna(t)	لعنة	____ لعن	cursing, damnation, being cursed.	____, execration, imprecation.
ulaanizi(N)	laạn/ laạna(t)	لعن لعنة	____	see ulaanifu.	____
ulaghai(N)	laghu(n) laghw(un)	لغو	خداع احتيال دجل / غش خدعة حيلة	fraud, deception, imposture, swindle.	nonsence, null, blunder, mistake, nugatory.
ulaini(N)	luyu:na(t)	ليونة	____	softness, gentleness.	____, companionableness.
ulainifu(N)	luyu:na(t)	"	____	see ulaini.	____
ulamaa(N) (mwana chuoni)	ụlama:ā ạ:lim	علماء	عالم	Islamic teacher, educated (in Islam).	learned, erudite, scholar, scientist.

Swahili word	Transcription of Arabic word	Arabic word	Arabic word in Swahili sense	Swahili usage	Arabic usage.
ulaya(N)	wila:ya(t)	وِلا يَة	___ أُرُوبَا	<u>Europe</u>,** district(usu. wilaya)	___
uledi(N)	wulaid	وُلَيْد	غُلامُ السَّفِينَة	cabinboy.	boy.
umaarufu(N) (umashuhuri)	maaru:f	مَعْرُوف	___, شُهْرَة سُمْعَة	fame, renown, well-known.	___, benefit.
umahiri (N)	maha:ra(t)	مَهَارَة	___	skill, cleverness, deftness.	___,proficiency.
umalaya(N)	mula:ã(t)	مُلاءَة	بَغَاء	prostitution.	bedsheat, sheet.
umaskini(N)(ufukara)	maskana(t)	مَسْكَنَة	___ فَقْر	poverty, misery, distress, indigence.	___, humbleness.
umati(N) (halaiki)	ùmma(t)	أُمَّة	حَشْدٌ مُرِيدُون، أتبَاع	large gathering, crowd, followers, adherents.	see umma.
umma(N) (jumla ya watu)	ùmma(t)	أُمَّة	___ شَعْب	people, nation.	___, folk, race, tribe.
umri(N) (uzima) (maisha)	ùmr	عُمْرٌ	___	age, time, period, time of life.	___
umurua(N)	muru:ã(t)	المُرُوءَة	___	see mrua.	___
unabii(N) (Rel.) (kazi ya utume)	nubu:ã(t)	النُّبُوءَة	___, النُّبُوَّة	Prophecy.	___
unadhifu(N)	nadha:fa (t)	النَّظَافَة	___	cleanliness, orderliness, neatness.	___, tidiness.
unafiki(N)	nifa:q	النِّفَاق	___	hypocrisy, deceit, dissimulation.	___, dissemblance.
unaibu(N)	nia:ba(t)	نِيَابَة	___	deputyship, representation, replacement.	___, substitution, prosecution.

Swahili word	Transcription of Arabic word	Arabic word	Arabic word in Swahili sense	Swahili usage	Arabic usage.
unajimu(N) (elimu ya nyota)	tanji:m	التَّنْجِيم	___	astronomy, astrology.	___
unajisi(N)	naja:sa(t)	نَجَاسَة/نجس	___ نجس	uncleanliness, defilement, impurity, desecration.	___, dirt, squalor, filth.
unanasi(N) [Persian]*	ánana:s	أنناس	لِيف/ نَسِيج الأَننَاس	fiber of the pine apple plant.	*
uneemefu(N)	naị:m	نَعِيم	فَيْض وَفْرَة	Profusion, plenty, abundance.	comfort, amenity, ease, happiness.
unidhamu(N)	niḍha:m	نِظَام	___	discipline.	___, see nidhamu.
uradi(N) (Rel.) (nyiradi)	àura:d	الأَوْرَاد	___	Prayer said at Islamic burial.	specified time devoted to private worship.
urafiki(N)	rifqa(t)	رِفْقَة	___, صَدَاقَة	friendship, friendliness.	___, kindness, gentleness.
urahisi(N)	rukhs	الرُّخْص	___, زَهِيد مُنْخَفِض	lowprice, cheapness, bargain, cheaply, easily.**	___, inexpensiveness.
uraia(N) (hali ya kuwa raia)	raạwiya(t)	رَعَوِيَّة	___	citizenship, nationality.	___
uraisi(N)	riã:sa(t)	رِئَاسَة	___	presidency, presidentship	___
urasharasha(N) (rasharasha)	rasha:sh	رَشَاش (رَشّ)	___	light rain, drizzle, sprinkle.	___, dribble.
urekebisho(N)	tarki:b	تَرْكِيب	___, صِيَانَة تَعْدِيل / تَكْيِيف	repair, orientation, adjustment.	preparation, fitting.
urithi(N)	irth	الإرْث	___ الوِرَاثة	inheritance, heritage, bequast, legacy.	___,
urudishaji(N)	radd	الرَّدّ	إِعَادَة/ تَجْدِيد	restoration, reconstruction,** rehabilitation.**	___, return, rejection, reimbursement.
urujuani(N) (also urujuwani)	ùrjuwa:n	الأُرْجُوَان	___	purple, (violet-colour).	___
usaa(N) (usaha)	àwsa:kh	أَوْسَاخ	قَيْح / صَدِيد	see usaha.	___

Swahili word	Transcription of Arabic word	Arabic word	Arabic word in Swahili sense	Swahili usage	Arabic usage.
usafari(N) (also usafiri)	safar	سَفَر	نَقْل ,___	travel, trip, journey, travelling, <u>transport</u>.	___, tour.
usafi(N)	ṣafa:ā	صَفَاء	___	purity, cleanliness, neatness, truthfulness, orderliness, frankness.	___, happiness, sincerity, cheerfulness, honesty.
usafiri(N)	safar	سَفَر	نَقْل / وَسِيلَة ___	see usafari.	___
usafirishaji(N)	safar (root)		اِنْتِقَال تَرْحِيل ,___ نَقْل / مُوَاصَلَات وَسِيلَة نَقْل	dispatch, conveyance, transport, transportation, export, communication, custom, duty.	see usafari.
usafishaji(N)	taṣfiya(t)	تَصْفِيَة	تَنْقِيَة ___ تَطْهِير نَظَافَة	cleaning, purification,	___, clearance, clarification, fittering.
usafisho(N)	taṣfiya(t)	"	___	see usafishaji.	___
usaha(N)	âwsa:kh	أَوْسَاخ	قَيْح / صَدِيد	pus, suppurate, matter, discharge.	dirt, filth, squalor.
usahaulifu(N)	sahw(un)	سَهْوٌ	نِسْيَان ,___	absentmindedness, forgetfulness.	___, inattentiveness, negligence, inattention.
usahihi(N)	ṣahi:ḥ	صَحِيح	دِقَّة ,___ ضَبْط / صِحَّة	correctiness, rightness, precision, faultlessness, accuracy, truthfulness.	___
usajili(N)	tasji:l	تَسْجِيل	___	registration, documentation.	___, anthentication.
usalama(N)	sala:ma(t)	سَلَامَة	أَمْن ,___	safety, security.	___
usalata(N) (also usaliti)	tasalluṭ tasli:ṭ	تَسَلُّط تَسْلِيط	___	see usaliti.	___

Swahili word	Transcription of Arabic word	Arabic word	Arabic word in Swahili sense	Swahili usage	Arabic usage.
usaliti(N)	tasalluṭ tasli:ṭ	تَسَلُّط تَسْلِيط	———	harshness, sarcasm, adulteration, mixing.	predominance, mastery command, authority.
usani(N)	sana:ạ(t) sanạ(t)	صَنْعَة/صِنَاعة	——— حِدَادَة	forging.	workmanship, work.
usanifu(N)	tasni:f	تَصْنِيف	———	skill, craft, art of composing, art.	classification, categorization, assorting, compilation, composition, writing.
usanii(N)	sanaạ(t)	صَنَاعَة/ صَنْعَة	———	see sanaa.	———
usawa(N)	mustawa: musa:wa: (t)/tasa: wi(n)	مَسْتَوَى مُسَاوَاة تَسَاوٍ	———	equality, similarity, likeness, fairness, balance, level.	———
usawanisho(N) (rare)	taswiya(t)	تَسْوِيَة	——— تَرْتِيبٌ تَنْظِيمٌ تَعْدِيلٌ	arrangement, demarcation, alignment.	___, leveling, settlement, equalization, adjustment.
usawazishaji(N)		تَسْوِيَة	———	see usawanisho.	———
usawazishaji wa Irabu (ling.)	taswiya(t) /ura:b	مِنْ تَسْوِيَة وَمِنْ اِعْرَاب	——— (اِعْلَال)	vowel harmony.	see "usawazishaji" and "Irabu".
ushabiki(N)	Ishtiba:k	اشْتِبَاك	فَخٌّ / شَرَك	cunning, snare, cleverness, strage.	entanglement, complication, involvement, clash.
ushahidi(N)	shaha:da (t)	شَهَادَة	———, بُرْهَان اثْبَات	proof, evidence, confirmation, martydom, testimony.	____, witness, deposition, certificate, attest.
ushairi(N)	shiịr	شِعْر	———, قَصِيدَة	poetry, art of poetry, high skill, beauty.	———
ushari(N) (ugomvi) (ugobo) (ubokozi)	sharr	شَرٌّ	———	evil, mischief, disaster, malice.	___, harm, calamaty.

Swahili word	Transcription of Arabic word	Arabic word	Arabic word in Swahili sense	Swahili usage	Arabic usage.
usharifu(N)	sharaf	شَرَف	———	excellence, dignity, respectabitily.	———
ushawishi(N)	tashwi:sh	تَشْوِيش	——— إِغْرَاء	entice, allurement, agitation, temptation.	confusion, disturbance, confounding, ailment.
usheha(N) (kazi ya sheha)	shiya:kha (t)	شِيَاخَة	———	position of status as a chief, councillor, respected special position, place reserved for elders at a funeral.**	position, or dignity of a sheik.
ushetani(N)	shaiṭana (t)	شَيْطَنَة	———	devilry, reckless daring.	———, dirty, trick, villainy.
ushirika(N)	sharika(t)	شَرِكَة	———, تَعَاوُن شَرَاكَة / اشْتِرَاك	co-operation, partnership sharing, commission, community of interests, common nature, intimate union	———, company, corporation companionship, communion.
ushirikiano (N) (umoja)	musha:raka(t)	مُشَارَكَة	———, اتِّحَاد	participation, partnership, co-operation, union.	———, collaboration.
ushirikina (N)(Rel.)	shirk ishra:k	شِرْك اشْرَاك	———	polytheism, idolatry.	———
ushirikishaji (N)	ishtira:k musha:raka(t)	اِشْتِرَاك مُشَارَكَة	———	see ushirika.	
(a) **ushoga**(N)	shauq	شَوْق	صَدَاقَة	friendship between women only.	longing, yearning, wish, desire, craving.
(b) **ushoga**(N)	shauq	"	خُنْث	see uhanithi.	———
ushtaki (N)	shakwa:	شَكوَى	———	accusation, prosecution arraignment.	———, complaint suffering, grievance.

Swahili word	Transcription of Arabic word	Arabic word	Arabic word in Swahili sense	Swahili usage	Arabic usage.
ushujaa(N) (uhodari) (ujasiri)	shaja:ạ(t)	شَجَاعة	____	courage, bravery, heroism.	___,boldness, valiance, valor, audacity.
ushuru(N)	ụshu:r	عُشُور	____	taxation, tax, duty, customs, rent.	tithes, (predial, personal) tithes, tax.
usia(V) **ka/wa/sha/ana**	waṣṣa:	وَصَّ	____	direct, advice, charge, order, commission, instruct, bequeath something to some one.	____, bid, councel recommend, commend, entrust, enjoin, decree.
usia(N) (also wasia)	waṣia	وَصِيَّة	____	see wasia.	____
usihiri(N)	siḥr	سِحْرٌ	____	see sihiri.	____
usimulizi(N)	samar	سَمَر	____	see simulizi.	____
usiri(N) (rare)	sūr	سُؤْر	تَأْخِير	stay, delay,tarry linger, lose time, detention, lagging behind.	rest, remnant, leftover, remainder.
usitawi(N)	istiwa:ā	اِسْتِوَاء	نَجَاح نَشَاط / اِزْدِهَار	success, flourishing condition, healthy, development, full activity.	straightness, evenness levelness, equality.
usitawishaji(N)	mustawa: istiwa:	مَسْتَوَى اِسْتِوَاء	نَجَاح / اِزْدِهَار حَيَوِيَة / تَطَوُّر نَشَاط	(1) prosperity, success, progress. (2) development, vitality.	level, standard, niveau.
usitawishi(N)	mustawa;	مُسْتَوَى	____	see usitawishaji.	____
ustaarabu(N)	istiạra:b	اِسْتِعْرَاب	تَحَضُّر تَمَدُّن	civilazation, education, refinement, goodmanners.	Arabization.
ustadh(N) (ZNZ)[(1)] (D.S.M.)[Persian]*	ụsta:dh	الأُسْتَاذ	____	teacher, professor, also title for respect.	____

(1) ustadh[Persian]* = skill in any art or profession.

Swahili word	Transcription of Arabic word	Arabic word	Arabic word in Swahili sense	Swahili usage	Arabic usage.
ustahamilifu(N)	taḥammul	تَحَمُّل	———	see ustahamilivu.	———
ustahamilivu(N)	taḥammul	"	——— اِحْتِمَال	endurance, patience, pertinacity, perseverance.	see stahamilivu.
ustahiki(N)	istiḥqa:q	اِسْتِحْقَاق	———	worthiness, honour, respect, regard.	see stahiki.
ustahili(N)	istiḥla:l	اِسْتِحْلَال	———	merit, worthiness, deservingness.	see stahili
ustahimilifu(-vu)(N)	taḥammul	تَحَمُّل	———	see stahamilivu.	———
ustahivu(N)	istiḥya:a	اِسْتِحْيَاء	———	politeness, respect, courtesy, consideration, attentiveness.	———
ustawi(N)	istiwa;a	اِسْتِوَاء	———	see usitawi.	———
(a) usufi(N) (Rel.)	taṣa<u>w</u>uf	تَصَوُّف	———	life of dervish,[Per.]*, lonely existance, retirement, hermit.	———
(b) usufi(N)	ṣu:f	(مِنْ الصُّوف)	القَبَك	kapok, wood, cotton wool, swab, wadding.	*
usufii(N)	taṣa<u>w</u>uf	تَصَوُّف	———	see usufi(a).	———
usufu(N)	ṣu:f	صُوف	———	see usufi(a) and (b).	———
usuli(N) (asili) (Ling.)	uṣu:L	أُصُول (ج)	——— الخَلْفِيَة الجُذُور الاِجْتِمَاعِيَة أو السِّيَاسِيَة لِحَادِثَةٍ أَوْ وَضْع	background.	origins, sources, roots, principles, elements, fundamentals.
usultani(N)	salṭana(t)	سَلْطَنَة	———	sultanship,sultanate[Ar]*.	———
usulubu(N)	ṣalb	صَلْب	———	see sulubu.	———

Swahili word	Transcription of Arabic word	Arabic word	Arabic word in Swahili sense	Swahili usage	Arabic usage.
usuluhi(N)	sulḥ	الصُّلْح	____	agreement, reconciliation concord, mediation, satisfaction.	____
usuluhifu(N)	sulḥ	"	____	see usuluhi.	____
usuluhishi(N)	iṣṭila:ḥ	اِصْطِلاح	____	see usuluhisho.	____
usuluhisho(N)	iṣṭila:ḥ	"	____ اِتّفاق اِنْسِجام / تَسْوِيَة مُعاهَدَة	agreement, reconciliation, convention.	____, practice, usage (colloquial ling.).
usuluhivu(N)	ṣulḥ	صُلْحٌ	____	see usuluhi	____
uswahili(N) (lugha nzuri)	sawa:ḥil	سواحل	بِلاد أَوْ عادات وتَقاليد وأخلاق السَواحِليّين	the Swahili country, manner of the Swahilis.	coasts.
utaabishaji(N) (utesaji)	taab	تَعْب	____	fatigue, distress, trouble, ado, toil.	____, nuisance, discomfort, tiredness.
utabibu(N)	taṭbi:b	تَطْبِيب	____ مُعالَجة	medical science, treatment, profession of a doctor.	medical profession, healingart, medical practice.
utabiri(N)	taabi:r	تَعْبِير	____، علم الفلك	interpretation, exposition/explanation, announcement, prediction.	____, expression, declaration, utterance.
utaifishaji(N)	ta:ifa(t)	طَائِفَة	تَأْمِيم	nationalization.	see taifa.
utajiri(N)	tija:ra(t)	تِجارَة	غِنَى / ثَرْوَة	riches, capital, possessions, wealth, status of a merchant.	____, affluence, commerce, trade, traffic.
utakalifu(N)	takalluf	تَكَلُّف / تَكْلِيف	جَهْد / هَمٌّ (زَمْل)	discomfort, weariness.	imposition, charging with a duty, tasking.
utalii(N)	istiṭla:a	اِسْتِطْلاع	سِياحَة	tourism.	study, investigation, exploration, curiosity.

Swahili word	Transcription of Arabic word	Arabic word	Arabic word in Swahili sense	Swahili usage	Arabic usage.
utamaduni(N)	tamaddun	تمدُن	____	civilazation, refinement	____
utamani	tamani(n)	تَمَنٍ	____ , رغبة	see tamani.	____
utamanifu(N)	tamani(n)	تَمَنٍ	____	see tamani.	____
utamu(N)	taąm	طَعْمٌ	____ تكمة مذاق حلوٌ حلوٌ	flavour, sweet taste, sweetness, pleasantness.	taste, flavor, savor, relish.
utanashati(N)	nasha:ṭ	نَشَاط	اناقة صفاء نظافة	cleanness, neatness, freshness.	briskness, activeness, animation, vivacity.
utani(N)	1. ȧwṭa:n 2. mauṭin	أَوْطَان مَوْطِن	مُعَاشَرَة صَدَاقة / نسب وَضْعٌ وَطَنِي / نَوْعٌ مِنَ المِزَاحِ بَيْنَ القَبَائِل	kinship, membership in tribe or race, clanship, familiar, friendship.	1.home, fatherland, national home, 2.native country, locality, district, region, zone, residence, habitat.
utaratibu(N) (taratibu)	tarti:b	تَرْتِيب	____	see taratibu.	____
utawala(N)	tawlia(t)	تَوْلِيَة / تَوَلّ	____ إدارة حُكْم / سُلْطَة	reign, rule, discipline.	____, investiture.
uthabiti(N)	thaba:t	ثَبَات	____ , موقف شجاعة	firmness, strength, stability, courage, resolution.	____, constancy, steadiness.
uthibitisho(N) (ushahidi)	ithba:t	إِثْبَات		proof, evidence, confirmation, support, firmness, honesty, effectiveness, decisive.	___, establishment attestation, affirmation, verification, documentation.
utii(N)	iṭa:ạ(t)	إِطَاعَة / طَاعَة	____ , خُضُوع	obedience. discipline	____
utiifu(N) (hali ya kutii)	ita:ą(t) ta:ą(t)	إِطَاعَة طَاعَة	____ , خُضُوع	see utii.	____
utimilifu(N) (ukamilifu)	itma:m	إِتْمَام	____ , تَمَام	perfection, consummation, completeness.	____, realization, fulfillment, conclusion.

Swahili word	Transcription of Arabic word	Arabic word	Arabic word in Swahili sense	Swahili usage	Arabic usage.
uwakili	tawki:l	تَوْكِيل	تَمْثِيل , ____	stewardship, condition of agent, representation.	____
uwaziri(N)	tawzi:r	تَوْزِير	مَقَامُ أَوْ رُتْبَةُ أَوْ عَمَلُ الوَزِيرِ	ministership.	____.
uyabisi(N) (rare)	ya:bis	يَبَاس	____	dryness, hardness.	____
uzani(N)	åwza:n	أَوْزَان	____	weight, weighing.	____
uzinifu(N) (uasherati)	zina:	الزِّنَا	____	adultery, fornication.	____
uzinzi(N)	zina:	"	____	see uzinifu.	____
uzulu(V)	azal(a)	عَزَل	____	dismiss, remove from office, degrade, depose, dethrone, discharge, cause to obdicate, isolate [Ar.]*	____, separate. segregate, detach, release, cut off.
		V			
vibaraka(N) (pl.of. kibaraka).	baraka(t) (root)	(مِنْ بَرَكَة)	عَمِيل / جَاسُوس	stooges (see kibaraka).	____
vibiriti(N) (pl. of kibiriti)	kibiri:t	كِبْرِيت	____	see kibiriti.	____
vitabu(N) (pl. of kitabu)	kita:b	كِتَاب	كُتُب	books(see kitabu).	____
volkeni(N) (mtetemeko wa ardhi)	burka:n	بُرْكَان	____	volkano[Ar.]*.	____

Swahili word	Transcription of Arabic word	Arabic word	Arabic word in Swahili sense	Swahili usage	Arabic usage.
waadhi(N) also maui-dha) (Rel.)	waaḍh	وَعْظ	——	sermon, moral, solemn, exhortation.	____, warning, admonition, para-enesis.
wadhifa(N) (madaraka)	wadhi:fa (t)	وَظِيفَة	——	position, job, post, of-ficialship, officialdom, duty, task.	____, assignment.
wafiki(V) (kubali) **ia/ika/iwa**	wa:faq(a)	وافَق	——	see afiki.	____
wahi(V) (diriki) (weza)	wakha:	وخى (تَوَخّى)	—— أدرك	be in time, be prompt to act.	to intend, purpo-se, aim, have in mind, have in view, aspire, strive.
wahidia(N) (tec)	wa:ḥid	واحدٌ	أُحادِىّ	monolingual.	sole, only, one.
wahyi(N) (Rel.)	waḥyu(n)	وَحْيٌ	——	inspiration, revelation.	____
waidhi(V) (hubiri) **ia/ika/isha/iwa/iana**	waaḍh(a)	وَعْظٌ	—— نُصْح حَضّ	to preach, exhort.	____, caution, admonish.
wajibika(V) (lazimi-ka) **ia/iwa/iana.**	wajab(a)	وَجَبَ	——	to be necessary, requisi-te, obligatory, imposed, enjoined duty.	____, indispensable, to be incumbent.
wajibu(N)	wa:jib	واجِب	——	necessary, requisite, ob-ligatory.	____, proper, adequate, duty.
wajihi(N)(prov.)	wajḥ	وَجْه	——	the appearance, surface, exterior.	____, face, countenance.
(a) **wakala**(N)	tawki:l	تَوكيل	——	agent, deputy, authoriza-tion.	____, power of attonney, full power.
(b) **wakala**(N) (ma-) (ajenti)	waka:la(t)	وَكالَة	——	agency, representation, deputyship, appointment, commission.	____, proxy, full power.

Swahili word	Transcription of Arabic word	Arabic word	Arabic word in Swahili sense	Swahili usage	Arabic usage.
wakati (N) (pl. nyakati)	waqt	وَقْت	——	time, period of time, season opportunity, point of time.	——
wakfu (N)	waqf	وَقْفٌ	——	religious endowment, wakf.	——
wakili (N)	waki:l	وَكِيل	—— مُحَامٍ، (مُحَامِي)	advocate, a lawyer, attorney, defense counsel.	——
wakti (N) (also wakati)	waqt	وَقْت	——	see wakati.	——
wala (conj.)	wa/la	وَلَا (وَ / لَا)	——	"wa" means (and), and "la" means (not), neither ...... nor.	——
walakini (N) (dosari) (kasoro) (ila)	wa/lakin	وَلَكِن	خَلَل / نَقِيصَة عِلَّة / عَيْب	(1) defect, a lacking, (2) nevertheless, not withstanding.	"wa" means (and) "lakin" (lakini) means (but), (yet) (hower). and even if, although, though.
walau (adv.) (hata kama) (japo) (ingawa)	wa/lau	وَلَوْ	——	even, anyhow, though, at least, notwithstanding, at any rate.	
walii (N) (ma-) (mtawa) (msufii)	waliyyu(n)	وَلِيٌّ	——	dervish, saint, a holy person.	——
wallahi! (adv.)	wallahi	وَاللّٰهِ (قَسَمٌ)	——	to swear by name of God.	——
waraka (N) (nyaraka) (barua) (ankara) (hati)	waraq a(t)	وَرَقَة	وَثِيقَة وَرَقَةٌ تُقَدَّمُ فِي وَرْشَةِ عَمَلٍ	a written communication, deed certificate, document, title deed.	paper, leaves, foliage, leafage, banknotes.
wardi (N)	ward	وَرْدٌ	——	see waridi.	——
waridi (N)	"	وَرْدٌ	—— وَرْدَة	a rose.	roses, flowers, blooms, blossoms.
warithi (N) (ma-)	wa:rith	وَارِث	——	see mrithi.	——

Swahili word	Transcription of Arabic word	Arabic word	Arabic word in Swahili sense	Swahili usage	Arabic usage.
warsha(N) (jopo)	warsha(t)	وَرْشَة	____	workshop.	____
wasaa(N) (muda)	wasaạ	وَسَعٌ / وَسْعَة	____ , فُرْصَة	opportunity, space, roominess, vastness, wideness leisure.	____
wasalaam(adv.)	wa-ssalaam	وَالسَّلَام	____	word used in the end of letter to show the end of explanation.	____, (and) that is all.
wasalaamu(adv.)	"	"	____	see wasalaam.	____
wasia(N)	waṣia(t)	وَصِيَّة	____	direction, advice, order, counsel, admonition, exhortation, testament, last will, recommendation.	___, instruction, injuction, command bequest, legacy.
wasii(N) (ma-)(rare)	waṣiyy(un)	وَصِيٌّ	____	trustee, executor.	____, authorized agent, commissioner, regent.
wasili(V) (fika) **ia/ ika/isha/iwa/iana.**	waṣal(a)	وَصَل	____	reach, arrive, come to, get to, cause to arrive, recieve.	___, unite, combine, link, join, connect.
wasiwasi(V) (wahaka)	waswa:s	وَسْوَاس	____ وَسْوَسَة	doubt, disquiet, scruple, infatuation, insinuation, suspicion, anxiety, temptation, disturbance.	___, devilish, wicked, thoughts, whisper, misgiving.
wastani(adv.) (kadiri) (kiasi)	wasṭa:ni muṭawassiṭ wasaṭ	وَسْطَانِي مُتَوَسِّط وَسَط	____	average, middling, moderate, intermediate, medium, middle	____, mediate, medial.
wazi(N) (dhahiri) (bayana)	wa:ḍiḥ	وَاضِح	____ ظَاهِر	open, bare, evident, clear, manifest, plain, obvious.	___, visible, lucid, distinct, patent.
waziri(N)	wazi:r	وَزِير	____	minister.	____
wilaya(N)	wila:ya(t)	وِلَايَة	____	district, province, parish.	____
witiri(N)	witr	وِتْرٌ / وَتْرِيٌّ	____ فَرْدِي	odd(of a number).	____

Swahili word	Transcription of Arabic word	Arabic word	Arabic word in Swahili sense	Swahili usage	Arabic usage.
witri(N) (also witiri)	witr	وِتْر / وِتْرِى	____ فَرْدِى	see witiri.	____
wizara(N)	wiza:ra(t)	وِزَارَة	____	ministry.	____
worodha(N) (also orodha)	arḍ	عَرض	____	see orodha.	____
wosia(N) (also wasia)	waṣiya(t)	وَصِيَّة	____	see wasia.	____
		Y			
yaani(conj.)	yaạni:	يَعْنِى	____	that is, to mean, that is to say.	____
yabisi(N) (-kavu) (rare)	ya:bis	يَابِس	____	dry, hard.	____
yahe(N)	ya/akhi	يَا أَخِى	____	brother, friend, the ordinary people.	my dear friend/ brother.
yahudi(N) (ma-) (myahudi)	yahu:diy	يَهُودِى	____	a Jew, Hebrew.	____
yailahi!	ya/ila:hi	يَا إِلَهِى	____	my God! ____	____
yakhe(N)	ya/ȧkhi:	يَا أَخِى	____	see yahe.	____
yakini(N)	yaqi:n	يَقِين	____	truth, proof, convintion, strong belief, certainly, assuredly, assurance.	____, certitude, positively, surely, axioms.
yakuti(N) (johari) (kito)	ya:qu:t	يَاقُوت	____	ruby, sapphire, conundum.	____, topaz [Lat.]*.

Swahili word	Transcription of Arabic word	Arabic word	Arabic word in Swahili sense	Swahili usage	Arabic usage.
(a) **yamkini**(N)(yumkini)	yumkin	يُمْكِن	____ اِمكَانِيّة	possibility.	to be possible.
(b) **yamkini**(adj.)	mumkin	مُمْكِن	____	probable, likely, possible.	____, maybe.
(c) **yamkini**(V)	yumkin	يُمْكِن (ف)	____	be possible.	____
yarabi!	ya/Rabbi	يَا رَبّ	____	my Lord(God).	____
yasmini(N)	yasmi:n	يَاسْمِين	____	see asmini.	____
yatima(N) (ma-) (mwana mkiwa)	yati:m	يَتِيم	____	orphan, a fatherless, a motherless, parentless.	____
Yesu(N)	yasu:ụ	يَسُوع	____	Jesus, Christ.	____
yumkini(N)	yumkin	يُمْكِن	____	see yamkini(a).	____
yumkini(adj.)	"	"	____	see yamkini(b).	____
yumkini(V)	"	"	____	see yamkini(c).	____
		Z			
zabibu(N)	zabi:b	زَبِيبٌ	____ عِنَب كَرْمَة	raisin, <u>grape**</u>.	____, grapes (dried).
zabuni(N) (mnadi)	zabu:n	زَبُون	زِبَانَة	clientele, patronage, custom.	customer, buyer, client, patron.
Zaburi(N) (Rel.)	zabu:r	الزَّبُور	____	psalm, the psalter.	____
zafarani(N)	zaạfara:n	زَعْفَرَان	____	saffron, crocus.	____
zahali(N)	zaḥl	زَحْل	____ (اِسْمُ كَوْكَبٍ)	planet saturn.	____

Swahili word	Transcription of Arabic word	Arabic word	Arabic word in Swahili sense	Swahili usage	Arabic usage.
zahanati(N) (dispensari) [Turkish]*	ijzakha:na (t)	اِجْزَخَانَة	مُسْتَوْصَف	dispensary.	pharmacy.
zaibaki(N) (zebaki) [Persian]*	ziịbaq	زِئْبَق	____	mercury, quicksilver.	____
zaidi(adv.)	za:i̲d	زَائِد	____	more, more than, in addition, besides.	___, increasing, growing, additional, extra, exceeding, immoderate.
zaini(V) (shawishi) (danganya) **ia/ika/isha/iwa/iana**.	zayyan(a)	زَيَّن	____	persuade to wrong, deceive, cheat.	____
zaituni(N)	zaitu:n	زَيْتُون	____	an olive.	____
zaka(N) (Rel.) (zakati) (sadaka)	zaka:(t)	زَكَاة	____	tithe, alms.	____, purity, honesty, justification, vindication, charity.
zakari(N) (taboo)	dhakar	ذَكَر	____	penis, see dhakari.	____, the male member.
zama(N)	zaman	زَمَن	___, وَقْت	see zamani.	____
zamani(N) (adv.)	zaman zama :n	زَمَن زَمَان	___, زِمَان وَقْت	(1) time, period, epoch, era, (2) long ago, the past, <u>already,** before</u>,** in ancient days.	___, duration, stretch of time, for sometime.
zandiki(V) [Persian]*	zandaq(a)	زَنْدَق	____ نَافَق	be hypocrite, be an atheist.	___ be a freethinker.
zawadi(N)	zawa:d	زَوَاد	____	gift, present, keepsake,	provisions.
zebaki(N)	ziịbaq	زِئْبَق	____	see zaibaki.	____
zeituni(N) (zaituni)	zaitu:n	زَيْتُون	____	see zaituni.	____

Swahili word	Transcription of Arabic word	Arabic word	Arabic word in Swahili sense	Swahili usage	Arabic usage.
ziada(N) (nyongeza)	ziya:da(t)	زِيَادَة	___ إِضَافَة مُلْحَق	addition, increase, supplement, bonus, augmentation.	___, allowance, surplus, excess, extra.
(a) **ziara**(N)	ziya;ra(t)	زِيَارَة	___	visit, go on a visit to, tomb, monument.	___
(b) **ziara**(N)(Rel.)	"	"	___	visit, pilgrimage.	*
zidi(V) (kuwa zaidi) (ongezeka) **ia/ika/isha/iwa/iana.**	za:d(a)	زَادَ	___ أَضَافَ	become more, increase, grow, be more and more, multiply.	___, augment.
zidisha(V) **ia/ika/wa** (ongeza)	zawad(a)	زَوَّدَ / زَايِد	___	cause to be more, greater.	___, to exceed, make offer, raize.
zidisho(N) (ma-)	ziya:da(t)	زِيَادَة	___	see ziada.	___
zikiri(N)	dhikr	ذِكْر	___	see dhikiri.	___
zinaa(N)	zina:	الزِّنَا	___ البِغَاء	adultery, fornication, whoredom, prostitution.	___
zini(V) **ia/ika/isha/iwa.**	zana:	زَنَى (ف)	___	to commit adultery, whore, fornicate.	___
(a)**-zinifu**(adj)(-enye tabia ya kuzini)	za:ni(n)	زَانٍ	___	see mzinifu.	___
(b) **zinifu**(adj.)	zina:wi	زِنَاوِي	___ خَاصٌّ بِالزِّنَا	adulterous, lecherous, lascivious, sexually immoral.	___
zubu(N) (rare) (taboo)	zubb	زُبّ	___ ذَكَر	see zakari.	___
zuri(N) (ushahidi wa uwongo) (kiapo cha uongo)(rare)	zu:r	الزُّور	___	false, perjury, swearing, untruth.	___, false hood, false testimony.
zuru(V)	za:r(a)	زَارَ	___	visit, pay a visit.	___

REFERENCES : (Dictionaries)

Swahili - Swahili

1. Johnson, F. Kamusi ya Kiswahili (Swahili - Swahili Dictionary) London, Sheldon Press, (1939).

2. Samson, R.H. Ufundi (wa) Magari (M.A), Leiden (Uholanzi) (1988).

3. TUKI Kamusi ya Kiswahili Sanifu Oxford University Press, Dar es Salaam (1981).

Swahili - English, English - Swahili

1. Johnson, F. A Standard Swahili - English Dictionary, Oxford University Press, Nairobi, (1987).

2. Johnson, F. A Standard English - Swahili Dictionary, Oxford University Press, Nairobi, Dar es Salaam, (1984).

3. Krapf, L. Dictionary of the Swahili Language. Trubner and Co. Ludgate Hill, London (1882).

4. Ohly, R. Primary Technical Dictionary English - Swahili, I.P.I. (UDSM), Dae es Salaam, (1987).

5. Prins, A.H.J. A Swahili Nautical Dictionary Chuo cha Uchunguzi wa Kiswahili, Dar es Salaam (1968).

6. Rechenbach, C.W. Swahili - English Dictionary The Catholic University of America Press. Washington D.C. 20017 (1967).

7. Snoxall. R.A. A Concise English - Swahili Dictionary. Oxford University Press, Nairobi, Dar es Salaam (1985).

English - English

1. Annandale, The Concise English Dictionary, Blackie and son Limited London (Undated).

2. Hornby, Oxford Student's Dictionary of Current English. Oxford University Press, London (1984).

3. Hardford, S.A. and Herberg, M. Shorter Latin Dictionary Langenscheidt KG, Berlin (1966).

Swahili - French

1. Sacleux, C.S. Dictionnaire Swahili - Francais, Tome 1 Institut D'Ethnologie Paris (1939).

Arabic - English, English - Arabic

1. Baalbaki, M. <u>AL-Mawrid</u> (A Modern English - Arabic Dictionary, Dar El ILm-LiL-Malayeen Beirut, Lebanon (1984).

2. Baalbaki, M. <u>Al-Mawrid Al-Caareeb</u> (Baalbaki's Pocket Dictionary), Dar El - ILm Lil - Malayeen Beirut, Lebanon (1982).

3. Cowan, J. M. <u>Arabic - English Dictionary</u>, Spoken Language Services, Inc. New York (1976).

4. Elias, A. E. Elias' <u>Modern Dictionary</u>, (Arabic - English), Cairo, Egypt.

<u>French - Arabic</u>

1. Abdul-Noor, J. and Idriss, S. <u>AL-Manhal Dictionnaire</u>, Francais - Arabe. Beirut (1977).

ARABIC REFERENCES

أَهَمُّ المَرَاجِعِ العَرَبِيّةِ

ابنُ مَنظور :
لِسَانُ العَرَبِ (١٥) مجلداً ! دار بيروت ــ بيروت (١٩٥٥م)

الطَّاهِرُ الزاوِي : مُخْتَارُ القَامُوس ، طرابلس الغرب

لويس مَعْلُوف : المُنْجِد فِي اللُّغَة والأَدَبِ ، المطبعة الكاثوليكية بيروت (١٩٥٦م)

مَجْدُ الدِّين مُحَمَّد بن يعقوب الفيروز آبادى : القَامُوس المُحِيط ،
مطبعة مصطفى البابى الحلبى مصر (١٩٥٢م)

مُحَمَّدُ بن أبى بكر عبد القادر الرّازِى :
مُخْتَارُ الصِّحَاح ، دار ومكتبة الهلال بيروت ــ لبنان (١٩٨٣م)

APPENDICES

THE INTERNATIONAL PHONETIC ALPHABET

(Revised to 1979)

CONSONANTS

		Bilabial	Labiodental	Dental, Alveolar, or Post alveolar	Retroflex	Palato-alveolar	Palatal	Velar	Uvular	Labial-Palatal	Labial-Velar	Pharyngeal	Glottal
(pulmonic air-stream mechanism)	Nasal	m	ɱ	n	ɳ		ɲ	ŋ	ɴ				
	Plosive	p b		t d	ʈ ɖ		c ɟ	k g	q ɢ		k͡p g͡b		ʔ
	(Median) Fricative	ɸ β	f v	θ ð s z	ʂ ʐ	ʃ ʒ	ç ʝ	x ɣ	χ ʁ		ʍ	ħ ʕ	h ɦ
	(Median) Approximant		ʋ	ɹ	ɻ		j	ɰ		ɥ	w		
	Lateral Fricative			ɬ ɮ									
	Lateral (Approximant)			l	ɭ		ʎ						
	Trill			r					ʀ				
	Tap or Flap			ɾ	ɽ				ʀ				
(non-pulmonic air-stream)	Ejective	pʼ		tʼ				kʼ					
	Implosive	ɓ		ɗ				ɠ					
	(Median) Click	ʘ		ʇ ʗ									
	Lateral Click			ʖ									

DIACRITICS

- ̥ Voiceless n̥ d̥
- ̬ Voiced s̬ t̬
- ʰ Aspirated tʰ
- ̤ Breathy-voiced b̤ a̤
- ̪ Dental t̪
- ̹ Labialized t̹
- ̡ Palatalized ƫ
- ~ Velarized or Pharyngealized ɫ, ɫ
- ̩ Syllabic n̩ l̩
- ͡ or ‿ Simultaneous sf (but see also under the heading Affricates)
- ˔ or ̝ Raised e˔, ẹ, e̝ w
- ˕ or ̞ Lowered e˕, ę, e̞ ʁ
- ̟ Advanced u̟, u+
- ̠ or - Retracted i̠, i-, t̠
- ̈ Centralized ë
- ~ Nasalized ã
- ˞, ʴ, ʳ r-coloured aʴ
- ː Long aː
- ˑ Half-long aˑ
- ̯ Non-syllabic ŭ
- ˒ More rounded ɔ˒
- ˓ Less rounded y˓

OTHER SYMBOLS

- ɕ, ʑ Alveolo-palatal fricatives
- ʆ, ʓ Palatalized ʃ, ʒ
- ɼ Alveolar fricative trill
- ɺ Alveolar lateral flap
- ɧ Simultaneous ʃ and x
- ʃˢ Variety of ʃ resembling s, etc.
- ɪ = ι
- ʊ = ɷ
- ɜ = Variety of ə
- ɚ = r-coloured ə

VOWELS

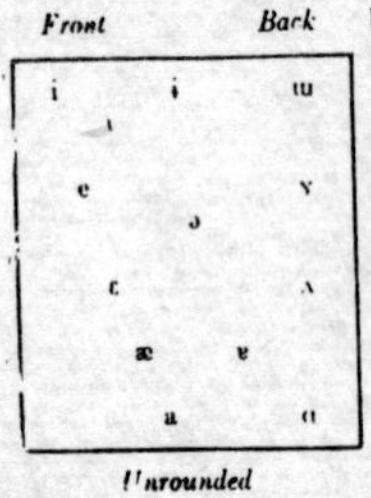

Close
Half-close
Half-open
Open

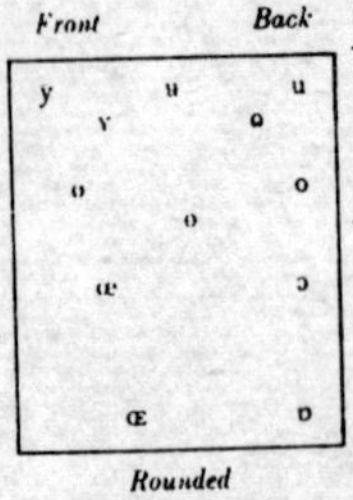

STRESS, TONE (PITCH)

ˈ stress, placed at beginning of stressed syllable: ˌ secondary stress: ˉ high level pitch, high tone: ˍ low level: ˊ high rising: ˏ low rising: ˋ high falling: ˎ low falling: ˆ rise-fall: ˇ fall-rise.

AFFRICATES can be written as digraphs, as ligatures, or with slur marks; thus ts, tʃ, dʒ: ʦ ʧ ʤ: t͡s t͡ʃ d͡ʒ.
c, ɟ may occasionally be used for tʃ, dʒ.

Utenzi wa Rasil-Ghuli Ms 711

Mnukuzi P. Ridhiwani

(1) Awali Bismilahi / jina la mola ilahi
Pweke asiye shabihi / ndiye wahidi kahari

(2) Arahamani rahimi / ndiye hayul kayumi
mwenye enzi ya dawami / alipendalo hujiri

(3) Huwa lhahu jalali / ndiye muenzi mudhili
Ndiye hakimu adili / ndiye mjuvi wa siri

(4) Huwa lhahul manani / mtukufu mwenye shani
Khalikal insani / biunathi wa dhukuri

(5) Huwa lhahul jabari / al-wahidul kahari
Al kabirul ghafaru / mudabiril umuri

(6) Ndiye karibu mujibu / ndiye ghafari dhunubu
Ndiye satari uyubu / ndiye rahimu shakuri

(7) Huwa lhahul khalaki / ndiye muumba riziki
Kaweneza makhluki / wakuu hata swaghiri

(8) Sharika wa gharibia / suheli wa kibulia
Kaweneza wote pia / wali bara na bahari

(9) Alhah alhah nduu zangu / tumuabudu mungu
Mumba nti ra mbingu / majabali na shajari

(10) Tumuhimidi jalali / ni jawabu afudhali
Na kuswalia Rasuli / Muhamadil bashiri

(11) Tuswalie masharafu / tumwa wa mola Latwifu
Kesho tupate wokofu / twepukane na sairi

(12) Tumswaliye habibu / asa ikawanaswabu

أعوذ بالله من الشيطان الرجيم بسم الله الرحمن الرحيم

(1) أول بسم الله / جن لمول إله / پويك اسي شبيه / ندي واحد قهار

(2) الرحمن الرحيم / ندي حي القيوم / موين عزي يدوام / اليپندال هجير

(3) هو الله الجلال / ندي معنز مذل / ندي حكيم عديل / ندي مجوو و سير

(4) هو الله المنان / متكوفو موين شان / خلق الانسان / بأنات وذكور

(5) هو الله الجبار / الواحد القهار / الكبير الغفار / مدبر الامور

(6) ندي قريب مجيب / ندي غفار ذنوب / ندي ستار عيوب / ندي رحيم شكور

(7) هو الله الخالق / ندي مومب رزق / كوينز مخلوق / وكوو امت صغير

(8) شرق وغربي / سهيل وقبلي / كوينز وت پي / ولي بار نبحار

(9) الله الله ندو زاڠ / تمعبد مڠو / مومب نت نمبڠ / مجبال نشجار

(10) تمحميد جلال / نجواب افضال / نكصلي رسول / محمد البشير

(11) تصلي مشرف / تومه و مول لطيف / كيشو تپات وكوف / توپكان نسغير

(12) تصلي حبيب / عاسي يكاونصب / [illegible] / [illegible]

[illegible]

[illegible]

SWAHILI PROVERBS	APPENDIX (C)	
Abdi hana hiari (p.226)	A slave has no choice.	لا خيارَ للعَبْدِ
Baada ya dhiki faraja (p.364)	After hardship, relief.	بَعْدَ الضِّيقِ فَرَجٌ (إنَّ مَعَ العُسْرِ يُسْرًا)
Dhamiri ni dira (p. 247)	The conscience is a compass.	الضَّمِيرُ بُوصَلَة
Fadhili ni utumwa (p.225)	Favours enslave.	الفَضِيلَةُ تَسْتَعْبِدُ القُلُوبَ
Ghururi za duniani huzijua Jahimuni (p.509)	The delusion of this world, one usually knows them in hell.	الغُرُورُ لاَ يَحِسُّ بِهِ الفَرْدُ إلاَّ فِي جَهَنَّمَ
Haraka haraka haina baraka (p.289)	Haste, haste has no blessing.	فِي العَجَلَةِ النَّدَامَةُ وَفِي التَّأَنِّي السَّلاَمَةُ
Ihsani haiozi (305)	Kindness does not rot (go bad).	مَنْ يَفْعَلِ الخَيْرَ لاَ يَعْدَمْ جَوَازِيَهُ لاَ يَذْهَبُ العُرْفُ بَيْنَ اللهِ وَالنَّاسِ
Jitihadi haiondoi kadari (P.36).	Effort does not annual the power of God	الحَذَرُ لاَ يُنْجِي مِنَ القَدَرِ
Kama unataka kuua nyoka mpige kichwani. (p.184)	If you want to kill a snake hit it on the head.	إِذَا أَرَدْتَ قَتْلَ ثُعْبَانٍ فَاضْرِبْهُ فِي رَأْسِهِ .
Kifo hakina kinga (p.138)	Death has no defence.	" أَيْنَمَا تَكُونُوا يُدْرِكْكُمُ المَوْتُ وَلَوْ كُنْتُمْ فِي بُرُوجٍ مُشَيَّدَةٍ "
Kila mtu lazima asaliwe, hata mudhinifu (p.248)	Every man must be prayed for, even a sinner.	كُلُّ إِنْسَانٍ يَنْبَغِي أَنْ يُدْعَى لَهُ (بِالخَيْرِ) حَتَّى المُذْنِبِ .

Mahaba ni tamu, mahaba ni sumu (p.)	Love is sweet, love is poison.	المَحَبَّةُ لَذِيذَةٌ والمَحَبَّةُ سُمٌّ (أَيْضًا)
Nadhari njia ya peponi (p.472)	Good judgement (planning) is the road to success.	التَخْطِيطُ طَرِيقُ النَّجَاحِ
Pahala pa itifaki ikrahi haipiti (p.173)	In a place where good is done, bad deeds are seen at once.	(جَاءَ الحَقُّ وَزَهَقَ البَاطِلُ إنَّ البَاطِلَ كَانَ زَهُوقًا).
Rafiki hakiki, wakati wa dhiki (p.228)	He that helps you in need, is trully your friend.	الصَّدِيقُ عِنْدَ الضِّيقِ.
Subira ni ufunguo wa faraji (p.295)	Patience is the key to tranguility. (Time cures pain).	الصَّبْرُ مِفْتَاحُ الفَرَجِ.
Tajiri huwa fakiri (p. 406)	A rich man can become a poor man.	قَدْ يُمْسِي التَّاجِرُ فَقِيرًا
Ujadidi wa juhudi (p.107)	Newness of the ancestors. There is nothing new under the sun.	الجَدِيدُ هُوَ الجُهْدُ (لَيْسَ تَحْتَ الشَّمْسِ جَدِيدٌ)
Utahara wa Jumaa utake Hamisi (p. 258)	After the purification of Friday try for Thursday. One should try to strive for a good life every day.	لَا تُعَجِّلْ إلَى غَدٍ مَا يُسْتَطَاعُ عَمَلُهُ اليَوْمَ.
Waarabu wa Pemba hujuana kwa vilemba (p.74)	The Arabs of Pembe know each other by the turban.	عَرَبُ الجَزِيرَةِ الخَضْرَاءِ (بِيمْبَا ـ زِنْجِبَار) يَعْرِفُونَ بَعْضَهُم البَعْضَ بِالعَمَائِم.

Waswahili hujuana kwa vilemba

The Swahili can tell each other by the turban they wear.

السَوَاحِلِيّونَ (السَاحِلِيُونَ) يَعْرِفُونَ بَعْضُهُمْ البَعْض بِالعَمَائِم •

Zani haina hazana: ni ukuba (p.174)

hazana = hazina, treasure

ukuba = bad smell.

The crime admits of no hiding. it brings its retribution in the future. Adultry is not a treasure, [one conceals] it is a punishment for later.

مَهْمَا تَكُنْ عِنْدَ امْرِئٍ مِنْ خَلِيقَةٍ
وَإِنْ خَالَهَا تَخْفَى عَلَى النَّاسِ تُعْلَمِ •

From Swahili Proverbs

Scheven University Press of America, Inc. Washington D.C. 20036 (1981).

COMMERCE AND ECONOMICS (BIASHARA NA UCHUMI)

APPENDIX (D)

Suluhisho	Arbitration
Msuluhishi	Arbitrator
Shughuli saidizi	Auxillary function
Bidhaa wastani	Average stock
Hawala	Bank draft
Chati mhimili	Bar chart
Faida sawia	Comparative advantage
Riba tata	Complex interest
Wakili	Consignee
Mali	Consignment
Hati ya mali	consignment note
Mwakilishaji	Consignor (also consigneer)
Bidhaa za kawaida	Consumption goods
Inayobadilishika	Convertible currency
Gharama na nauli	Cost and freight
Tarehe ya ahadi	Date of maturity
Uwasilishaji	Delivery
Mahitaji/Matakwa	Demand

(From toleo la No.3 (1978)

Administration/management (Uendeshaji/uongozi)	APPENDIX (E)
Idara ya Taratibu za Taaluma	Academic programme dept
Manufaa	Advantage
Kubali/kubaliana [makubaliano]	Agree(agreement)
Nyaraka	Archive(s)
Msuluhishi(wa)	Concilliator(s)
Iktisadi/uwekevu	Economy
Dahili/Mdahalo	Debate
Muasisi(wa) (asisi)	Founder(s) (found)
udhibiti wa bei (etc.)	Price control

From (Toleo Na. 5 (1985))

APPENDIX (F)

Bunge	National assembly/Parliament
Bila ya majadiliano/mjadala	Without debate
Dua	Prayer/prayers
Haki	Rights/right
Hoja	Motion
Kanuni	Rule/rules
Katibu/mwandishi	Secretary

From "Toleo Na. 2 (1976)

TERMS OF LINGUISTICS **APPENDIX (G)**

English	Kiswahili
abstract noun (N)	nomino dhahania
abstract sound (N)	sauti dhahania
accent (N)	lafudhi
accentology (N)	elimu lafudhi
accomodation (N)	urekebishaji
actualization (N)	udhihirishaji
affinity (N)	uhusianolugha
algebric linguistics (N)	isimu algebra
alternant (N)	kibadala
alternation (N)	ubadilishaji
anaphoric substitute (N)	umbo mrejeo sabiki
anaphoric word (N)	umbo mrejeosabiki
ancestor language (N)	Lugha azali
aminate (adj.)	hisivu
antecedent (N)	kisabiki (vi)

(From the dictionary of "Kamusi Sanifu ya Isimu na lugha) TUKI: (1990)

APPENDIX (H)

From Lugha Yetu No. 27.17,30

Daftari ya rasilimali	Assets register
Fedha taslimu	Cash terms
Hesabu ya amana maalum	Fixed deposit account
Hesabu ya akiba	Saving account
Hesabu ya stakabadhi	Receipt(s) account
Hesabu ya udhibiti	Control account
Jumlisho (kinyume)	Additive inverse
Tabia shirikisha	Assign
Ukubalifu	Axion
Vikamilisho pembe mraba	Complementary angles
Dhana Taswira	Concept Image
Athari Maana	Impact Implication
Uhakiki wa thamani wastani	Mean value theorem
Zidisha	Multiply

From "Tafsiri Sanifu" Toleo la Na. 3 (1978)

APPENDIX (I)

Fizikia	Physics
amilifu	active
mizani	balance(s)
nuru/mwanga	light
husisha	relate
uhusiano	relation
uhusianifu	relationism
husianifu	relative
mahusiano	relationship
kasi husianifu	relative speed
uhusianishi	relativity
mdudu(wa)	insect(s)
maadui asilia	natural enemies
toxin (etc)	sumu

From Toleo No. 5 (1985)

APPENDIX (J)

RIADHA	ATHLETICS
Mhudumu wa habari	press steward
msajili	recorder
mtunza wakati	time keeper
mshiriki (washiriki)	participant (participants)
Duara (miduara)	Circle (circle)
Mwanariadha (wanariadha)	athlete (atheletes)
adhabu adhibu	punishment penalise
ishara	signal
msitari wa goli	goal line
sheria (kanuni)	law
uhalifu uaminifu	infringement honest
namba halali	legal number

APPENDIX (K)

From Different areas

kaimu katibu wa shirika	acting corporation secretary
msaidizi wa ustawi	welfare assistant
mkurugenzi wa idhaa	director for broadcasting
ridhaa	endorsement
kizidisho	multiplier
nyuzi witiri	odd degree
hawala ya posta	postal order
hatua wazi	open interval
mbadala	substitution
takwimu	statistics
uzani (etc.)	weight.